Medieval Jewish Philosophy

An Introduction

Medieval Jewish Philosophy

An Introduction

Dan Cohn-Sherbok

CURZON

First published in 1996
by Curzon Press
St John's Studios, Church Road, Richmond
Surrey, TW9 2QA

© 1996 Dan Cohn-Sherbok

Typeset by LaserScript, Mitcham, Surrey

Printed in Great Britain by
TJ Press Limited, Padstow, Cornwall

British Library Cataloguing in Publication Data
A catalogue record for this book is available from the British Library

Library of Congress in Publication Data
A catalogue record for this book has been requested

ISBN 0–7007–0414–0 (Cloth)
ISBN 0–7007–0453–0 (Paper)

Contents

Contents

Acknowledgements

I would like to acknowledge my indebtedness to a number of important books: Colette Sirat, *A History of Jewish Philosophy in the Middle Ages*, Cambridge, 1995 – this authoritative and seminal study provided a great deal of information as well as source material; I. Husik, *A History of Medieval Jewish Philosophy*, New York, 1952; *Encyclopaedia Judaica*, Jerusalem, 1972, Robert Seltzer, *Jewish People, Jewish Thought*, Macmillan, 1980. Those who seek more detailed information about the history of Jewish thought in the Middle Ages are strongly encouraged to read these works. This volume is designed simply to provide a bird's eye view of the fascinating richness of the medieval Jewish philosophical tradition.

Throughout the book an asterisk (*) has been used to indicate philosophers who are discussed elsewhere in this study.

Chronological Table

Mid 8th Century	Jewish Messianic Movements
762–767	Beginning of the Karaite Movement
820–890	David Al-Mukammis
830–860	Growth of Karaism
850–c. 932	Isaac Ben Solomon Israeli
882–942	Saadiah Gaon
10th–11th Centuries	Karaite academy in Jerusalem
fl. 1st half of 10th Century	Jacob Al-Kirkisani
fl. 1st half of 11th Century	Yusuf Al-Basir
1021–c. 1058	Solomon Ibn Gabirol
fl. 2nd half of 12th Century	Bahya Ibn Pakuda
c. 1075–1141	Judah Halevi
1089–ll64	Abraham Ibn Ezra
1096	Massacre of Rhineland Jews
fl. 1st half of 12th Century	Nethanel Ben Al-Fayyum Fayyumi
fl. 1st half of 12th Century	Abraham Bar Hiyya
fl. 1st half of 12th Century	Abu Al-Barakat
1110–1180	Abraham Ibn Daud
1146	Persecution of Spanish Jews by Almohades
1135–1204	Moses Maimonides
1182–1198	Expulsion of French Jews
1190	Massacre of Jews at York
c. 1150–1220	Joseph Ben Judah Ibn Aknin
c. 1160–1230	Samuel Ibn Tibbon
c. 1160–1235	David Kimhi
1186–1237	Abraham Ben Moses Maimonides
1240	Disputation of Paris
fl. 1st half of 13th Century	Jacob Ben Abba Mari Anatoli

fl. 1st half of 13th Century	Moses Ben Samuel Ibn Tibbon
1263	Disputation of Barcelona
c. 1286	Completion of Zohar
1290	Explusion of Jews from England
fl. 2nd half of 13th Century	Gershom Ben Solomon of Arles
c. 1225–1295	Shem Tov Ben Joseph Falaquera
fl. 2nd half of 13th Century	Isaac Albalag
fl. 2nd half of 13th Century	Levi Ben Abraham Ben Hayyim
fl. 2nd half of 13th Century	Judah Ben Solomon Ibn Malkah
1210–1280	Isaac Ben Abraham Ibn Latif
fl. 2nd half of 13th Century	Judah Ben Nissim Ibn Malkah
1240–c. 1291	Abraham Ben Samuel Abulafia
fl. 2nd half of 13th Century	Zerahiah Ben Shealtiel Gracian
fl. 2nd half of 13th Century	Hillel Ben Samuel
1280–c. 1325	Judah Ben Moses Ben Daniel Romano
c. 1261–1328	Immanuel Ben Solomon of Rome
c. 1270–1340	Yedayah Ha-Penini
fl. 1st half of 14th Century	Nissim Ben Moses of Marseille
c. 1270–1340	Abner of Burgos
1288–1344	Levi Ben Gershom
fl. 1st half of 14th Century	Isaac Pulgar
fl. 1st half of 14th Century	Joseph Caspi
fl. 1st half of 14th Century	Shemariah Ben Elijah
1348–1349	Black Death Massacres
fl. 2nd half of 14th Century	Moses Ben Joshua Narboni
1413–1414	Disputation of Tortosa
fl. 1st half of 15th Century	Joshua Lorki
fl. 1st half of 15th Century	Isaac Ben Moses Levi
fl. 1st half of 15th Century	Hasdai Crescas
fl. 1st half of 15th Century	Hoter Ben Solomon
1361–1444	Simon Ben Zemah Duran
fl. 2nd half of 15th Century	Joseph Albo
1400–1460	Joseph Ben Shem Tov Ibn Shem Tov
fl. 2nd half of 15th Century	Abraham Ben Shem Tov Bibago
1420–1494	Isaac Ben Moses Arama
1437–1509	Isaac Abrabanel
c. 1460–93	Elijah Ben Moses Abba Delmedigo
1492	Expulsion of Jews from Spain
c. 1460–1523	Judah Ben Isaac Abrabanel

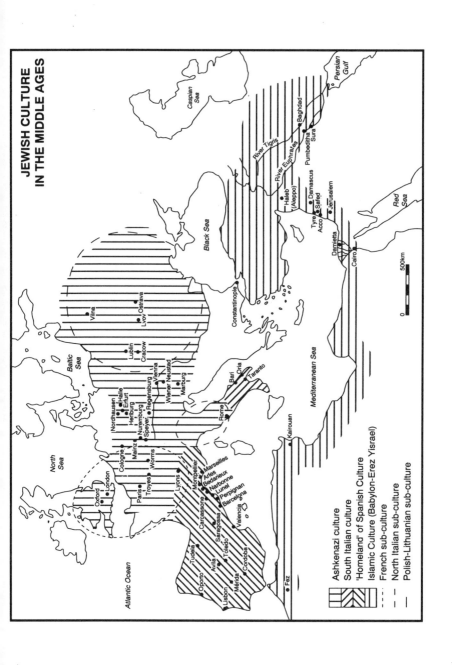

JEWISH CULTURE
IN THE MIDDLE AGES

Ashkenazi culture

South Italian culture

'Homeland' of Spanish Culture

Islamic Culture (Babylon-Erez Yisrael)

French sub-culture

North Italian sub-culture

Polish-Lithuanian sub-culture

Atlantic Ocean

North Sea

Baltic Sea

Black Sea

Caspian Sea

Mediterranean Sea

Red Sea

Persian Gulf

River Tigris

River Euphrates

0   500km

Oporto

Lisbon

Mérida

Ávila

Toledo

Córdoba

Valencia

Tudela

Saragossa

Barcelona

Perpignan

Carcassone

Lunel

Narbonne

Bedaneux

Arles

Marseilles

Montpellier

Lyons

Troyes

Paris

Worms

Cologne

Oxford

London

Mainz

Speyer

Nuremburg

Hertburg

Nordhausen

Erfurt

Halle

Regensburg

Marburg

Wiener Neustad

Vienna

Cracow

Lublin

Vilna

Lvov

Ostrawa

Rome

Bari

Oria

Taranto

Kairouan

Fez

Cairo

Damietta

Constantinople

Tyre

Acco

Safed

Jerusalem

Damascus

Haleb
(Aleppo)

Baghdad

Sura

Pumbeditha

For Lavinia

Introduction

What is Jewish philosophy? The answer depends on how philosophy is understood. There is no doubt that the ancient Israelites reflected philosophically on the origin of the universe and the nature and activity of God. Thus the Hebrew Bible begins with an account of creation and God's dealings with human creatures, and the Five Books of Moses continue the history of ancient Israel from the time of the patriarchs to the death of Moses. The rest of Scripture traces the development of the Jewish people through conquest and settlement, the rise of monarchy, the fall of the Northern and Southern Kingdoms, and the return of the exiles. In this panormaic epic God is depicted as preoccupied with the destiny of his chosen people in the unfolding of his providential plan.

In a similar vein the rabbis of the Tannaitic period (between the first century BCE and the second century CE) and the Amoraic period (between the second and sixth centuries CE) continued such speculation about the Deity and his relationship to the cosmos. Such theological reflection embraced a wide range of topics including: God's unity, omniscience, omnipotence, and goodness; Israel and its mission to the nations; the concept of the Messiah and redemption; and the purpose and scope of the moral law. In the Mishnah and the Midrash as well as in both the Palestinian and Babylonian Talmuds, the sages engaged in theological and philosophical activity within a Jewish framework. In addition, Jewish mystical texts contain abstruse theorizing about the process of creation and the nature of the Godhead.

Yet, such literary sources – both biblical and rabbinic – do not strictly speaking constitute Jewish philosophy. In no case is there a rational, systematic attempt to present an explanation of the nature of God. Biblical and rabbinic literature is therefore far removed from

1

Greek philosophical reflection as found in the works of such writers as Plato and Aristotle. Although the ancient Israelites and the rabbis pondered the most fundamental metaphysical issues, their speculations were fragmentary in character. In this light, it would be misleading to describe pre-medieval Jewish thought as Jewish philosophy; rather, it consists of unsystematic reflections on the most fundamental problems of the universe as seen in a religious context. The only exception to this pattern of Jewish theological writing is the work of the 1st century thinker Philo who lived in Alexandria. In a series of works Philo attempted to integrate Greek philosophy and Jewish teaching into a unified whole: by applying an allegorical method of interpretation to Scripture, he explained the God of Judaism in Greek philosophical categories and reshaped Jewish notions about God, humanity and the world.

The evolution of medieval Jewish philosophy was hence a late development, preceded by centuries of religious speculation contained in both biblical and rabbinic sources. The cultural milieu in which it originated was dominated by Hellenistic ideas filtered through both Christian and Muslim interpreters. In the 4th century BCE Alexander the Great encouraged the spread of Hellenistic civilization; after his death Alexandria (the capital of the Ptolemies in Egypt) and Antioch (the capital of Syria under the Seleucids) became centres of Greek learning. When Syria became a Roman province in the 1st century BCE, these traditions were perpetuated, and they continued when Christianity became the religion of the empire. Similarly, in the Orient where Islam became the dominant faith Greek texts were translated into Arabic and exerted a profound influence on Muslim thought.

Indirectly, then, Greek writers became the teachers of the Jews; this was so particularly in Muslim lands where Jews followed the lead of Arab thinkers in formulating their own philosophical systems. In particular, Islam as propounded by theologians known as the Mutakallimun exerted an important influence on Jewish thinkers of the early Middle Ages. According to these Islamic theologians, reason was perceived as a major source of knowledge alongside the authority of the Koran and the Sunna (traditional teachings about Mohammed). The aim of these thinkers was to purify the faith by freeing it from distortion. As a school their efforts were directed to demonstrate the creation of the world, divine providence, and the reality of miracles in opposition to Aristotelians who subscribed to the eternity of motion, denied God's knowledge of particulars, and argued for the unchanging character of natural law.

2

In the view of these Muslim thinkers, God creates continually and is therefore not restrained by natural law. Thus when natural phenomena occur, it is a mistake to believe that each event is preceded by a cause. Rather, God himself is the direct cause of each occurance. Hence, rain falls because God willed it to do so not because of laws governing nature, and the ground is wet because of God's decree. If God willed that the ground should remain dry after a rainfall, it would be so. On this basis, miracles cease to be mysterious – they are simply events brought about by God for specific purposes. Similarly, the theory of creation was demonstrated by this explanation of the phenomena of nature.

The oldest sect of the Mutakallimun, the Mu'tazila, were however not known primarily for such physical theories; instead, their conceptions of the unity of God and divine justice singled them out from other schools of Islamic thought. Of central importance was their understanding of the passages in the Koran where God is described anthropomorphically. In their opinion, when the Koran speaks of God's eyes, ears, or hands, or when God is depicted as seeing, hearing or standing, these expressions do not denote any corporeal presence: such descriptions, they argued, must be understood metaphorically. In a similar vein, they maintained that when attributes are ascribed to God, they should be conceived as different from his essence. This is so because if such attributes were eternal, there would be more than one eternal being, and God would cease to be a strict unity. The only way to defend the pure unity of God is to say that God has no positive attributes. Thus God is omnipotent, omniscient, all good, etc, but not because he possesses these characteristics as attributes.

The other major issue which concerned the Mu'tazila was the justice of God. Previous Muslim thinkers defended the absolute freedom of the will, insisting on justice as the sole motive of God's dealings with human beings. God, they argued, must be just and cannot act otherwise. Regarding the question whether actions are good in themselves, they maintained that an act is good because God wills it so. The Mu'tazila, however, believed in the absolute character of an action: what makes an act good or bad is reason, and it is because an act is inherently good that God commands it. conversely, an act is forbidden because of its inherent evil.

The doctrines of the Mu'tazila were of crucial importance for the history of Jewish philosophical reflection because of their influence on early medieval Jewish thinkers. Writing in the 12th century, for example, Moses Maimonides emphasized the impact of these Muslim writers on Jewish thought:

> You will find that in the few works composed by the Geonim and the Karaites on the unity of God and on such matter as is connected with this doctrine, they followed the lead of the Mohammedan Mutakallimun . . . It also happened, that at the time when the Mohammedans adopted this method of the Kalam, there arose among them a certain sect, called Mu'tazila. In certain things our scholars followed the theory and the method of the Mu'tazila (in Husik, 1966, xxiv)

In addition to the Mu'tazilite kalam, a number of medieval Jewish philosophers were deeply influenced by two systems of Greek thought: Aristotelianism and Neoplatonism. Aristotelian philosophy was based on the assumption that the world can be known only through observation; its advocates contend that such knowledge is attained through the study of speculative and practical sciences. According to tradition, the speculative sciences are divided into physics, mathematics and metaphysics; practical sciences consist of ethics, economics and politics. Logic, on the other hand, serves as the instrument of all scientific inquiry. Within the Aristotelian system, physics is concerned with the analysis of the changes that take place in the world – these are explained by means of four causes: material, efficient, formal and final.

The world itself is subdivided into the celestial and sublunar domains. In the sublunar region entities are classed as minerals, plants and rational beings which are all composed of matter and form. Here generation and corruption take place, and everything is reducible to the four elements of earth, water, air and fire. Within the celestial region, however, generation and corruption does not occur – everything is immortal and the only motion is that of the celestial spheres. This celestial domain is composed of the fifth element consisting of spheres in which are set the sun, moon, planets and fixed stars. Each sphere itself is composed of a body directed by an incorporeal soul and intelligence. At the centre of the universe is the earth around which all the spheres revolve.

All organic beings – plants, animals and human beings – are governed by the internal principle of motion, namely the soul. In human beings the soul possesses a wide range of faculties: nutrative, sensory, appetitive, and rational. The highest faculty is reason and the purpose of life is to improve its capacities. This faculty begins as the

4

Potential Intellect, and through a variety of exercises, it becomes the Actual Intellect, and finally the Acquired Intellect. As far as human knowledge is concerned, the Active Intellect is the primary agent – in Jewish and Islamic texts it is identified with the lowest of the celestial intelligences. Further, the Active Intellect produces prophecy in those who have acquired the correct preparation. In this philosophical system, metaphysics is conceived as the study of being including God and the incorporeal intelligences which are identified as angels. Morality is understood as the acquisition of the moral and intellectual virtues; these moral virtues are attained by following the mean and serve as a prerequisite for achieving the intellectual virtues.

The second philosophical system that influenced Jewish philosophers of the Middle Ages was Neoplatonism. In its various forms, Neoplatonism embraced the doctrine of emanation, asserting that the world emanated from God in a manner analogous to the emanation of rays from the sun or springs of water from a fountain. To insure the unity of God, Neoplatonic thinkers believed in a first emanation which they identified either as Wisdom (logos) or as a Divine Will. Using the concept of macrocosom (world) and microcosom (man), they argued that there are a number of spiritual substances such as Intellect, Soul and Nature which stand between this first emanation and the world. Moreover, some Neoplatonists maintained that there are spiritual substances that are composed of matter and form.

In its different manifestations, Neoplatonism affirmed that there is a fundamental separation between God and creation. Thus, God can only be described by negative attributes. In positing the distinction between the Creator and the world, some Neoplatonists insisted that the world proceeds by necessity from God and is contemporaneous with him; others argued that the world is the product of God's will. In their view of humanity, Neoplatonists believed in the duality of body and soul: the soul's origin is in the upper realm, and it is compelled to join the body. The purpose of life is to liberate the soul from the body, enabling it to return to its source in the celestial realm.

Given the formative impact of biblical and rabbinic theology on the evolution of medieval Jewish philosophy, this survey commences in Chapter 1 with an outline of the history of Jewish life and thought prior to the Middle Ages. Since medieval writers frequently refer to various aspects of the Jewish tradition, this background information provides a framework for their discussion. Beginning with a brief examination of the development of biblical Judaism, this chapter highlights the major features of biblical thought as it emerged from the time of the patriarchs to the destruction of the Second Temple in 70 CE. This is followed by a description of the evolution of rabbinic Judaism as well as the Jewish mystical tradition. Finally, the chapter concludes with an examination of the origins of medieval Judaism and its historical development.

Chapter 2 continues with a discussion of the evolution of medieval philosophical reflection from the 9th to the 11th century beginning with Karaite scholars who were critical of the anthropomorphism contained in rabbinic sources. During this period Jewish writers were profoundly influenced by the teachings of the Muslim schools, and in their attempt to defend Judaism from internal and external attack they frequently sought to adapt Mu'tazilite kalam as a mode of defense. In addition to such philosopical apologetics based on the speculations of Muslim thinkers, rabbinic scholars also employed features of Aristotelianism and Neoplatonism as well as astrological theorizing in expounding their interpretations of the Jewish tradition.

In the 12th century the major currents of Islamic thought, Aristotelianism, Neoplatonism and astrological speculation continued to exert a profound influence on Jewish thinkers. As Chapter 3 illustrates, throughout this century upholders of traditional Judaism sought to explain the meaning of the Torah in the light of these traditions. With the composition of Moses Maimonides' *Guide for the Perplexed*, such theorizing reached a climax. The central purpose of this work was to resolve the confusion into which Jewish thinkers had fallen by illustrating that Scripture must be interpreted in a figurative sense. Such an understanding of the meaning of the Torah, however, roused considerable hostility in the Jewish world leading to the condemnation of Maimonides' writing in the following century.

Chapter 4 continues this historical survey of medieval Jewish thought by focusing on the dissemination of Jewish texts by such figures as Judah Ibn Tibbon and his son Samuel. In this century Jewish philosophy underwent various transformations: in Islamic lands Jewish writers continued to be influenced by Muslim thought while making use of Maimonides' *Guide*; in Provence Maimonidean exegesis became well established; in Spain mystical sources exerted a profound influence on the direction of philosophical theorizing; and finally in Italy, Latin scholasticism played a major role in the development of a Maimonidean exegetical tradition.

As Chapter 5 illustrates, in the 14th century Jewish thinkers engaged in vigorous activity in Provence, Spain and the Byzantine empire. Throughout this century astrological exploration as evidenced in the writings of Abraham Ibn Ezra gained widespread allegiance. In addition, the works of Moses Maimonides as well as the Islamic philosopher Averroes continued to be viewed as the foundations for speculative thought as did the philosophical works of Gersonides which were composed at the beginning of this century. During the latter half of the 14th century, the translations of Latin medical texts and logical treatises attracted considerable attention. In addition, kabbalistic theories as found in traditional rabbinic sources came to play an important role in the evolution of medieval Jewish thought.

In the final century covered in this book, Jewish philosophy continued to undergo considerable change and development. The persecutions of the 14th century profoundly affected Jewish life and thought in the 15th century. In attempting to make sense of the changes that had occurred in the Jewish world, various thinkers argued that Aristotelian thought had undermined the Jewish faith and led the way to the rejection of the tradition. Foremost among those who levelled this accusation was Shem Tov Ibn Shem Tov. In his opinion, Jewish thought was more dangerous than the writings of the ancient Greeks. Yet while such figures within the Jewish community enveiged against the influence of such philosophical enquiry, others sought to defend Judaism on the basis of metaphysical and scientific investigation.

Chapter 1

Jewish Life and Thought Before the Middle Ages

The history of Jewish thought began with the emergence of the Hebrews as a separate people in the 13th century BCE. From what is known of Mesopotamian civilization, it appears that the authors of the Hebrew Scriptures drew on elements of ancient Near Eastern myths, refashioning them in the light of their own religious ideas In Scripture God is presented as the creator of the universe who chose the Jews and guides them to their ultimate destiny. After rescuing the nation from captivity in Egypt, he led them to the land he had promised to the patriarchs. Yet because of the iniquity of the Jewish people, both the Northern and Southern Kingdoms were devastated by foreign invaders. Later during the early rabbinic period, the sages engaged in speculation about a wide variety of topics – these discussions are recorded in various Midrashic collections. In addition, Jewish mystics formulated abstruse theological doctrines as well as recondite cosmological theories. This tradition of religious reflection continued into the Middle Ages, serving as a background for the evolution of philosophical reflection about the nature and activity of God.

Biblical Judaism

The development of Jewish religious thought began in the 2nd millennium BCE; following successive empires of the ancient world, the Jews emerged as a separate people. Distancing themselves from previous civilizations that had worshipped many Gods, the Jewish nation believed in one invisible God who created Heaven and Earth. How did such a religious view arise in a polytheistic context? According to some scholars, this radical break can be traced back to Abraham's discovery that the concept of universal justice must rest

9

on the belief in one supreme God. Other scholars see Moses as the principal architect of Israelite monotheism; these writers point out that before Moses there was evidence of monotheistic belief in the religious reforms of the Egyptian Pharaoh Akhenaton in the fourteenth century. In this light Moses is seen as following the path of this Egyptian revolutionary figure. Another interpretation of the origins of monotheism views monotheistic belief as emerging out of monolatry (the belief in one God despite the existence of other gods).

In any case, it is clear that by the ninth century BCE the ancient Israelites viewed the Canaanite gods as powerless. This was certainly the opinion of the prophet Elijah who when confronting the prophets of Baal proclaimed: 'The Lord He is God; the Lord He is God' (1 Kings 18:39). By the time of the prophet Jeremiah (several decades before the Babylonian exile), monotheism appears to have taken a firm hold on the Israelite community. In the words of Jeremiah: 'Their idols are like scarecrows in a cucumber filed, and they cannot speak; they have to be carried for they cannot walk. Be not afraid of them, for they cannot do evil, neither is it in them to do good.' (Jeremiah 10:5). Such a conviction is reflected in the Book of Psalms where the psalmist declares that God rebukes the other gods for their injustice and deprives them of divine status and immortality:

God has taken his place in the divine council;
In the midst of the gods he holds judgment;
How long will you judge unjustly,
and show partiality to the wicked? Selah.
Give justice to the weak and the fatherless;
maintain the right of the afflicted and the destitute.
Rescue the weak and the needy;
deliver them from the hand of the wicked –
They have neither knowledge, nor understanding, they walk about in darkness;
all the foundations of the earth are shaken –
I say, 'You are gods,
sons of the Most high, all of you;
nevertheless you shall die like men,
and fall like any prince.'
Arise, O God, judge the earth,
for to thee belong all the nations!

(Psalm 82)

On this view, the God of Israel is the true God, the creator of all things who guides history and will eventually be recognized by all.

According to the biblical narrative in Genesis, Abraham was the father of the Jewish nation. Originally known as Abram, he came from Ur of the Chaldeans, a Sumerian city of Mesopotamia near the head of the Persian Gulf. Together with his father Terah, his wife Sarai, and his nephew Lot, he travelled to Haran in northern Syria. There God called upon him to go to Canaan: 'Go from your country and your kindred and your father's house to the land I will show you. And I will make of you a great nation' (Genesis 12:1–2). During a famine in Canaan, he went first to Egypt and then preceded to the Negev, finally settling in the plain near Hebron. Here he experienced a revelation which confirmed that his deliverance from Ur was an act of providence. Later God made a covenant with Abraham symbolized by an act of circumcision (Genesis 17:11). Some years later God tested Abraham's dedication by ordering him to sacrifice Isaac, only telling him at the last moment to desist.

Similar divine disclosures were made to subsequent patriarchal figures. Isaac's son Jacob, for example, had a vision of a ladder rising to Heaven and heard God speak to him, promising that his offspring would inherit the land and fill the earth:

> And he dreamed that there was a ladder set up on earth, and the top of it reached to Heaven; and behold, the angels of God were ascending and descending on it! And behold, the Lord stood above it and said, 'I am the Lord, the God of Abraham your father and the God of Isaac; the land on which you lie I will give to you and your descendants; and your descendants shall be like the dust of the earth.'
>
> (Genesis 28:12–14)

The history of Abraham, Isaac and Jacob is followed by the cycle of stories about Jacob's son Joseph who was sold into slavery in Egypt. There the Jewish clan flourished, but eventually a Pharaoh who did not know Joseph (Exodus l:8), oppressed and persecuted the Hebrew people. In response God resolved to free his people, sending Moses as their deliverer. Revealing himself to Moses, the Lord commanded that he deliver the chosen people from Pharaoh's harsh bondage:

> I am the God of your father, the God of Abraham, the God of Isaac, and the God of Jacob . . . I have seen the affliction of my people who are in Egypt, and have heard their cry because of

11

their taskmasters. I know their sufferings . . . Come, I will send you to Pharaoh that you may bring forth my people, the sons of Israel, out of Egypt.

(Exodus 3:6–7, 10)

After escaping from the Egyptians, the Israelites wandered for forty years in the desert. During this period God called Moses up to the top of Mount Sinai where he revealed his covenant. The people were commanded to wash and purify themselves for two days; on the third day they came to the foot of the mountain amongst thunder, lightning and the sound of a ram's horn to hear God's voice. Subsequently, under he leadership of Joshua, the Jewish people conquered and settled the land that had been promised to them by God. In a more settled existence the Covenant expanded to include additional legislation. Mosaic law consisted largely of unconditional statements of principle, but as time passed other provisions were needed for every kind of situation. Many of these provisions were required for an agricultural community, and seem to date back to the time of the judges.

Although the nation was ruled over by a series of judges, the people clamoured for a king to protect them from foreign powers. When some tribes suggested to Gideon that he deserved such a role, he declared that it was impossible for all the nation to be ruled by both God and a human king (Judges 8:22–3). Later Samuel warned about the dangers of kingship, cautioning the people to remain loyal to the Covenant: 'If you will fear the Lord and serve him and hearken to his voice and not rebel against the commandment of the Lord, and if both you and the king who reigns over you will follow the Lord your God, it will be well; but if you will not hearken to the voice of the Lord, but rebel against the commandment of the Lord, then the hand of the Lord will be against you and your king (1 Samuel 12:13–15).

Such forebodings proved to be correct; repeatedly the leaders of the nation and the Jewish people as a whole violated the Covenant, evoking a hostile reaction from generations of prophets who warned both the Northern and Southern Kingdoms of the consequences of disobedience. In the North, for example, the eighth century prophet Amos proclaimed that Israelite society had become morally corrupt. Many Israelites had become rich, but at the expense of the poor. Shrines like Bethel were full of worshippers, but such ritual was empty. The 'Day of the Lord', Amos announced, would be a time of punishment for sinfulness. His later contemporary Hosea echoed these dire predictions: Israel had gone astray and would be punished. In line with such prophecy, the Northern Kingdom was devastated in 722 BCE by invading Assyrian forces.

In the Southern Kingdom, prophets such as Isaiah were deeply concerned about the violation of Covenantal law. In his view, the collapse of the Kingdom of Israel was God's punishment for sinfulness, and he foresaw a similar fate for Judah. A contemporary of Isaiah, the prophet Micah also criticized the people for their iniquity and foretold destruction:

> Hear this, you heads of the house of Jacob
> and rulers of the house of Israel,
> who abhor justice and pervert equity . . .
> because of you Zion shall be plowed as a field;
> Jerusalem shall become a heap of ruins.
>
> (Micah 3:9, 12)

After the fall of the Southern Kingdom in 586 BCE, many Jews were transported to Mesopotamia where they lamented the loss of their homeland. With the defeat of the Babylonians by the Persians, however, such dire circumstances were reversed by King Cyrus who permitted the nation to return to Zion. The Temple was rebuilt and religious reforms were enacted. This return to the land of their fathers led to national restoration and a renaissance of Jewish life.

In the centuries that followed, all Jews professed allegiance to the Torah; nonetheless, the Jewish community in Judaea was divided into various sects. According to the first century CE historian Josephus, the three most important groups were the Sadducees, the Pharisees and the Essenes. In all likelihood the Sadducees consisted of a small group of influential individuals including the hereditary priests who controlled Temple worship – for these Jews there was no reason to interpret and expand the written law, and they rejected any speculation about a future life. The Pharisees, however, believed in the resurrection of the body and the World to Come; moreover, they were anxious to make biblical law applicable to contemporary circumstances by offering oral expositions of the text. This procedure, they believed, had been commanded by God to Moses on Mt Sinai when he received the written commandments. The third sect of this period was the Essenes; the most important characteristic of this group concerned their lifestyle – rejecting the corruption of town life, they congregated in semi-monastic communities. In their community rule and war rule (Manual of Discipline), they described a cataclysmic end of the world which would be preceded by a struggle between good and evil in which Israel would emerge victorious.

The period following Herod's death at the end of the first century BCE was a time of intense anti-Roman feeling among the Jewish population of Judaea as well as in the diaspora. Eventually such hostility led to war only to be followed by defeat and destruction, once again, of the Jerusalem Temple. In 70 CE thousands of Jews were deported. Such devastation, however, did not quell the Jewish hope of ridding the Holy Land of its oppressors. In the second century a messianic rebellion led by Simeon Bar Kochba was crushed by Roman forces, who killed multitudes of Jews and decimated Judaea. Yet despite this defeat, the Pharisees carried on the Jewish tradition through teaching and study.

Early Rabbinic Judaism

Following the Bar Kochba War, Hadrian outlawed Judaism throughout the land, but after his death in 138 CE prohibitions against the religion were rescinded. As far as the Jews were concerned, their defeat under Bar Kochba initiated a conciliatory policy toward the Roman authorities resulting in the flourishing of rabbinic learning. The centre of Jewish life was transferred to Galilee, and under the disciples of Rabbi Akiva, the Sanhedrin reassembled at Usha. The outstanding scholars of this period included Simeon ben Gamaliel II, Eleazar ben Shammua, Jose ben Halafta, Judah bar Illai, Simeon bar Yohai and Meir. Under these sages, the Sanhedrin emerged as the decisive force in Jewish life; through its deliberations the legal decisions of previous generations were systematized and disseminated.

By the third century economic conditions in Galilee improved and the Jewish population attained a harmonious relationship with the Roman administration. The most important Jewish scholar of this period was Judah ha-Nasi whose main achievement was the redaction of the Mishnah. This volume consisted of the discussions and rulings of scholars whose teaching had been transmitted orally. According to the rabbis, the law recorded in the Mishnah was given orally to Moses along with the written law:

> Moses received the Torah from Sinai, and handed it down to Joshua and to the Elders, and Elders to the Prophets, and Prophets to the men of the Great Assembly.
>
> (Avot 1:1)

14

This view implies that there is an infallible chain of transmission from Moses to the leaders of the nation and eventually to the Pharisees.

The Mishnah itself is almost entirely legal in content, consisting of six sections (or orders) comprising a series of chapters (known as tractates) on specific subjects. The first order (Seeds) begins with a discussion of benedictions and required prayers and continues with the other tractates dealing with various matters (such as the tithes of the harvest to be given to priests, Levites and the poor). The second order (Set Feasts) contains twelve tractates dealing with the Sabbath, Passover, the Day of Atonement and other festivals as well as shekel dues and the proclamation of the New Year. In the third second (Women) seven tractates consider matters affecting women (such as betrothal, marriage contracts, and divorce). The fourth section (Damages) contains ten tractates concerning civil laws, property rights, legal procedures, compensation for damage, ownership of lost objects, treatment of employees, sale and purchase of land, Jewish courts, punishments, criminal proceedings, etc.). In addition, a tractate of rabbinic moral maxims (Sayings of the Fathers) is included in this order. In the fifth section (Holy Things) there are eleven tractates on sacrifical offerings and other Temple matters. The final section (Purifications) treats in twelve tractates the various types of ritual uncleanliness and methods of purification.

The Sanhedrin which had been so fundamental in the compilation of this work met in several cities in Galilee, but later settled in the Roman district of Tiberius. The Nasi remained the head of the Sanhedrin, but other scholars established their own schools in other parts of the country where they applied the Mishnah to everyday life together with old rabbinic teachings (beraitot) which had not been incorporated in the Mishnah. By the first half of the fourth century Jewish scholars in Israel had collected together the teachings of generations of rabbis in the academies of Tiberius, Caesarea and Sepphoris. These extended discussions of the Mishnah became the Palestinian Talmud. The text of this multi-volume work covered four sections of the Mishnah (Seeds, Set Feasts, Women and Damages), but here and there various tractates were missing. No doubt the discussion in these academies included matters in these missing tractates, but it is not known how far the recording, editing and arrangement of these sections had progressed before they were lost. The views of these Palestinian teachers had an important influence on scholars in Babylonia, though this work never attained the same prominence as that of the Babylonian Talmud.

During this period those Jews who had been exiled in Babylonia participated in a similar scholarly enterprise. While post-Mishnaic scholars in Israel engaged in learned debate about the application of Jewish law, the third century teacher Rav founded an academy at Sura and his contemporary Samuel was simultaneously head of another Babylonian academy at Nehardea. After Nehardea was destroyed in an invasion in 259 CE, the school at Pumbeditha became a dominant academy of Jewish learning. By the sixth century Babylonian scholars completed the redaction of the Babylonian Talmud – an editorial task began by Rav Ashi in the fourth century at Sura.

This massive work parallels the Palestinian Talmud and is largely a summary of the Amoraic discussions that took place in the Babylonian academies. Both Talmuds are essentially elaborations of the Mishnah though neither commentary contains material on every Mishnah passage. The Palestinian Talmud treats thirty-nine Mishnaic tractates whereas the Babylonian deals with slightly fewer (thirty-seven), but the Babylonian Talmud is 2,500,000 words, nearly four times the size of the Palestinian Talmud. The text itself consists largely of summaries of rabbinic discussions: a phrase of Mishnah is interpreted, discrepancies resolved, and redundancies explained. In this compilation conflicting opinions of earlier sages are contrasted, unusual words explained, and anonymous opinions identified.

Frequently individual teachers cite specific cases to support their views and hypothetical eventualities are examined to reach a solution to the discussion. Debates between outstanding scholars in one generation are often cited, as are differences of opinion between contemporary members of an academy or a teacher and his students. The range of Talmudic exploration is much broader than that of the Mishnah itself and includes a wide range of rabbinic teachings about such subjects as theology, philosophy and ethics. This non-legal material is usually presented as digressions and comprises about one third of the Babylonian Talmud.

Unlike the Mishnah and Talmud which consist largely of legislation presented without explicit references to Scriptural sources, Midrash (rabbinic commentary on Scripture) focuses on the contemporary relevance of specific biblical texts. The early legal Midrash consists of commentaries on the legal verses of the Bible such as the *Mekhilta* on Exodus and the *Sifrei* on Numbers and Deuteronomy. Narrative Midrash, on the other hand, derives from sermons given by sages in synagogues and academies and includes such texts as *Midrash Rabbah* (a series of commentaries on the Pentateuch and the Hagiographa: the

Song of Songs, Ruth, Lamentations, Ecclesiastes and Esther). Though the rabbis were not speculative philosophers, they nevertheless expressed their theological views in these works and attempted to apply this teaching to daily life.

In the interpretation of Scripture the rabbis employed both direct and explicit exegesis where the Biblical text is commented upon or accompanied by a remark as well as indirect exegesis where a Scriptural passage is cited to support an assertion. As an example of the first type, it was common practice among the rabbis to clear up a possible confusion about the meaning of a Biblical verse. In a Midrash on Psalms, for example, Simlai (third century CE) explained that the fact that Psalm 50 begins with the words 'The Mighty One, God the Lord speaks' does not signify that God has a trinitarian nature. Rather 'all three appelations are only one name, even as one man can be called workman, builder, architect. The psalmist mentions these three names to teach you that God created the world with three names, corresponding with the three good attributes by which the world was created.'

The rabbis also frequently reinforced their exhortations by a Biblical sentence which expressed their sentiments. Such a homiletical use of Scripture was illustrated in the first century BCE by Simeon ben Shetach, who declared in a Midrash on Deuteronomy:

> When you are judging, and there come before you two men, of whom one is rich and the other poor, do not say, 'The poor man's words are to be believed, but not the rich man's.' But just as you listen to the words of the poor man, so listen to the words of the rich man, for it is said, 'Ye shall not be partial in judgement.' (Deuteronomy 1:17)

Turning to the method of indirect exegesis, it was a frequent practice in rabbinic literature to draw deductions from Scriptural texts by means of a number of formal hermeneutical rules. Hillel the elder who flourished about a century before the destruction of the second Temple, is reported to have been the first to lay down these principles. Hillel's seven rules were expanded in the second century CE by Ishmael ben Elisha into thirteen by sub-dividing some of them, omitting one, and adding a new one of his own. The first rule (the inference from minor and major) states that if a certain restriction applies to a matter of minor importance, we may infer that the same restriction is applicable to that which is of comparatively minor importance. Conversely, if a certain allowance is applicable to a thing

17

of major importance, we may infer that the same allowance pertains to that which is of comparatively minor importance. In the Mishnah, for example, we read that the Sabbath is in some respects regarded as being of more importance than a common holiday. If therefore a certain kind of work is permitted on the Sabbath, we may infer that such work is more permissible on a common holiday; conversely, if a certain work is forbidden on a common holiday, it must be all the more forbidden on the Sabbath.

Another rule of indirect exegesis (rule six) was intended to solve a problem by means of a comparison with another passage in Scripture. For example, in the Talmud the question why Moses had to hold up his hands during the battle with Amalek (Exodus 17:11) is answered by referring to Numbers 21:8. There the text states that in order to be cured from snakebite the Israelites were to look at the fiery serpent raised up in the wilderness. The hands of Moses could no more bring victory than could the brass serpent cure those who had been bitten. but the point is that, just as in the case of the fiery serpent, it was necessary for the Israelites to lift up their hearts to God in order to be saved.

Such methods of exegesis were based on the conviction that the Bible is sacred, that it is susceptible of interpretation and that, properly understood, it guides the life of the worthy. By means of this process of explanation of God's revelation, the rabbinic authorities were able to infuse the tradition with new meaning and renewed relevance. The literary outpouring of the first few centuries of Pharisaic Judaism bears witness to the fervent conviction that God's eternal word can have a living message for each generation of Jewry.

Rabbinic Theology and Ethics

Unlike the Mishnah which consists of legislation presented without explicit reference to a Scriptural source, rabbinic narrative focuses on the contemporary relevance of specific Biblical texts. The early halachic (legal) Midrashim consist of commentaries on the legal verses of the Bible such as the *Mekhilta* on Exodus and the *Sifrei* on Numbers and Deuteronomy. Narrative Midrashim, on the other hand, derive from sermons given by the sages in synagogues and academies. Though the rabbis were not speculative philosophers like the Greeks, they nevertheless expressed their theological views in these works and attempted to apply this teaching to daily life. This

Midrashic literature along with the narrative sections of the Talmud serves as the basis for reconstructing the theology of early rabbinic Judaism.

Within these texts the rabbis expressed their theological views by means of stories, legends, parables and maxims based on Scripture. According to the sages of the Midrashim and the Talmud, God's unity was of paramount importance; repeatedly they pointed out that though God has many different Hebrew names in the Bible, he is always the same. In the light of this belief, rabbinic literature condemns idolatry even more vigorously than the Bible. Thus a Midrash on Numbers proclaims: 'He who renounces idolatry is as if he professed the whole Law.' For the rabbis God is a transcendent creator, yet he is imminent as well. As the Talmud explains, he is near to all who call upon him: 'God is far and yet he is near . . . For a man enters a synagogue and stands behind a pillar, and prays in a whisper, and God hears his prayer, and so it is with all his creatures. Can there be a nearer God than this? He is as near to his creatures as the ear to the mouth.'

The view of the rabbis regarding God's omniscience and human free will was summarized in a statement by Akiva in the second century CE: 'All is foreseen but freedom of choice is given; and the world is judged with goodness, and all is in accordance with thy works.' Here it is asserted that although God knows all things, human beings have nevertheless been accorded free will and as a consequence they will be judged on the basis of their actions. But such judgement is tempered by mercy as a Midrash on Leviticus records: 'In the hour when the Israelites take up their ram's horns, and blow them before God, he gets up from the throne of judgement and sits down upon the throne of mercy and he is filled with compassion for them, and he turns the attribute of judgement into the attribute of mercy.'

For the rabbis God is concerned with all humankind but the Jewish people play a special role in the divine plan. Israel's love of God is reciprocated by God's tender loving concern. In the words of Simeon bar Yohai (second century CE): 'Like a king who entrusted his son to a tutor, and kept asking him, "Does my son eat, does he drink, has he gone to school, has he come back from school?" So God yearns to make mention of the Israelites at every hour.' It is out of this love that God has entrusted his chosen people with the Torah; the purpose of Israel's election is to sanctify God's name and be a holy people dedicated to his service. As one Midrash explains: 'It says in Leviticus 11:45, "For I am the Lord who brought you up out of the land of

Egypt, to be your God: you shall therefore be holy, for I am holy." That means, I brought you out of Egypt on the condition that you should receive the yoke of the commandments.'

The Torah also played a central role in the rabbinic depiction of the Afterlife. This conception was a significant development from Biblical Judaism in which there was no explicit doctrine of eternal salvation. According to rabbinic sources, the World to Come is divided into several stages. First, there is the period of messianic redemption which is to take place on earth after a period of decline and calamity and will result in the complete fulfilment of every human aspiration. Peace will reign throughout nature; Jerusalem will be rebuilt, and at the close of this era the dead will be resurrected and rejoined with their souls, and the final judgment will come upon all humanity. Those Jews who have fulfilled the precepts of the law and are thereby judged righteous will enter into Heaven (Gan Eden) as well as gentiles who have lived in accord with the Noachide laws (the laws which Noah and his descendents took upon themselves).

These central themes within rabbinic theology do not exhaust the scope of rabbinic speculation. In addition, early rabbinic authorities discussed a wide variety of religious issues including martyrdom, prayer, charity, atonement, forgiveness, repentance and peace. Within rabbinic sources, the sages expressed their profound reflections on human life and God's nature and activity in the world. Unlike the legal precepts of the Torah and the rabbinic expansion of these Scriptural ordinances, these theological opinions were not binding on the Jewish community. They were formulated instead to educate, inspire and edify those to whom they were addressed. Study of the Torah was a labour of love which had no end, a task whose goal was to serve the will of God.

In addition to such theological speculation, the rabbis were preoccupied with moral matters. In their view, moral precepts are grounded in the will of God; hence the Torah serves as the blueprint for ethical action, and it is through the admonitions of the rabbis in Midrashic and Talmudic sources that the Jewish people were encouraged to put the teachings of the law into effect in their everyday lives. In this context, a number of distinctive characteristics of Jewish morality are expressed in the tradition. First, rabbinic ethics require that each person be treated equally. Rabbinic sources show a constant concern to eliminate arbitrary distinctions between individuals so as to establish a proper balance between competing claims. On the basis of the Biblical view that everyone is created in the image of God, the rabbis declared that false and irrelevant distinctions must not be introduced to disqualify human beings from the right to justice.

A second characteristic of Jewish morality is its emphasis on human motivation. The Jewish faith is not solely concerned with actions and their consequences; it also demands right intention. The rabbis explained: 'The Merciful One requires the heart.' It is true that Judaism emphasizes the importance of action, but the rabbis also focus attention on rightmindedness: inner experiences – motives, feelings, dispositions and attitudes – are of supreme moral significance. For this reason the rabbis identified a group of negative commandments in the Torah involving thought. The following are representative examples: 'Thou shalt not take vengeance, or bear any grudge against the sons of your own people' (Leviticus 19:18). 'There are six things which the Lord hates . . . a heart that devises wicked plans.' (Proverbs 6:16, 18). 'Take heed lest there be a base thought in your heart' (Deuteronomy 15:9). In the Mishnah the rabbis elaborated on this concern for the human heart: in the second century CE Eliezer said, 'Be not easily moved to anger', and Joshua said, 'The evil eye, the evil inclination, and hatred of his fellow creatures drives a man out of the world.' Levitas of Yavneh said, 'Be exceedingly lowly of spirit.'

Thirdly, connected with right thought is the Jewish emphasis on right speech. Rabbinic sources insist that individuals are morally responsible for the words they utter. Evil words spoken about one person by another could arouse hatred and enmity and destroy human relations. The rabbis considered slander to be a particular evil: 'Whoever speaks slander is as though he denied the fundamental principle (existence of God). The Holy One, blessed be He, says of such a person who speaks slander, "I and he cannot dwell together in the world."' There was also a positive aspect to this emphasis on human speech. Just as the rabbis condemned false utterance, they urged their disciples to offer cheerful greetings. Anger could be soothed with gentle words and reconciliation could be brought about.

A fourth dimension of Jewish morality concerns the traditional attitude toward animals. According to the rabbis, human beings are morally obliged to refrain from inflicting pain on animals. We read, for example, of Judah ha-Nasi (2nd century CE): Judah was sitting and studying the Torah in front of the Babylonian synagogue in Sephhoris, when a calf passed before him on its way to the slaughter and began to cry out as though pleading, 'Save me!' Said he to it, 'What can I do for you? For this you were created.' As a punishment for his heartlessness, he suffered toothache for thirteen years. One day, a weasel ran past his daughter, who was about to kill it, when he said to her, 'My daughter, let it be, for it is written, "and his tender mercies are over all his works".' Because Judah prevented an act of cruelty, he was once again restored to heath.

A final aspect of Jewish ethics is its concern for human dignity; the rabbis put a strong emphasis on the respect due to all individuals. The Torah's concern for human dignity even includes thieves. Johanan ben Zakkai pointed out in the first century CE that, according to the law, whoever stole a sheep should pay a fine of four times the value of the sheep; whoever stole an ox must pay five times its value. Those who stole sheep had to undergo the embarrassment of carrying the sheep off in their arms, and the Torah compensated them for this indignity, but those who stole oxen were spared such embarrassment because they could simply lead the ox by its tether.

These specific qualities of Jewish ethics illustrate their humane orientation to all of God's creatures. Throughout rabbinic literature, Jews were encouraged to strive for the highest conception of life in which the rule of truth, righteousness and holiness would be established among humankind. Such a desire is the eternal hope of God's people – a longing for God's kingdom. The coming of God's rule requires a struggle for the reign of justice and righteousness on earth. The Kingdom is not an internalized, spiritualized, other-worldly concept, rather it involves human activity in a historical context.

The Mystical Tradition

Within rabbinic sources the sages also engaged in mystical speculation based on the biblical text. These doctrines were frequently of a secret nature; in a Midrash on Genesis it is reported that these mystical traditions were repeated in a whisper so they would not be overheard by those for whom they were not intended. Thus in the third century Simeon ben Jehozedek asked Samuel Nahman: 'Seeing that I have heard you are adept at aggadah, tell me how light was created.' He replied in a whisper, upon which the other sage retorted. 'Why do you tell this in a whisper, seeing that it is taught clearly in a Scritural verse?' The first sage responded: 'Just as I have myself had it whispered to me, even so I have whispered it to you.' Such knowledge was restricted to a select group of scholars. In the same century, Judah, for example, said in the name of Rab that God's secret name could only be entrusted to one who is 'modest and meek, in the midway of life, not easily provoked to anger, temperate, and free from vengeful feelings.'

In their mystical reflections, the first chapter of Ezekiel played an important role in early rabbinic mysticism. In this Biblical text the divine chariot (Merkavah) is described in detail, and this Scriptural source served as the basis for rabbinic speculation about the nature of the Deity. It was the aim of the mystic to be a 'Merkavah rider' so that he would be able to penetrate the heavenly mysteries. Within this contemplative system, the rabbis believed that the pious could free themselves from the fetters of bodily existence and enter paradise. A further dimension of this theory is that certain pious individuals can temporarily ascend into the unseen realm and having learnt the deepest secrets may return to Earth. These mystics were able to attain a state of ecstasy, to behold visions and hear voices. As students of the Merkavah they were the ones able to attain the highest degree of spiritual insight. A description of the experiences of these Merkavah mystics is contained in Hekhalot (heavenly hall) literature from the later Gaonic period (from the seventh to the eleventh centuries CE). In order to make their heavenly ascent, these mystics followed strict ascetic disciplines, including fasting, ablution and the invocation of God's name. After reaching a state of ecstasy, the mystic was able to enter the seven heavenly halls and attain a vision of the divine chariot.

Closely associated with this form of speculation were mystical theories about creation (Maaseh Bereshit). Within rabbinic courses scholars discussed the hidden meanings of the Genesis narrative. The most important early treatise, possibly from the second century CE, which describes the process of creation is *The Book of Creation (Sefer Yetsirah)*. According to this cosmological text God created the universe by thirty-two mysterious paths consisting of twenty-two letters of the Hebrew alphabet together with ten emanations (sefirot). Of these twenty-two letters we read: 'He hewed them, combined them, weighed them, interchanged them, and through them produced the whole creation and everything that is destined to come into being.'

These letters are of three types: mothers, doubles and singles. The mothers (Shin, Mem, Aleph) symbolize the three primordial elements of all existing things: water (the frist letter of which is Mem in Hebrew) is symbolized by Mem; fire (of which Shin is the most prominent sound) is represented by Shin; air (the first letter of which in Hebrew is Aleph) is designated by Aleph. These three mothers represent in the microcosm (the human form), 'the head, the belly and the chest – the head from fire; the belly from water, and the chest from the air that lies in between.'

In addition to these three mother letters, there are seven double letters (Beth, Gimel, Daleth, Caph, Peh, Resh, Tau) which signify the contraries in the universe (forces which serve two mutually opposed ends). These letters were 'formed, designed, created and combined into the stars in the universe, the days of the week, and the orifices of perception in man . . . two eyes, two ears, two nostrils, and a mouth through which he perceives by his senses.' Finally, there are twelve simple letters (He, Vav, Zayin, Chet, Tet, Yod, Lamed, Nun, Samek, Ayin, Tsade, Kof) which correspond to man's chief activities – sight, hearing, smell, speech, desire for food, the sexual appetite, movement, anger, mirth, thought, sleep and work. The letters are also emblematic of the twelve signs of the zodiac in the heavenly sphere, the twelve months, and the chief limbs of the body. Thus man, world and time are linked to one another through the process of creation by means of the Hebrew alphabet.

These recondite doctrines are supplemented by a theory of divine emanation through the ten sefirot (emanations). The first of the sefirot is the spirit of the living God; air is the second of the sefirot and is derived from the first – on it are hewn the twenty-two letters. The third sefirah is the water that comes from the air: 'It is in the water that he has dug the darkness and the chaos, that he has formed the earth and the clay, which was spread out afterwards in the form of a carpet, hewn out like a wall and covered as though by a roof.' The fourth of the sefirot is the fire which comes from water through which God made the heavenly wheels, the seraphim and the ministering angels. The remaining six sefirot are the six dimensions of space – north, south, east, west, height, and depth.

These ten sefirot are the moulds into which all created things were originally cast. They constitute form rather than matter. The twenty-two letters, on the other hand, are the prime cause of matter: everything that exists is due to the creative force of the Hebrew letters, but they receive their form from the sefirot. According to this cosmological doctrine, God transcends the universe; nothing exists outside of him. The visible world is the result of the emanation of the divine: God is the cause of the form and matter of the cosmos. By combining emanation and creation in this manner, the *Sefer Yetsirah* attempts to harmonize the concept of divine imminence and transcendence. God is imminent in that the sefirot are an outpouring of his spirit, and he is transcendent in that the matter which was shaped into the forms is the product of his creative action.

The mystical texts of early rabbinic Judaism were studied by Jewish settlers in the Rhineland from approximately the ninth century. During the twelfth and thirteenth centuries these authorities – the Hasidei Ashkenaz – delved into Hekhalot literature, the *Sefer Yetsirah*, as well as the philosophical works of such scholars as Saadiah Gaon and various Spanish and Italian Jewish Neo-Platonists. Among the greatest figures of this period were the twelfth-century Samuel ben Kalonymus of Speyer, his son Judah ben Samuel of Regensburg, and Eleazar ben Judah of Worms. Though the writings of these and other mystics were not systematic in character, their works do display a number of common characteristics.

In their studies these mystics were preoccupied with the mystery of divine unity. God himself, they believed, cannot be known by human reason – thus all anthropomorphic depictions of God in Scripture should be understood as referring to God's glory which was formed out of divine fire. This divine glory – kavod – was revealed by God to the prophets and is made manifest to mystics in different ways through the ages. The aim of German mysticism was to attain a vision of God's glory through the cultivation of the life of pietism which embraced devotion, saintliness and contemplation. The ultimate sacrifice for these pietists was martyrdom, and during this period there were ample opportunities for Jews to die in this way in the face of Christian persecution. Allied to such a manifestation of selfless love of God was the emphasis on a profound sense of God's presence in the world; for these sages God's glory permeates all things.

Parallel with these developments in Germany, Jewish mystics in southern France engaged in mystical speculation about the nature of God, the soul, the existence of evil and the religious life. In twelfth century Provence the earliest kabbalistic text, the *Bahir*, reinterpreted the concept of the sefirot as depicted in the *Sefer Yetsirah*. According to the *Bahir*, the sefirot are conceived as vessels, crowns or words that constitute the structure of the divine realm. Basing themselves on this anonymous work, various Jewish sages of Provence engaged in similar mystic reflection. Isaac the Blind, the son of Abraham ben David of Posquières, for example, conceived of the sefirot as emanations of a hidden dimension of the Godhead. Utilizing Neo-Platonic ideas, he argued that out of the infinite (Ayn Sof) emanated the first supernal essence, the Divine Thought, from which came the remaining sefirot. Beings in the world beneath, he believed, are materializations of the sefirot at lower degrees of reality. The purpose of mystical activity is to ascend the ladder of emanations to unite with Divine Thought.

In Gerona the traditions of Isaac the Blind were broadly disseminated. one of the most important of these Geronese kabbalists was Azriel ben Menahem who replaced the Divine Thought with the Divine Will as the first emanation of the Ayn Sof. The most famous figure of this circle was Moses ben Nahman (Nahmanides) who helped this mystical school gain general acceptance. His involvement in kabbalistic speculation combined with his halachic authority persuaded many Jews that mystical teachings were compatible with rabbinic Judaism. In his commentary on the Torah he frequently referred to kabbalistic notions to explain the true meaning of Scripture.

During the time that these Geronese mystics were propounding their kabbalistic theories, different mystical schools of thought developed in other parts of Spain. Influenced by the Hasidei Ashkenaz and the Sufi traditions of Islam, Abraham ben Samuel Abulafia wrote meditative texts concerning the technique of combining the letters of the alphabet as a means of realizing human aspirations toward prophecy. As an admirer of Maimonides, he believed his system was a continuation and elaboration of the teaching of the *Guide for the Perplexed*. Another Spanish kabbalist, Isaac Ibn Latif, also attempted to elaborate ideas found in Maimonides' *Guide*. For ibn Latif, the Primeval Will is the source of all emanation. Adopting Neo-Platonic concepts, he argued that from the first created thing emanated all the other stages, referred to symbolically as light, fire, ether, and water. Each of these, he believed, is the subject of a branch of wisdom: mysticism, metaphysics, astronomy and physics. According to ibn Latif, kabbalah is superior to philosophy – the highest intellectual understanding reaches only the 'back' of the Divine whereas the 'face' is disclosed only in supra-intellectual ecstasy.

Other Spanish kabbalists were more attracted to Gnostic ideas. Isaac ha-Kohen, for example, elaborated the theory of a demonic emanation whose ten spheres are counterparts of the holy sefirot. The mingling of such Gnostic teaching with the kabbalah of Gerona resulted in the publication of the major mystic work of Spanish Jewry, the *Zohar*, composed by Moses ben Shem Tov de Leon in Guadalajara. Although the author places the work in a second century CE setting, focusing on Simeon bar Yochai and his disciples after the Bar Kochba uprising, the doctrines of the *Zohar* are of a much later origin. Written in Aramaic, the text is largely a Midrash in which the Torah is given a mystical or ethical interpretation.

The Emergence of Medieval Jewry

By the sixth century the Jews had become largely a diaspora people. Despite the loss of a homeland, they were unified by a common heritage: law, liturgy and shared traditions bound together the scattered communities stretching from Spain to Persia and Poland to Africa. During the eighth century messianic movements appeared in the Persian Jewish community which led to uprisings against Muslim authorities. Such revolts were quickly crushed, but an even more serious threat to traditional Jewish life was posed by the Karaites. This group was founded in Babylonia in the 760s by Anan ben David, who had earlier been passed over as exilarch. According to some scholars, Anan's movement absorbed elements of an extra-Talmudic tradition and took over doctrines from Islam. The guiding interpretative principle formulated by Anan, 'Search thoroughly in Scripture and do not rely on my opinion', was intended to point to Scripture itself as the sole source of law. Jewish observances, the Karaites insisted, must conform to Biblical legislation rather than rabbinic ordinances.

During the same century that Karaism began to challenge rabbinic Judaism, the Muslim empire began to undergo a process of disintegration. When Abbasid caliphs conquered the Ummayads in 750 CE, Spain remained independent under a Ummayad ruler. As the century progressed, the Abbasids began to lose control of the outlying territories. After 850 Turkish troops managed to gain control over the Abbasids and the caliph became essentially a figurehead behind which Turkish generals exerted power. In 909 Shi'ite Muslims took control over North Africa; in 969 they conquered Egypt and Israel. By the end of the tenth century the Islamic world was divided into a number of separate states pitted against one another.

The disappearance of the political unity of the Islamic empire was accompanied by a decentralization of rabbinic Judaism. The rabbinic academies of Babylonia began to lose their hold on the Jewish academic world; in many places yeshivot (rabbinic schools) were created in which rabbinic sources were expounded. The growth of these local centres of learning enabled individual teachers to exert their influence on Jewish learning independent of the academies of Sura and Pumbeditha. The locality in which the local rabbinate asserted itself was the Holy Land. Tiberias was the location of the rabbinical academy there as well as the centre of the Masoretic scholars such as the families of Ben Asher and Ben Naphtali who produced the standard tradition (Masorah) of the Bible by adding vowels and punctuation to the Hebrew text. By the ninth century the rabbinic academy moved to Ramleh and then to Jerusalem; this institution was supported by the Turkish communities of Egypt, Yemen and Syria, but due to Turkish and Christian invasions its influence waned in the eleventh century.

Egyptian Jewry also underwent a transformation during this period. Under the Fatimids Jewish life prospered in Egypt, and by the end of the tenth century a yeshiva had been established in Cairo. Kairouan had also become a centre of scholarship: at this time academies were established by distinguished Talmudists and affluent Jewish families who supported Jewish scientists and philosophers. The city of Fez also reached a degree of eminence, producing one of the most important rabbinic scholars of the period, Isaac Alfasi who compiled an influential code of Jewish law. But it was in Spain that the Jewish community attained the greatest level of achievement. In the tenth-century Spanish royal court the Ummayad caliphs, Abd Al-Rahman III and Hakam II employed the Jewish statesman Hisdai ibn Shaprut as court physician, administrator and diplomat. In addition he acted as head of the Jewish community and patron of Jewish scholarship. Cordoba, the capital of the Ummayad caliphate, became a vibrant centre of Jewish civilization, attracting poets, grammarians and yeshiva students from throughout the diaspora.

As the Ummayad caliphate began to disintegrate in the eleventh century, small Muslim principalities were often at odds with one another. Several of the rulers of these states used Jewish courtiers, such as Samuel ibn Nagrela of Granada in their adminstrations. This figure was knowledgeable about mathematics and philosophy, writing in Hebrew and Arabic; in addition, he served a vizier of Granada for thirty years. In commemoration of his own miliarty victiories he composed Hebrew poetry as well as an introduction to the Talmud. Other scholars of the period lived in Seville, Saragossa, Toledo, Calatayud and Lucena, which became reknowned for its Jewish academy.

In 1086 the life of Spainish Jewry was shaken when the Almoravides from North Africa were invited to Spain to lead an attack on Christian communities in the north and persecuted the Jewish population. Soon, however, Jews were restored to their former positions and the next generation saw outstanding poets, philosophers, Biblical commentators, theologians, and rabbinic authorities. But in the middle of the twelfth century the golden age of Spanish

Jewry came to an end. Fearing Christian conquest, the Almohades – a Berber dynasty from Morocco – came to defend the country and simultaneously persecuted the Jewish population. Jews were forced to convert to Islam, and academies and synagogues were closed. Some Jews practised Judaism in secret; others escaped to the Middle East or migrated to Christian Spain. At the beginning of the thrirteen century the dominance of the Almohades came to an end when Christian kingdoms managed to seize control of most of the former Muslim territories in Spain.

In other parts of the Muslim empire, Jews faced changing circumstances during these centuries. In the mid-twelfth century, during the Almohade persecution, some Spanish Jews migrated to Egypt, including the philosopher Moses Maimonides. In Israel a small Jewish community survived during the Crusades and was augmented by Jewish pilgrims who went to the Holy Land. Babylonian Jewry continued after the death of the last important gaon, Hai bar Sherira in 1038 but the Mongol invasions in the middle of the thirteenth century had devestating consequences for the region.

The Muslims, however, did not manage to conquer all of Europe in their campaigns in the seventh century – many countries remained under Christian rule as did much of the Byzantine empire. The early Jewish communities in western Europe lived in small, self-contained groupings and engaged in local trades. The Jews of each town constituted a separate unit since there was no equivalent of an exilarch (as in Muslim lands) to serve as the official leader of the Jewish population. Instead, each community (kahal) set its own rules and adminsitered local courts, in a form of self-government which was the Ashkenazic adaption to the feudal structure of medieval Christian Europe.

In this environment Jewish study took place in a number of important centres such as Mainz and Worms in the Rhineland and Troyes and Sens in northern France and produced such leading scholars as Rabbenu Gershom of Mainz and Solomon ben Isaac of Troyes (Rashi). In subsequent generations, the study of the Talmud reached great heights: in Germany and northern France scholars known as the tosafists utilized new methods of Talmudic interpretation. In addition, Ashkenzaic Jews of this period composed religious poetry modelled on the liturgical compositions (piyyutim) of fifth and sixth century Israel.

Despite this effloresence of Jewish learning, Jews in Chritian countries were subject to frequent oubursts of anti-Jewish sentiment.

In 1095 Pope Urban II proclaimed the First Crusade – an act which stimulated mobs in the Rhineland in 1096 to attack Jews in towns such as Worms and Mainz. Jews in these communities willing martyred themselves as an act of sanctification rather than convert to the Christian faith. These massacres at the end of the century were not officially authorized by the state, and Jews who had converted under duress were subsequently allowed to return to the Jewish tradition.

In the following two centuries the Jewish community of Christian Europe became increasingly more involved in moneylending as the Christian guilds forced Jews out of trade. The practice of usury intensified anti-Semitism especially by those who were unable to pay back loans. Added to this economic motive, Christians in the Middle Ages persecuted the Jews on religious grounds: the Jew was stereotyped as a demonic Christ-killer and murderer. As early as 1144 in Norwich, England, the Jewish community was accused of killing Christian children at Passover to use their blood in the preparation of unleavened bread. Later the same accusation was made in Blois, France, in 1171 and in Lincoln, England, in 1255. Another frequent charge against the Jews was that they defamed the host in order to torture Jesus' body. Further, Jews were also regarded with enmity since they obtained Church property through defaulted loans. Such factors led the fourth Lateran Council in 1215 to strengthen the Church's restrictions regarding the Jewish people.

In the same century Dominican priests were active against the Jewish community. In 1240 they participated in a disputation about the Talmud in Paris with leading Jewish scholars; as a result of the debate, the Talmud was condemned and all copies burned. Expulsion of the Jews from countries in which they lived also became a dominant policy of Christian Europe. In 1182 the king of France, Philip Augustus, expelled all Jews from the royal domains near Paris, cancelled nearly all Christian debts to Jewish moneylenders, and confiscated Jewish property. Though the Jews were recalled in 1198, they were burdened with an additional royal tax, and in the next century they increasingly became the property of the king. In thirteenth-century England the Jews were continuously taxed and the entire Jewish population was expelled in 1290, as was that in France by Philip IV some years later. At the end of the thirteenth century in Germany, the Jewish community suffered violent attack. Subsequently in the next century, Jews were blamed for bringing about the Black Death by poisoning the wells of Europe, and from 1348 to 1349 Jews in France, Switzerland, Germany and Belgium suffered at the hands of their Christian neighbours. In the following two centuries, Jewish massacre and expulsion became a frequent occurance.

Chapter 2

9th–11th Centuries

In the Hellenistic period the Jewish philosopher Philo attempted to integrate Greek philosophy and Jewish teaching into a unified whole. By applying the allegorical method of interpretation to Scripture, he explained the God of Judaism in Greek philosophical categories and reshaped Jewish notions about God, human beings and the world. Philo was the precursor of medieval Jewish philosophy which attempted to combine alternative philosophical systems with the received biblical tradition. The beginnings of this philosophical development took place in ninth century Babylonia during the height of the Abbasid caliphate when rabbinic Judaism was challenged by Karaite scholars who criticized the anthropomorphic views of God in Midrashic and Talmudic sources. Added to this internal threat was the Islamic contention that Muhammad's revelation in the Koran superseded the Jewish faith. In addition Zoroastrians and Manichaeans attacked monotheism as a viable religious system. Finally some gentile philosophers argued that the Greek scientific and philosophical world view could account for the origin of the cosmos without reference to an external Deity. In combatting these challenges, Jewish writers were influenced by the teachings of Muslim schools (kalam) of the eighth to the eleventh centuries. In their attempt to defend Judaism from internal and external assault, a number of thinkers sought to adapt the Mu'tazilite kalam as a line of defense, and as time passed also employed other aspects of Graeco-Arabic thought including Aristotelianism and Neoplatonism as well as astrological theories in their expositions of the Jewish faith.

David Al-Mukammis

Born c. 900 David Ibn Marwan Al-Raqi Al-Shirazi (also known as David ha-Bavli or David Al-Mukammis) was one of the first Jewish philosophers of the Middle Ages. According to the Karaite scholar *Jacob Al-Kirkisani, he was a Jew who contemplated converting to Christianity while a student of the Christian philosopher, Nonnus, who lived at Nisibis. But when he gained a greater knowledge of the Christian faith, he composed two tracts critical of Christianity. Yet it is not known for certain whether he converted or not. In any event, Al-Mukammis translated Christian commentaries on Genesis and Ecclesiastes as well as studies of different religions and sects.

Discussing Al-Mukammis' contribution to early medieval Jewish thought, Al-Kirkisani writes:

> Da'ud ibn Marwan al-Rakki, known as Al-Mukammis, has written a fine book containing a commentary on Genesis, which he translated from the commentaries of the Syrians. But in some places he did not say all that needed to be said about the intended meaning of the Sacred Text, while in other places he was guilty of foolish verbosity for which there was no need. Another scholar of our own time also composed a fine book on this subject in which he followed a method similar to that of Da'ud. We shall extract the best part of both works and we shall add thereto that which they, in our opinion, have neglected to mention or have failed to explain adequately.
>
> (in Nemoy, 1932, 54)

A manuscript which contains most of his religious views, *Twenty Treatises*, is extant in the St. Petersburg library but only a small section of the Arabic original of this text has been published; this corresponds to one of the sections of a partial Hebrew translation of a work forming a section of Judah ben Barzillai al-Bargeloni's commentary on the *Sefer Yetsirah (Book of Creation)*. Al-Mukammis' study deals with topics including knowledge and truth, substance and accident, the existence of God, God's unity and attributes, prophecy, and the divine commandments.

Those sections of the extant parts of this work reveal that Al-Mukammis was influenced by the Mu'tazilites (even though he embraced some of the theories of Greek philosophers). In his view, the attributes of God are not independent of his essence, thereby making God into a multiplicity. Rather God and his attributes are a single unity; it is due to the limitations of human language that require the faithful to describe God in such terms. According to Al-Mukammis, positive attributes should be understood negatively: they should be perceived as implying what God is not as opposed to what he is.

For Al-Mukammis, God is a perfect unity, not in the sense that that a genus or a species is one, but as being devoid of plurality. He is first and last, the cause and ground of all things. Concerning God's essence, Al-Mukammis points out that some say it is not permissible to ask what God is because any answer would in some sense limit the Deity. Others, however, stress that although it is permitted to pose such a question because Scripture provides an authoritative response, this is no way poses a limit to his nature. On this account, God should be understood as first and last, visible and hidden, without beginning or end. He is living, but not through acquiring life independently. God is not sustained by food; nor is he wise through acquiring the attribute of wisdom. He hears although he has no ears; he sees without eyes; he is understanding and a true judge. This conception is derived from God's own testimony as recorded in the Bible.

On this view, we should not assume that the expressions 'living', 'wise', 'seeing', 'hearing' and so forth when applied to God mean the same as when attributed to human beings. Thus when we say that God is living we do not mean that there was a time when he was not in existence, or that there will be a time when he will be no more. Similarly God's wisdom is not like ours – it lacks beginning or end, and is not subject to error. God's attributes are totally unlike ours because he is inherently different from anything which has been formed.

On the basis of this conception of divine attributes, it is a mistake to think that the expression 'God is living' means that God has the attribute of life. There was no time when God was not living and then acquired life. Rather, the life that makes God living is eternal, and as a result God was always living and will continue to be so throughout all time. Such a life through which God lives is not distinct from his being. Christians are therefore guilty of distorting God's true nature by introducing external beings alongside him (the Holy Spirit and the Son). If we say that God's life is a part of his being, we are undermining his simplicity – God's life is identical with his being.

This explanation can be made clearer by various illustrations: the body lives through the soul; when the body dies it dies even though the soul does not live through anything else. Instead, the soul lives through itself. Similarly, angels live through their own being: this is why souls and angels are called 'spirits'. A spirit is fine, light and incomposite; as a result, its life cannot be the result of anything distinct from its being which would render it composite.

The claim that souls and angels live through their own being should not be interpreted as suggesting that they were uncreated. Rather, such a view implies that the being bestowed upon them by God is different from what he has given bodies. Bodies need souls to give them life whereas the soul itself is living. Similarly, with regard to material objects: the sun shines with its own light not with light which has been acquired; myrrh is fragrant through itself, not through something else; the eye sees with its own power, but human beings see through their eyes; the tongue does not speak using another tongue, but humans need tongues by which to speak. So when we say of God that he is living, he lives not through a life which is distinct from his being. This conclusion applies to all the other divine attributes which are depicted in Scripture.

Al-Mukammis continues this discussion by adding that just as God's attributes are identical with his being, so the various attributes ascribed to God (such as wise, seeing, hearing, knowing) are not different from each other in meaning – otherwise they would imply that God is composite. The reason we use these various terms is to indicate that God does not possess their opposites. Thus if we say that God is living, we mean that he is not dead. Aristotle maintains that it is more suitable to apply negative attributes (as opposed to positive attributes) to God; others contend that we must not describe the Creator in positive terms since this would endow him with bodily form. Yet speaking of him negatively, we imply positive characteristics without causing offence.

Turning from this discussion of divine attributes, Al-Mukammis focuses on the subject of reward and punishment. In his opinion, reward should be understood as the soul's tranquility and infinite joy in the world; punishment, on the other hand, consists of the soul's disquiet and sorrow as retribution for enjoying evil pleasures. According to Al-Mukammis, God executes justice with equity. It is appropriate, he argues, that the promises of reward and punishment are consequent upon acts of obedience and disobedience. Only in this way will the soul learn self-control. So by commanding human beings to do what is worthy, God has seen fit to delineate what will befall them if they remain faithful to his word or, conversely, what they will be compelled to endure if they violate his commands. In this way God has provided a means whereby the faithful can find pleasure and joy in their obedience, and the unobservant may be afflicted with fear and sorrow. In this context Al-Mukammis insists that the reward of the righteous as well as punishment for the wicked will be without end.

Due to the paucity of information, it is difficult to determine Al-

Mukammis' influence on Jewish thought. Although he was used extensively by the Karaite philosopher Al-Kirkisani, little is known of his impact on subsequent medieval philosophy. None the less, it is possible that he may have served as a link between Jewish and Christian explanations of creation since there are striking parallels between early Christian interpretations of this doctrine in the writings of such thinkers as St Augustine and what is found in Jewish commentaries of the thirteenth and fourteenth century.

Isaac Ben Solomon Israeli

In the evolution of Jewish thought, Isaac Israeli was the first writer after *Philo to integrate Greek notions into the Jewish religious tradition. Born in Egypt in c. 855, he emigrated to Kairouan, capital of the Maghreb, at about the age of 50; there he was appointed court physician by Ubayd Allah al-Mahdi, founder of the Fatimid dynasty. While still in Egypt, the Jewish philosopher *Saadiah Gaon addressed several letters to him regarding philosophical and scientific issues. It appears that he never married and died possibly before 932 (although it is possible that he lived until 955). According to tradition, Israeli declared that four of his books – Book on Fevers, Book of Aliments and Drugs, Book on Urines, and Book on the Elements – would secure his reputation. In any event, his medical texts were translated into Hebrew and Latin and continued to be used until the end of the Middle Ages.

Despite his eminence as a medical authority, his reputation as a philosopher was less general. According to *Maimonides, he was simply a doctor. Whatever the correct evaluation, Israeli was preoccupied with Neoplatonic ideas in his various philosophical works. In formulating his theories, he made use of the works of Al-Kindi, an Arab philosopher of the early ninth century who had access to numerous Greek texts, as well as a treatise by an anonymous Neoplatonic philosopher. In addition, he borrowed from Aristotelian thought the concept of the four sublunary elements as well as the quintessence of which the spheres are composed. His surviving works include:

1 The Book of Definitions. This is perhaps the best known of his philosophical studies. It was quoted by Moses Ibn Ezra in The Book of the Garden; other citations are found in the Arabic work, The Aim of the Wise. Two Latin translations

date from the twelfth century, while Nissim ben Solomon's Hebrew translation was in all likelihood made before 1200, and another Hebrew translation was made somewhat later.

2 *The Book of Substances.* This work, discovered in St. Petersburg, appears to have been written in Arabic characters, although the extant manuscripts are in Hebrew.

3 *The Book on Spirit and Soul.* This is preserved in a Hebrew translation and is possibly part of a larger work; it is the only one of Israeli's studies that refers to the Bible.

4 *The Book on the Elements.* This exists in two Hebrew translations, one of which was made by Abraham Ibn Hasdai at the request of David Kimhi.

5 *Chapter on the Elements.* This has been attributed to Israeli by several modern scholars even though the texts contains an attribution to Aristotle.

In expounding his views, Israeli locates himself in the Aristotelian tradition by focusing on Aristotle's four types of inquiry. Yet it is clear from the contents of Israeli's works that he stands firmly within the Neoplatonic tradition. According to Neoplatonic theory, the universe is structured hierarchically. Between God who is perfect and the imperfect lower world are placed essences that join the immaterial God with the material domain. In Israeli's view, the First Matter and the First Form both emerge from God: these then engender the Intellect. From the Intellect emanates the world of souls (the rational soul, the animal soul, and the vegetative soul). This is followed by the world of the spheres, and then the sublunary world with four elements and their compounds. At the centre of this complex is earth which is a mixture of the four elements (earth, water, air and fire). The spheres which are made of a more perfect substance – the quintessence – revolve around the earth, and by these movements form compounds.

In expounding this theory, Israeli cites Aristotle as a source for understanding the nature of First Matter and First Form:

Aristotle the philosopher and master of the wisdom of the Greeks said: 'The beginning of all roots is two simple substances: one of them is first matter, which receives form and is known to the philosophers as the root of roots. It is the first substance which subsists in itself and is the substratum of diversity. The other is substantial form, which is ready to impregnate matter. It is perfect wisdom, pure radiance, and clear splendour, by the conjunction of which with first matter the nature and form of intellect came into being, because it (intellect) is composed of them (matter and form).

(in Altmann and Stern, 1958, 119)

Distancing himself from those Neoplatonists who view First Form and Matter as emanating from God, Israeli argues that they were created ex nihilo. The Intellect then emanates from the conjunction of First Matter and First Form. Israeli goes on to explain that the mode of action of the Intellect and the souls differs from both the spheres and sublunary world. The first is a creation in which nothing is lost of the essential light. It is from the shadow of this light that inferior beings are formed. Beginning with the spheres, the action of nature generates as well as corrupts; the source of this action is diminished and changed by the action which affects bodies with opposite qualities.

In the realm below the celestial sphere, all plants and animals are produced from the elements – fire, air, water and earth – in which one of these four elements predominantes. Only human beings are created of the four elements joined together in a harmonious relationship. Further, Israeli contends that every being which is composed of elements receives a soul in accordance with its nature. Hence, all beings are endowed with souls. As a result, the light that originates in the Intellect penetrates the domain of living beings down to the mineral world. The greater the distance between the light and its source, the darker it becomes even though it does not disappear altogether:

Regarding the quality of the emanation of the light from the power and the will, we have already made it clear that its beginning is different from its end, and the middle from both extremes, and this for the following reason: when its beginning emanated from the power and the will, it met no shade or darkness to make it dim and coarse – while its end met various imperfections and obscurities which made it dim and coarse; the middle partook of both extremes.

(*Ibid.*, 88)

In Israeli's opinion, the rational soul is the highest degree of the soul; for this reason, human beings are able to distinguish good and evil and are thereby capable of being rewarded or punished for their actions. The animal soul, however, is of an inferior character – it comes into being from the shadow of the rational soul and therefore is distant from the Intellect. Its characteristic is movement and locomotion; unlike human beings, animals lack discernment and as a consequence do not merit either reward or punishment. The vegetative soul is the most inferior since it arises from the shadow of the animal soul. It lacks perception as well as locomotion, and it is capable only of nourishment, growth and procreation.

In formulating this scheme, Israeli does not absolutely separate the three degrees of the soul: animals (such as dogs and birds) can exhibit intelligence like human beings, and some plants (like musk) exude perfume. Such capacities are the result of the inclinations of various souls toward each other – the rational soul can incline toward the animal soul which desires physical gratification; likewise, animal souls can exhibit rational characteristics. Nonetheless, the rational soul is capable of attaining perfection; as such, it seeks what is good and true:

> One who is ruled by the rational soul will be intelligent, discriminating between things spiritual and corporeal, exceedingly humble, occupied with (the search for) truth and beautiful things, and shunning things which are blameworthy.
>
> (*Ibid.*, 138)

In a universe where the rational soul aspires to its source, prophecy is reserved for the few; it is possessed only by those who serve as God's messengers:

> For when the Creator wishes to reveal to the soul what He intends to innovate in this world, He makes the intellect the intermediary between Himself and the soul, even as the prophet is an intermediary between the Creator, blessed be He, and the rest of His creatures.
>
> (*Ibid.*, 135)

These individuals function as divine intermediaries who are sent by God to bring the divine word to human beings.

Here Israeli compares revelation to the psychological process of dreaming. While asleep, the forms which are received by the sensus communis are more exalted because they are removed from the material domain; they arise from activity of the intellect which provides an impetus to the rational activity of the imaginative faculty. Both prophetic dreams and other forms of dreaming are hence of the same kind, utilizing the same psychological mechanism. Yet, prophecy originates in God's will to disclose himself to human beings. As such, the prophetic dream requires interpretation which can only be accomplished by individuals who are endowed with the highest form of the rational soul:

When, therefore, the cogitative faculty of the person concerned is spiritual, pure, luminous, and hardly obscured by shells and darkness, intellect will cause its light and brilliance to emanate upon it and make known to it its own properties and forms, and spiritual messages; it will also enlighten it as to the properties and forms of the soul and its faculties, and as to the differences between its spiritual forms and corporeal ones. Then these forms will be completely purified of all shells adhering to them, and it (cogitation) will interpret those dreams without fault.

(*Ibid.*, 137)

According to Israeli, the imagination enables a person to reach the spiritual realm, even though it clothes such knowledge in corporeal terms which must subsequently be eliminated. Imagination is the medium of both dreams and prophecy. The Divine Word offers the means of interpreting God's disclosure; in Israeli's view, only the philosopher is able to decipher such heavenly communications and thereby fulfil God's word. As he writes:

Some of His words therein are unambiguous, self-evident, in no need of elucidation and interpreation. Yet there are others which use corporeal expressions, and are doubtful and in need of elucidation and commentary ... The Creator ... put His message in spiritual, unambiguous words to serve as a guide and true teacher to those endowed with intellect and understanding so as to enable them to reach an understanding of the meaning of those messages which are couched in corporeal and ambiguous terms.

(*Ibid.*, 139)

These sages are needed by those who are incapable of percieving the the Divine Word. Through their interpretations, those who are incapable of understanding the nature of divine truth by themselves will be enlightened and draw near to the source of purity. God thereby places himself within the reach of all those who search after him with purity of heart.

Saadiah Gaon

As we have seen, medieval Jewish philosophers were influenced by the teachings of Muslim schools (kalam) of the eighth to the eleventh centuries; in particular the contributions of one school of Muslim thought (the Mu'tazilite kalam) had a profound effect on the development of Jewish thought. These Islamic scholars maintained that rational argument was vital in matters of religious belief and that Greek philosophy could serve as the handmaiden of religious faith. In their attempt to defend Judaism from internal and external assault, rabbinic authorities frequently adapted the Mu'tazilite kalam as an important line of defense.

Preeeminent among such thinkers, Saadiah Gaon (Saadiah ben Joseph al-Fayyumi) was born in 882 in Pithom (in Upper Egypt). At the age of twenty he published a Hebrew dictionary; three years later he issued a polemic against Karaism. After living in Palestine and Aleppo, Syria, he settled in Babylonia where he engaged in a bitter dispute with the Palestinian gaon Aaron Ben-Meir about fixing the dates of the Holy Days. Subsequently he was appointed gaon of the Babylonian academy at Sura which had fallen into decline. Under Saadiah, Sura underwent a major revival, attracting students from throughout the Jewish world. In time, however, Saadiah became embroiled in a controversy with the exilarch David Ben Zakkai, who had appointed him. When David Ben Zakkai sought to replace Saadiah as gaon, Saadiah appointed a different exilarch. The quarrel between these two leaders split Bagdad Jewry, but seven years later the elders of the community arranged a reconciliation and Saadiah was reinstated.

As gaon of the Babylonian academy, Saadiah wrote treatises on a wide range of subjects: he produced grammatical and lexicographical studies, translated almost the entire Bible into Arabic, composed a book of prayers as well as liturgical poems, introduced a scientific methodology and a new interpretation of the study of the Talmud, defined and codified numerous questions of Jewish law, expounded important decisions in response to questions from diaspora communities, composed Talmudic commentaries, wrote works on the calendar and biblical and rabbinic chronology, and elaborated a rational theology.

In his major philosophical work, *The Book of Beliefs and Opinions*, Saadiah attempts to refute the religious claims of Christians, Muslims and Zoroastrians. Basing his approach on the teachings of the kalam, he argues that there are four sources of knowledge: sense experience, intuition of self-evident truths; logical inference and reliable tradition. This fourth category, derived from the first three is reliable tradition, the mainstay of civilization – it was given by God to human beings to provide guidance and protection against uncertainty since the vast majority of humanity is incapable of engaging in philosophical speculation.

Only the Torah, Saadiah maintains, is of divine origin – it was revealed by God to the prophets and transmitted in written and oral form. Adapting the teaching of the Mu'tazilites, Saadiah argues that religious faith and reason are fully compatible. On this basis, he attempts to demonstrate that God exists since the universe must have had a starting point. Time, he believes, is only rational if it has a beginning because it is impossible to pass from an infinite past to the present. The divine Creator, he asserts, is a single incorporeal Being who created the universe out of nothing.

In connection with God's unity, Saadiah – like the Mu'tazilite philosophers and along with *David Al Mukkamis – assumes that if God has a plurality of attributes, this implies He must be composite in nature. Thus, he argues, such terms as 'life', 'omnipotence', and omniscience' should be understood as implications of the concept of God as Creator rather than attributes of the Deity. The reason we are forced to describe God by means of these descriptions is because of the limitations of language, but they do not in any way involve plurality in God. In this light Saadiah argues that the anthropo-morphic expressions in the Bible must not be taken literally since this would imply that God is a plurality. Hence when we read in the Bible that God has a head, eye, ear, mouth, face or hand, these terms should be understood figuratively. Similarly, when human activity is attributed to God or when he appears in a theophany such depictions should not be interpreted in a literal way.

Turning to the nature of human beings, Saadiah contends that men and women possess souls which are substances created by God at the time when bodies are brought into being. The soul is not pre-existent nor does it enter the body from the outside; rather, it uses the body as an instrument for its functions. When it is connected to a corporeal frame the soul has three central faculties (reason, spirit, and desire), yet it is incapable of activity if it is divorced from the body. As for the sufferings which the soul undergoes because of its bodily connection, some are due to its negligence whereas others are inflicted for the soul's own good so that it may later be rewarded.

In order to lead a fulfilled life, humans have been given commandments and prohibitions by God. These consist of two types: the first embraces such acts as reason recognizes as good or bad through a feeling of approval or disapproval which has been implanted in human beings. We perceive, for example, that murder is wrong because it would lead to the destruction of humanity and would also frustrate God's purpose in creating the world. The second group of ordinances refers to acts which are intrinsically neither right nor wrong, but are made so by God's decree. Such traditional laws are imposed on human beings essentially so that we may be rewarded for obeying them. Nevertheless, these laws are not arbitrary; they have beneficial consequences as well. For instance, laws of ceremonial purity teach humility and make prayer more precious for those who have been prevented from praying because of their ritual uncleanliness. Since these traditional laws are not inherently rational in character, divine revelation is necessary to supplement humanity's rational capacity.

Turning to the issue of divine miracles. Saadiah contends that faith does not depend on such occurances; rather miraculous events strengthen religious conviction. Thus here, too, reason and faith are interrelated:

> The reason for our belief in Moses lies not in wonders or miracles only, but the reason for our belief in him and all the other prophets lies in the fact that they admonished us in the first place to do what was right, and only after we heard the prophet's message and found it was right did we ask him to produce miracles in support of it. If he performed them we believed in him, but if we hear his call and at the onset found it to be wrong, we do not ask for miracles, for no miracle can prove the impossible.
>
> (Altmann, 1965, 113)

Saadiah then goes on to discuss the freedom of the will. In his view, it would make no sense to believe that God gave human beings commandments and prohibitions if they were not able to make free choices. Like the Mu'tzilite philosophers, Saadiah argues that men and women are responsible for their deeds; otherwise there would be no sense in the concept of divine reward and punishment. The seeming conflict between omniscience and freedom of the will is resolved by appealing to the principle of causation. In Saadiah's opinion, God knows in advance the outcome of human choices, yet such knowledge in no way determines what will occur. Hence God's foreknowledge is not the cause of a person's action – rather God simply knows beforehand the outcome of one's free deliberation. In this connection Saadiah argues that divine legislation is needed to clarify the moral principles known by reason. The corpus of Jewish law cannot be abrogated; it is valid for all time: thus the Bible declares, 'I have set before you life and death . . . therefore choose life' (Deuteronomy 30:19).

Discussing Jewish beliefs concerning the afterlife, Saadiah asks why the righteous suffer and the wicked prosper. Here he summarizes the traditional solutions to this problem: the pious suffer as a punishment for their transgressions; the suffering of the righteous is a test and mode of purification. Yet because there is more suffering than happiness in the world, divine justice requires that the soul should be immortal so that there can be a proper recompense in the hereafter. In Saadiah's view, the soul is a pure, luminous substance that acts through physical embodiment. For this reason the body is not impure – it will be resurrected together with the soul so that the entire person can enjoy bliss in the World-to-Come. For Saadiah, since God created the world ex nihilo, there is no logical difficulty in believing that God can recreate the bodies of those who have died.

In Saadiah's scheme there are two final stages of human existence. The messianic period will be inhabited by the remnant of the righteous of Israel who wil be allowed to participate in the restoration of the monarchy. At this stage poverty, oppression and conflict will disappear. Eventually the World-to-Come will be established. The dead of all nations will be rewarded and recompense will take place through the medium of the divine light – the righteous will be illuminated with joy whereas the wicked will be consumed by fire. In presenting these theories Saadiah was the first Jewish thinker to offer a systematic treatment of rabbinic theology. Throughout his writing the central doctrines of Judaism were defended on biblical and rabbinic grounds; like the Mu'tazilites, he was determined to provide a rational interpretation of the faith.

Jacob Al-Kirkisani

Living in the first half of the 10th century, Jacob Al-Kirkisani (Abu Yusuf Yakub al-Qirqisani) was a Karaite scholar. His surname may have been derived from the ancient city of Circesium in Upper Mesopotamia. Although nothing is known of his personal life, he appears to have been acquainted with Islamic theological, philosophical and scientific texts; in addition, he demonstrates considerable knowledge of Jewish sources. Further, it appears that he was familiar with the New Testament, the Koran, and early Christian literature. Concerning his non-Karaite associates he refers to the Rabbinic sage

Jacob ben Ephraim and the Christian 'bishop' Yasu Sekha. Distancing himself from other Karaite propogandists, he did not engage in fierce exchanges with his rabbinic opponents; instead he offered a rational defence of his own position. As a champion of reason and common sense, his views are characterized by their moderation and rationality.

Kirkisani's major work, *Book of Lights and Watch Towers*, is a theoretical exposition of Karaite ideology. Divided into thirteen chapters, it begins with an historical and philosophical exposition of the history of Jewish sects, the validity of rational investigation in theology and jurisprudence, the refutation of the doctrines of various sects, and a treatise on the methods of interpreting the Law. These four chapters are of particular importance since they provide an invaluable source of information about the religious sects that existed in the tenth century.

In Kirkisani's view, rational speculation about theology is both permissible and desirable – it serves as the foundation of all religions and the source of all knowledge:

> The true procedure should be this: laws should be made along the lines of research and speculation only; whatever is proved by research and speculation to be necessary should be accepted as dogma, no matter who adheres to it, be it the Rabbanites, or Anan (the founder of Karaism), or anyone else . . . all knowledge should be derived by means of reason only.
>
> (in Nemoy, 1930, 320–1)

According to Kirkisani, God manifests himself through reason – which is given to each person – and by means of revelation. However, revelation is not unique to the Jews since Christians and Muslims assert that they too have received a divine disclosure. Only revelation, he insists, allows one to ascertain the authenticity of an alleged divine encounter. Hence it is necessary that the intellectual processes should be brought to bear on any prophetic tradition. Before accepting the validity of a particular prophecy, one must be persuaded that it was caused by God. In the first place then, one must demonstrate by means of reasoning that God exists. Thus, reason serves as the moral law that allows us to differentiate good from evil; it is because the moral law also applies to God that we are able to establish the existence of a benevolent Deity. Moreover, it is also reason that permits the allegorical interpretation of ambiguous passages in Scripture.

In the Bible, God addresses himself to mortals so as to make himself understood:

Scripture addresses mankind in a manner accessible to their understanding and about matters familiar to them from their own experience; this is what the Rabbanites mean when they say, 'The Law speaks with the tongue of men.' Thus when the Creator wished to describe Himself to the effect that nothing visible is hidden from Him, He described Himself as provided with eyes, because men are familiar with the sense of sight and know from their own experiences that its seat is the member of the body which is the eye, not because He really is provided with bodily members . . . The same applies to all matters of this sort.

(in Nemoy, 1932, 63–4)

Such rational speculation proves that a psychological process exists; the desire to know and inquire is present in all individuals and no person can be truly happy who is perceived as ignorant. The process of inquiry distinguishes human beings from all other species. Like animals, humans have rational souls, but they are different in so far as they have the capability to comprehend and communicate through language. By its nature, the human soul is able to comprehend the true definitions of things, and fit together the different pieces of knowledge attained through reason into a coherent whole. Thus, the human soul through its natural disposition can think, understand, and exercise choice. It is the capability to choose the good, to perceive past and future events, and to obtain what is required for physical survival, that constitutes the 'image and resemblance of God'.

In his presentation of human comprehension, Kirkisani argues that there are four sources of knowledge: (1) sense perception; (2) knowledge of what is self-evident; (3) demonstrative knowledge; and (4) traditionally transmitted knowledge. In making this claim, Kirkisani contends that revelation is in agreement with reason and perception – it is not a separate source of information:

These, then, are the rational proofs built upon the knowledge based on sense perception; and it is for this reason that King David, in describing the Law and stating that it is allied with both reason and perception says: 'The Law of the Lord is perfect' (Ps. 19:8–10); i.e., its perfection is due to its close connection with reason free from error. He says further: 'The commandments of the Lord are upright, rejoicing the heart', refering to the satisfaction felt by the human heart because of the truth of the premises and conclusions contained in his commandments; and further: 'The precept of the Lord is pure, enlightening the eyes, refers to the clarity and lucidity of the precept, caused by its freedom from ambiguities; and further: 'The fear of the Lord is immaculate, enduring forever', meaning that the word of the Law is firmly established in the face of disputes and attacks against it, and remains irrefutable.

(Ibid., 57–8)

In Kirkisani's view, Scripture demonstrates that the study of science and philosophy is not illegitimate. King Solomon, he points out, gained scientific knowledge in the same fashion as doctors and philosophers do. There is no conflict between the concept of creation and the laws of science and philosophy; rather they confirm one another. Scientific investigation, he continues, is a means for gaining knowledge of the truths of the Torah: just like religious belief, scientific discovery relies on human reason which is governed by the perception of sense data and the comprehension of what is self-evident.

Against the belief that science and philosophy can lead to heretical opinions, Kirkisani contends that such investigations can be embarked on by those who have a well-proportioned character, sound natural intellect, and the quest for truth. As far as the science of physics is concerned, Kirkisani argues that the three first elements – earth, water and air – were formed simultaneously; composite bodies were created from their mixture. As far as fire is concerned, there are two types: celestial and concrete. Celestial fire arises through this process:

Every moving body moves with it the body which is attached to it. The latter becomes hot by that movement. When the celestial sphere moves, it moves with it the air attached to it. This air, while moving with the sphere, becomes hot, and consequently becomes thinner and lighter. This (thinner and lighter air) is fire. This is why the fire is the highest element. This (process) is also demonstrated by sense perception, for when two solid dry bodies are rubbed forcefully against each other fire is produced in between them. (The reason for) that is that the few particles of air which exist between the two solid bodies heat and change into fire.

(in Sirat, 1995, 44)

Since such celestial fire is produced from the friction of two bodies, it was not mentioned in the Book of Genesis: the void has no existence and all the interstices between bodies are filled with air. Time is the duration of celestial movement even though it is not dependent upon such change. Even if celestial bodies did not move, time would exist. Just as time in its origin was not preceded by an anterior time, so the universe is not in a particular place; rather within the universe all bodies have a place.

Such doctrines serve as the basis for the Karaite refutation of anthropomorphism. According to Kirkisani, the Rabbanites are guilty of attributing humanlike characteristics to God:

> They attribute to him likeness and corporeality, and describe him with the most shameful descriptions; (they assert) that he is composed of limbs and has a (definite) measure. They measure each limb of his in parsangs. This is to be found in a book entitled *Shiur Komah*, meaning 'The measure of the stature', i.e., the stature of the Creator.
>
> (*Ibid.*, 45)

There are two reasons, Kirkisani maintains, why God cannot be a body: first a body has three dimensions; second, a body cannot create another body. God cannot be two since each of two gods would be limited by the other. Nor can he be three for a substance of three hypostases would indicate that Aristotelian definitions that only refer to the world of bodies could be ascribed to God. Nothing can be compared to God, and divine actions are of a different order from human acts. Commenting on the verse, 'Hear O Israel, the Lord is our God, the Lord is one', Kirkisani argues that rational investigation is in accord with revelation, providing a basis for our understanding of the unity of God. Like the Mu'tazilites, Kirkisani contends that God can only be defined by negative attributes; in his view, the only positive attribute that can be ascribed to God is his eternity.

Turning to the angelic hierarchies, Kirkisani describes four characteristics of angels: (1) they are confined to heaven; (2) they do not die, but like human beings they are intelligent and communicate through speech; (3) they do not need sustenance; (4) they are able to perform miracles. In Kirkisani's view, the celestial and terrestrial world are connected through prophecy – the prophet is selected by God for his religious qualities and thereby possesses special characteristics. The highest degree of prophecy is manifest in Moses' ministry: he was able to see God's glory and hear his voice; the second degree of prophecy involves spiritual inspiration initiated by the Holy Spirit. By this means David and the sons of Asaph composed the Psalms; and Solomon the Song of Songs, Ecclesiastes, and Proverbs.

The authenticity of a divine mission, he continues, is demonstrated by the performance of miracles that can only come from God.

Yusuf Al-Basir

Living in the first half of the 11th century, the Karaite scholar Yusuf Al-Basir lived in Iraq or Persia. Because he was blind, he was called Al-Basir ha-Roeh (the Seeing). Although a number of Karaite scholars confused him with Al-Kirkisani, it has been shown that Al-Basir lived 100 years after Al-Kirkisani since he refers to Samuel ben Hophni who died in 1036 as 'of blessed memory'. Despite his disability, he travelled extensively, presumably in order to spread Karaite doctrine. As one of the most significant Karaite writers of his day, he studied Talmud as well as rabbinic sources and was familiar with Islamic thought. In formulating his philosophical views, he was deeply influenced by the Mu'tazilites.

Al-Basir's most important work, *The Comprehensive Book* is general known in the Hebrew translation by Tobias ben Moses entitled: *Sefer ha-Neimot*. This work consisting of forty chapters was summarized by Al-Basir as *The Distinction* in thirteen chapters, also translated by Tobias ben Moses under the title: *Which Gives Wisdom to the Ignorant*. Concerning Al-Basir's other writings, it appears that only a manuscript about the precepts has been preserved.

In essence *The Comprehensive Book* is a work of kalam, similar to Islamic kalam texts. Like these Muslim thinkers, Al-Basir argues that there are five principles of the unity of God:

1 The establishment of atoms and accidents.
2 The establishment of the Creator.
3 The establishment of the Creator's attributes.
4 The rejection of those divine attributes which should not be applied to God.
5 The establishment of God's unity.

In accordance with the kalam, the argument for the unity of God is based on the distinction between atoms and accidents. All generated things are of two types: atoms of substance and atoms of accidents. Atoms of substance compose bodies and accidents reside in them:

> The thin things which you see (when looking) through the ray of sunlight are not like the atom which I have mentioned, for the atom is smaller. Those (thin things) are visible (to the the eye)

while the atom is not. However, God sees it, because He does not see with eyes. You should know, from now onwards, that when I mention in this book (the term) daq I mean that thing which is not divisible and not visible to the eye (i.e. atom of substance). It is that (same) thing which I called above hatika. (Consequently) when I mention (from now onwards) hatika, I mean one particle of the accidents which do not occupy any space or place, but rather occur and abide on an atom of substance.

(in Sirat, 1995, 55)

According to Al-Basir, atoms of substance are invisible whereas atoms of accident are both visible and audible. Paralleling the writings of the Mu'tazilites, Al-Basir goes on to define the voice as a succession of atoms. In this light, he discusses the problems connected with the concept of divine speech as it relates to God's attributes:

We omitted also the discussion of Divine Speech; although it is under dispute among the people. (We did so) for the following reasons: (a) the proof which demonstrates that God alone is eternal (at the same time) denies that He be speech, since speech (generally) is instructive by virtue of its being a composite sequence, of which the former parts inevitably precede the latter. A thing which is described in this way cannot be (other) than created. Therefore when God is said to be speaking, this does not constitute an Attribute which would be ultimately attributed to His Essence. Rather, this is related to Him by way of derivation from his creating the Speech, like 'doing good' or 'hitting'.

(*Ibid.*, 55)

Like Al-Basir, his disciple Jeshua ben Judah was influenced by the Mu'tazilites; most of his works, like his teacher's, were translated into Hebrew in the twelfth century by scholars who came from Constantinople to study Arabic under him. In the Karaite tradition, Al-Basir was regarded as a seminal authority, and other Karaite writers such as Judah Hadassi, Aaron ben Joseph ha-Rofe, Bashyazi and others frequently cite his halakhic opinions and scriptural interpretations. Subsequently Aaron ben Elijah of Nicomedia who lived in the 14th century often refers to Al-Basir in his work, *Etz Hayyim* (Tree of Life).

Solomon Ibn Gabirol

Beginning in the 11th century there appeared a number of Jewish writers in the Mediterranean West who made major contributions to the history of Jewish thought. The first Spanish Jewish philosopher, Solomon ben Judah ibn Gabirol, produced an influential work in the Neoplatonic tradition, *The Fountain of Life* as well as a religious poem, 'Kingly Crown', which had an important impact on later Jewish as well as Christian thinkers. Born in 1021 most probably in Malaga, Ibn Gabirol lived at Saragossa where he was educated. When he was a child, his father died, followed by his mother in 1045.

In his poetry, Ibn Gabirol provides a self-description: he was, he states, small, sickly, ugly, and of a disagreeable disposition. The most important of his friends appears to have been Jekuthiel ben Isaac ibn Hasan whom he praises for his erudition and worldliness. However due to Jekuthiel's courtly connections, he was assassinated in 1039. In consequence Gabirol's financial position deteriorated, and he was unable to find other patrons in Saragossa. It seems that he attempted to settle in other towns including Granada and Valencia where he died at an early age.

Ibn Gabirol's philosophical treatise, *The Fountain of Life*, contains no biblical quotations or allusions to the Jewish religious tradition except for scattered references to the early mystical work, the *Sefer Yetsirah* (*Book of Creation*). Like other Neoplatonic works, *The Fountain of Life* is written in the form of a dialogue no doubt in imitation of Plato. However, in contrast with the Platonic dialogues, the personalities of the master and his pupil are deemphasized – philosophical doctrines are explained by the master and the pupil's role is solely to put relevant questions to his teacher which provide the opportunity for an extended response.

Written in Arabic, the *Fountain of Life*, is divided into five treatises dealing primarily with the principles of matter and form. In the first treatise, Gabirol discusses matter and form as they exist in objects perceived by the senses as well as the underlying qualities of corporeal existence; the second contains a depiction of the spiritual matter that underlies corporeal form; the third deals with the existence of simple substances; the fourth concerns the form and matter of simple substances; the fifth treats universal form and matter as they exist in themselves. In expounding this metaphysical scheme, Gabirol adopts a Neoplatonic framework – in his view, God is the First Essence. Next in descending order of being is the divine will, followed by universal matter and form, the simple substances (intellect, soul and nature), and then the corporeal world.

In presenting his cosmological theories, Gabirol argues that both spiritual and corporeal substances are composed of two elements – form and matter; this duality leads to the differences between various substances. In some passages of the *Fountain of Life*, it appears that the forms are responsible for differentiating one substance from another, whereas in other sections matter seems to be the cause. In any event, Gabirol contends that matter is the substratum underlying the forms. All distinctions in the various substances are due to the differences between universal matter and form, which are the first created beings. Gabirol, however, appears to offer two different accounts of their creation: in one case universal matter is described as coming from the essence of God and form from the divine will; elsewhere both principles are described as the product of the divine will. Further, in some passages Gabirol contends that universal matter exists independently, but in other sections he argues in accordance with Aristotelianism that matter is akin to privation and exists only in potentiality.

Turning to the doctrine of forms, Gabirol suggests that all forms are contained in universal form. Matter and form do not exist independently: their first compound is intellect which is the initial spiritual substance from which the soul emanates which is similarly composed of matter and form. All spiritual or simple substances, he continues, emanate forces that give existence to substances below them in the order of being. Hence soul is emanated from intellect and is of three types: rational, animate and vegetative. There are also cosmic principles which exist in human beings. Nature is the last of the simple substances and emanates from the vegetative soul – from it emanates corporeal substance which is below nature in the chain of being. Corporeal substance is the substratum underlying nine of the ten Aristotelian categories; the tenth category – substance – is universal matter as it appears in the corporeal world, and the nine other categories are universal form as it appears in the corporeal world.

In order for souls to be linked to bodies, a mediating principle is needed: the principle which joins the universal soul to the corporeal world is Heaven; the principle combining the rational soul with the body is the animal spirit. The relation of the human body to the soul is like the relation between form and matter – the soul comprehends the forms but not matter since matter is unintelligible. The forms which always exist in the soul are intelligible; however, since the soul was deprived of knowledge due to its union with the body, these forms exist only in potentiality. Therefore God created the world and provided senses for the soul by means of which it can conceive concrete forms and patterns. It is through the comprehension of the sensible forms that the soul is able to apprehend ideas which in the soul emerge from potentiality to actuality.

In Gabirol's view all forms exist in a more subtle and simple fashion in the intellect than in the soul – there they are combined in a spiritual union. Intellect, he argues, consists of universal form and matter, and is at a lower plane – it is capable of conceiving of universal form and matter only with difficulty. Above the knowledge of form and matter there is a knowledge of the divine will which is identified with divine wisdom and divine logos. This will in relation to its activity should be conceived as identical with the divine essence, yet when considered with respect to its activity, it is separate. In its essence, the will is infinite, but with regard to its action, it is finite. Hence it is the intermediary between divine essence and matter and form even though it penetrates everything. In terms of its function, it is the efficient cause of all things, uniting form with matter; the will, however, which is the cause of all movement is in itself at rest. The First Essence, or God, cannot be known because it is infinite and lacks any similarity with the soul; nonetheless its existence can be demonstrated. For Gabirol, the highest aspiration is to attain knowledge of the purpose for which human beings were created: such knowledge can be achieved through an apprehension of the will as it extends to all form and matter as well as through an understanding of the will as it exists in itself. Such an awareness brings about release from death and attachment to the source of all things.

Such theoretical speculation about form and matter and the process of emanation is reflected in Gabirol's religious poem, *Kingly Crown*. Here he provides a description of the three worlds that present themselves to human thought: the divine world, the created universe, and man. Beginning with praise of God, the poem continues with a depiction of the hidden secrets of the divine:

This is the mystery of power, the secret and the foundation.
Thine is the name that is hidden from the wise, the strength that sustains the world over the chaos, the power to bring to light all that is hidden.

Thine is the mercy that rules over Thy creatures and the goodness preserved for those who fear Thee.

Thine are the secrets that no mind or thought can encompass, and the life over which decay has no rule, and the throne that is higher than all height, and the habitation that is hidden at the pinnacle of mystery.

Thine is the existence from the shadow of whose light every being was made to be and we said, 'Under His shadow we shall live'.

Thine are the two worlds between which Thou didst set a limit, the first for works and the second for requital.

Thine is the reward which Thou has set aside for the righteous and hidden, and

Thou sawest that it was good, and has kept it hidden.

(Ibn Gabirol, 1961, 27–28)

The end of the first part of the poem concludes with a series of statements about the topics dealt with in the Fountain of Life: God and his wisdom; the will; matter; form; and the combination of the two which forms all creation:

Thou art wise; and wisdom, the fountain of life, flows from Thee, and every man is too brutish to know Thy wisdom.

Thou art wise, pre-existent to all pre-existence, and wisdom was with Thee at nurseling.

Thou art wise, and Thou dist not learn from any other than Thyself, nor acquire wisdom from another.

Thou art wise, and from Thy wisdom Thou dist send forth a predestined Will, and made it as an artisan and a craftsman,

To draw the stream of being from the nothingness as the light is drawn that comes from the eye.

To take from the source of light without a vessel, and to make all without a tool and cut and hew and cleanse and purify.

That Will called to the nothingness and it was cleft asunder, to existence and it was set up, to the universe and it was spread out.

It measured the heavens with a span, and its hand coupled the pavilion of the spheres,

And linked the curtains of all creatures with loops of potency; and its strength reaches as far as the last and lowest creature – 'the uttermost edge of the curtain in the coupling'.

(*Ibid.*, 32–33)

Because Gabirol did not deal with the issue of the relationship between philosophy and faith and also since his work lacks Jewish content, his writings did not have a major impact on subsequent Jewish thought. Nonetheless, the *Fountain of Life* was quoted by such 12th Century Jewish scholars as Moses Ibn Ezra, Joseph ibn Zaddik, and *Abraham Ibn Ezra; in addition, his views were bitterly criticized by another 12th Century thinker,*Abraham Ibn Daud. In time, however, Gabirol's Neoplatonic theories were largely neglected by Jewish thinkers.

Bahya Ibn Pakuda

Little is known about Bahya Ibn Pakuda other than that in all likelihood he lived in Saragossa in the second half of the 11th century. In addition to religious poetry, he composed a philosophical tract, *Duties of the Heart*, in about 1090; this was translated into Hebrew by Judah Ibn Tibbon in 1161 and subsequently became immensely popular and profoundly influenced Jewish pietistic literature. A second translation was undertaken by Joseph Kimhi, and other versions followed in Arabic, Spanish, Portuguese, Italian and Yiddish. Later this work was translated into English, German and French. Although Pakuda's writing draws on Muslim mysticism and Arabic Neoplatonism, *Duties of the Heart* is Jewish in character. Throughout Bahya calls upon his readers to remain faithful to inner experience – divided into ten chapters, the book progressively leads the faithful to the love of God.

In the introduction, Bahya divides human obligations into two types: (l) duties of the members of the body – these obligations involve overt action; and (2) duties of the heart – these are comprised of inner responsiblities. The first category includes ritual and ethical practices which are prescribed by the Torah such as Sabbath regulations, prayer and charity; the second type consists of beliefs such as the conviction that there is one God, the need for love and fear of the Deity, the importance of repentance, and the centrality of ethical prohibitions (ie bearing a grudge and taking revenge). Bahya goes on to explain that he composed this treatise because such inner obligations had been largely neglected by previous thinkers as well as by his contemporaries who concentrated instead on outward acts. To redress this imbalance, Bahya seeks to supply a work which would complement the halakhic compendia which had been written for pious Jews.

The structure of Bahya's treatise was borrowed from Arab mystical tracts which lead the reader through ascending stages of man's inner life toward spiritual perfection and ultimately, union with the Divine. Each of its ten chapters is devoted to a particular duty; the subjects treated include the unity of God, the nature of the world which reveals God's handiwork, divine worship, trust in God, sincerity of purpose, humility, repentance, self-examination, asceticism, and the love of God.

The starting point of this spiritual journey is an awareness of God's unity; this belief, Bahya insists, is the fundamental principle of the faith:

> When we inquired as to what is the most necessary among the fundamental principles of our religion, we found that the wholehearted acceptance of the Unity of God – the root and foundation of Judaism – is the first of the gates of the Torah. By the acceptance of the Unity of God, the believer is distinguished from the infidel. It is the head and front of religious truth. Whoever has deviated from it will neither practise any duty properly nor retain any creed permanently.
>
> (Ibn Pakuda, 1962, 55)

Beginning with God's unity, Bahya argues that the Deity is neither substance nor accident – thus we cannot know God as he is in himself. Rather, it is only through his creatures that we can gain an apprehension of the Divine. Here Bahya follows the same method as *Saadiah Gaon and the kalam, proving the existence of the Creator on the basis of order in the cosmos. According to Bahya, God created the universe ex nihilo. From this observation, Bahya goes on to discuss God's nature. In his view, the unity of God is not undermined by the ascription to him of divine attributes. In this context Bahya distinguishes between essential attributes which are the permanent attributes of God – existence, unity, and eternity – and those attributes which are ascribed to God because of his action in the world. For Bahya, the essential attributes should be conceived as negative in character; they deny their opposites. The outcome of this discussion is that only two kinds of attributes are applicable to God: negative attributes and those which we can infer from God's activity as manifest in history.

This theological investigation provides the metaphysical background to Bahya's examination of the duties of the heart. To recognize God's unity with full devotion involves the quest to prove his existence and unity. On this basis, the pious can direct their hearts and minds to put such knowledge into action. Intellectual ascent to propositions about the Divine is therefore not of primary importance; rather, what matters is the translation of such understanding into concrete deeds. Study of the active attributes then is a precondition for living the religious life. It is one's duty to investigate the natural world so as to gain an appreciation of God's wisdom and goodness.

In Bahya's view, the variety of natural phenomena and the laws underpining the order of the world exhibit God's providential will. Above all this is humanity, the highest of all creatures. In the laws and ordinances given to human beings it is possible to discover God's benficence. In this context Bahya points out that all of us have a duty of attitude to those who have been of assistance; how much the more is the duty to appreciate God's favours which he has bestowed upon all persons. The only way in which we can repay God for his kindness is by submitting to his will and performing those acts which draw us near to him. To accomplish this, each individual must abstain from too much eating, drinking, and idleness; the quest for pleasure leads one from following God's laws. Similarly we must refrain from the quest for power.

In realizing their religious duty, human beings are not simply to follow the promptings of reason; rather, we possess a positive law which is designed to regulate human conduct. In presenting this interpretation of one's duty to God, Bahya differentiates between body and spirit. Bodily functions are located in the lower, earthly domain whereas spirit functions in the higher realms. The role of divine legislation is to nourish the spirit by restraining bodily appetites – this can be achieved through prayer, fasting and charity.

For Bahya, positive law is necessary because it encourages the middle course between asceticism and self-indulgence, regulating and defining human conduct. Further, it encourages new occasions for worship and thanksgiving as God continually bestows benefits to his chosen people. The law also prescribes actions which are not deducible by reason alone. These are the traditional, as opposed to the rational, commandments. In Bahya's view, positive law is necessary for the young, women and those of limited intellectual capacities. To worship God – not because the law prescribes such activity but because it is demanded by reason – constitutes a spiritual advance, and is reserved only for those of a prophetic or pious disposition.

Bahya stresses that one of the major duties of the heart is to trust in God. Leaving aside biblical injunctions, human reflection can lead one to such an attitude since in God alone are found the conditions necessary for such confidence. Only God has the power to protect and aid us – he is kind, generous and loving. Trust in God, he continues, is religiously advantageous – it leads to peace of mind and independence. In addition, by trusting in God a person can attain the freedom to devote himself to the service of God without being overwhelmed by worldly cares. It might be objected, however, that the suffering of the good and the prosperity of the wicked illustrate that such trust is misplaced. Although Bahya does not offer a solution to the problem of evil, he stresses that there are some possible explanations for this seeming discrepancy. The righteous may suffer because of a sin committed; alternatively, such suffering may simply occur so as to demonstrate the virtues of patience. Or a good person may be punished because he has not rebuked evildoers. Conversely, it is possible to account for the fact that the wicked flourish on different grounds.

Turning to the notion of personal sincerity, Bahya states that the duties of the limbs are imperfect unless they are accompanied by the intention of the heart. Motives must be sincere, and a person's aim should not be to obtain the favour of others or to gain honour. Instead, the observance of the commandments must be motivated by regard for God. In order to act in this way a person must have a sincere concept of God's unity, an appreciation of his acts in nature, a willingness to submit to his will, and an indifference to the opinions of society.

Humility, too, is of vital importance in human conduct. True humility, Bahya explains, is an attitude of total dedication, manifesting itself in a quiet spirit and modest behaviour. A humble person practices patience and forgiveness, and is intent on doing good to all people. Such an individual is able to endure hardship with resignation, and is unmoved by praise or blame. Yet Bahya notes that humility is compatible with a certain type of pride: that which leads to gratitude for the gifts that have been bestowed by God. According to Bahya, such humility before God is a necessary condition for true repentance; this can be achieved only by returning to God, expressing regret, discontinuing the sinful act, confessing one's failing, and promising not to repeat the action. In all this Bahya encourages the faithful to love God – this is the highest stage of human development and the goal of the religious life.

Chapter 3

12th Century

The writings of Jewish philosophers influenced by the Mu'tazilite kalam, Aristotelianism, Neoplatonism, and astrological theories provided a framework for the evolution of Jewish thought in the 12th century. Throughtout the writings of these 12th century thinkers, there was a quest to explain the nature of the Jewish faith in the light of secular thought; continually these thinkers sought to provide a rational basis for Jewish belief and practice. Such reflection cultimated in the philosophical system propounded by the greatest Jewish philosopher of this century, *Moses Maimonides. His *Guide for the Perplexed* was deliberately written for the intellectual elite. In the introduction to this work, he explains that his book is intended only for those whose study of logic, mathematics, natural science and metaphysics has led them to a state of perplexity about seeming contradictions between the Torah and human reson. The central aim of the *Guide* is to remove such confusion by providing a figurative interpretation of the biblical text. The controversy which raged about Maimonides' interpretation of the Jewish faith served as the basis for philosophical discussion in the following century.

Judah Halevi

Born in Tudela in c. 1075 Judah Halevi received an Arabic and Hebrew education. While a young man, he travelled to Granada where he won a poetry contest. During this period he came into contact with Moses Ibn Ezra as well as other great poets of Granada, Seville and Saragossa. However with the conquest of Andalusia by the Almoravides after 1090, he settled in Grenada. During the next two decades he travelled from town to town in Christian Spain, practising medicine at Toledo until his benefactor, Solomon Ibn Ferrizuel, was murdered. On his return to Muslim Spain, he went to Cordoba, Granada and Almeria. In addition, he made a journey with *Abraham Ibn Ezra to North Africa. After deciding to go to the Holy Land, he travelled to Alexandria in 1140; four months later he sailed to Palestine where he died several weeks later.

In addition to a variety of poetic works written in Hebrew, Halevi composed his best known work, the *Kuzari*. According to the author, this tract was written in order to combat the heretical views of the Jewish Karaite movement. The work itself describes the conversion to rabbinic Judaism of the King of the Khazars. Although a literary fiction, the *Kuzari* is based on historical fact – in the 10th century Hasdai Ibn Shaprut engaged in correspondence with the King of the Khazars who converted to the Jewish faith.

Book 1 of the Kuzari opens with an exposition of different ideologies: philosophical, Christian, Muslim and Jewish. Questioned by the king, the rabbi who represents the Jewish tradition states:

> I believe in the God of Abraham, Isaac, and Israel, who brought the children of Israel out of Egypt by means of signs and miracles, took care of them in the wilderness, and gave them the land of Canaan after crossing the sea and the Jordan by means of miracles. He sent Moses with his religious law by means of promises to whoever observed it and threats to whoever transgressed it.
>
> (*Kuzari*, I, 11)

Here the rabbi proclaims his faith in the Creator who chose Israel as his special people who watches over their destiny. In response the king argues that the rabbi believes in a national God because of the suffering of the Jewish people; due to historical circumstances, he is unable to envisage the Deity as the Lord of all creation. Undeterred by this criticism, the rabbi points out that the God of Judaism is not the God of the philosophers, but the God of faith. In his view, the way of the prophets is superior to that of philosophical reflection; in making this observation, Halevi is implicitly critical of Aristotelian metaphysics which he regards as misguided.

Continuing his presentation, the rabbi explains why he began his discourse by emphasizing God's role in the history of the Jewish people. This is because God's existence and providential care of the Jewish nation is proven – it is authenticated by Israel and the Egyptians who witnessed his intervention in the life of the nation. The king then states that if this is so, then Jewry has received an exclusive revelation from God. Agreeing with the king, the rabbi states that those who have converted to Judaism are not equal to born Jews in that they are incapable of receiving prophecy.

After discussing the preeminence of the prophets over ordinary humankind, the rabbi goes on to explain that all human beings accept a number of truths based on the insights of these gifted individuals. After a discussion of the concept of nature, the rabbi proceeds to explain how the Jewish people originated. Israel was not founded by a small community of like-minded individuals, but through God's intervention: God selected Moses to free the Israelites from bondage, and to forge them into a unified people. The miracles he performed on their behalf were crowned by the giving of the Law on Mt Sinai.

This historical narrative is interrupted by the king's observation that the nation was guilty of making a Golden Calf. How can one maintain that the Jewish people is superior to others given such disobedience? he asks. In defence, the rabbi stresses that this idolatrous act was undertaken by only a small segment of the community. And he adds that those elders who had a hand in its creation acted so as to distinguish the rebellious from believers so that those who worshipped the calf would be eliminated.

Persuaded by the sage's arguments, the king is ready to convert to the Jewish faith. Yet, the rabbi proceeds to deal with two further questions: why did God choose only one people rather than all human beings? and are reward and punishment reserved for the soul after the death of the body? From this point the dialogue between the king and the rabbi becomes a vehicle for the rabbi to enunciate his views. As the rabbi explains, God revealed himself by choosing a people, land and language. These acts constitute the only real proof of his existence. Hierarchically structured, the order of the universe consists of the prophets, Adam and his sons, Noah, and the people of Israel – this is superimposed on the mineral, vegetative, animal and rational realms. Such a scheme follows the general pattern of Aristotlian teaching.

In Halevi's opinion, the progression from union with the Intellect to union with the prophetic faculty is not a gradual and natural process. While it is possible to ascend to the Intellect through the study of philosophy, to reach the level of the prophets it is necessary to advance through the Torah. This path has been reserved for God's chosen people. Paralleling the selection of Israel is God's choice of the Holy Land as the place for prophecy to occur. In a similar vein, the Hebrew language occupies a central role in Halevi's thought. Hebrew, he writes, 'in its essence is more noble (than other languages) both traditionally and rationally. Traditionally, it is the language in which revelation was made to Adam and Eve and by means of it they spoke . . . Its superiority (may be shown) rationally by considering the people who utilized it insofar as they needed it for addressing one another, especially for prophecy, which was widespread among them, and the need for preaching, songs, and praises.' (Kuzari, II, 68) Further, Halevi asserts that the divine commandments – expressed through God's revelation to Moses – can only be perfectly observed in Israel; it is the means God uses to insure Israel's survival. Hence the king observes:

> I have reflected about the situation and I have seen that God has a secret means of giving you permanence. Indeed, He has certainly made the Sabbaths and the festivals become one of the strongest reasons for making permanent your esteem and splendour. The nations (of the world) would have divided you (among themelves), would have taken you as servants on account of your intelligence and your quickness, and they would certainly have made you soldiers also were it not for (the observance of these) times which you are so mindful of because they are from God.
>
> (Kuzari, III, 10)

The Kuzari ends with the Jewish sage's decision to leave the land of the Khazars in order to travel to Jerusalem. Such dedication to the Holy Land is reflected in Halvei's other works where he glorifies Zion. In one of his poems, he extols Jerusalem in the most glowing terms – these sentiments help to explain Halevi's own determination to go to Eretz Israel (the land of Israel) near the end of his life:

> If only I could roam through those places where God was revealed to your prophets and heralds! Who will give me wings, so that I may wander far away? I would carry the pieces of my broken heart over the rugged mountains. I would bow down, my face on your ground; I would love your stones; your dust would move me to pity. I would weep, as I stood by my ancestors' graves, I would grieve, in Hebron, over the choicest of burial places! I would walk in your forests and meadows, stop in 'Gilead, marvel at Mount Abarim . . . The air of your land is the very life of the soul, the grains of your dust are flowing myrrh, your rivers are honey from the comb. It would delight my heart

to walk naked and barefoot among the desolate ruins where
your shrines once stood; where your Ark was hidden away.

(in Carmi, 1981, 348–9)

Such lyricism highlights the rhapsodic character of Halevi's spiri-
tuality. Unlike other thinkers of the medieval period, he rejects the
philosophical approach of those thinkers who attempted to reconcile
Greek patterns of thought with the Torah. In place of such
speculation, he encourages his fellow Jews to rediscover the God of
the patriarchs. It is through such dedication to the faith, he contends,
that Jewry will be able to reclaim the past splendour of Jewish history
and rekindle hope for the coming of the Messiah.

Abraham Ibn Ezra

Born in Tudela in 1089, Abraham Ibn Ezra was a poet, grammarian,
exegete, philosopher, astronomer, astrologer, and doctor. Until 1140
he lived in Spain where he was a friend of such luminaries as Joseph
Ibn Zaddik, *Abraham Ibn Daud, Moses Ibn Ezra, and *Judah
Halevi. It appears that he traveled extensively (possibly to Egypt,
Palestine, Baghdad and India.) He composed most of his works
between 1140–6; during this period he also undertook journeys to
Lucca, Mantua and Verona. Subsequently he traveled to Provence,
and later Dreux and Rouen. In France he was acquainted with
Rabbenu Tam, the grandson of Rashi. According to various sources,
he died in Rome in 1164. His son Isaac, who may have been his only
survivor, converted to Islam.

Preeminent among Ibn Ezra's writings are his commentaries on the
Bible in which he alludes to various secret philosophical and
astrological theories; intrigued by such allusions, subsequent scholars
composed a variety of super-commentaries on these studies. In
addition, Ibn Ezra wrote numerous treatises on grammar, astrology,
and numbers. Because of the disparate nature of these works, it is
difficult to present a systematic exposition of his views. Nonetheless,
his commentaries on Scripture provide a framework for his thought.
At the very beginning of his commentary on Genesis, he explores
several issues connected with creation:

In the beginning God created the heaven and the earth. Most of
the commentators have said that created (bara) means to
produce a being out of nothing, according to Numbers 16:30: If
the Lord makes a new thing; but they have forgotten the verse:

And God created great whales (Genesis 1:21) ... and again: I create darkness (Isaiah 45:7). Darkness is the opposite of light, which is 'being'. Grammatically, the word to create is twofold, it can be written 'bara', as we have seen (= bet, resh, alef), or barah (hay instead of alef = bet, resh, hay) as in the verse: Neither did he eat bread with them (2 Samuel 12:17). The meaning of the verb is thus to cut, to decide, to set a precise limit, and let him who may understand, understand!

(in Sirat, 1995, 105)

Here Ibn Ezra seeks to demonstrate that the word bara can mean: (1) to create someting ex nihilo; (2) to create something out of something else; (3) to deprive existing things of being. Hence there is no necessity to understand Genesis 1:1 as implying creation out of nothing. Rather, Ibn Ezra contends that God formed the universe out of the four elements that constitute our world. Before creation God existed as did the world of intelligences (the eternal spheres and the four elements). Creation took place out of obedience to God's will through the circular movements of the spheres which were brought into existence by the intelligences. In Ibn Ezra's view, the spheres govern the lower world according to God's decree. True religion consists in recognizing the place assigned to the stars in the natural order; idolatry, however, occurs when the stars are perceived as having power of their own independent of God. The decree of the stars that regulates natural law is fixed; both bodies themselves and their movements and relations are eternally determined. To seek to alter this state of affairs is fruitless.

Addressing the question whether the intelligences, the spheres and the four elements are co-eternal, Ibn Ezra asserts that they did not have a temporal beginning even though they are caused by God. In speaking of God as the originator of all things, Ibn Ezra argues that he exists by himself and is self-sufficient. As the foundation of all, he bestows existence on everything. He is in everything, and his action is everywhere. In attempting to explain the relation between God, the world of pure forms and the lower world, Ibn Ezra uses the concept of species, genus and individual. All individuals in the lower world are part of a genus; each genus is contained within a species; and the characteristics of the species can be recognized in each of the individuals that belong to it. Simiarly, in arithmetic, one – which is the source of the indefinite series of numbers – potentially contains all of them and can be recognized in each of them. God, therefore, is the world; he contains the world in general but not in particular. He knows the world because he knows himself, more than if he knew it by individuals. Thus God knows all individuals, but not in their particularity. In his *Commentary on the Torah* (Genesis 18:21), he writes, 'The Whole (God) knows every part through the genera but not through the individual.'

In creation human beings occupy a special place: they are the only beings who possess immortal souls like the angels. Because humans are microcosms, they are able to know the whole world through self-knowledge. Yet revelation is needed in order to assist them on their return to their immortal origins. According to Ibn Ezra, revelation is of three types:

1 Revelation in Scripture and the giving of the law – all the commandments must be complemented by knowledge.
2 Intellectual knowledge which is bestowed on all human beings – this consists of moral and rational principles.
3 Revelation that leads to prophecy.

Explaining the nature of such divine communication, Ibn Ezra emphasizes the importance of an interior vision. Even in a spiritual vision, he contends, God does not speak directly to the prophet. Rather, an angel is used as God's messenger, and it appears that the angel who speaks is the prophet's own soul which has become united to pure forms. Such a notion, current among Neoplatonic writers, was based on the view that the soul has two faces, one turned upwards toward God and the other bending downwards toward the world.

For Ibn Ezra, worldly events are regulated by natural laws, dependent on the movement of the stars. Miracles take place when God intervenes in the course of these natural events. Disagreeing with the philosophers who dispute that miracles take place, Ibn Ezra contends that since we are unable to possess complete knowledge about the course of nature, it is impossible to determine what exceeds nature. Though the stars determine what takes place in the universe, their existence and the laws that govern their movements are divinely ordered. Thus, God is able to intervene whenever he wishes.

According to Ibn Ezra, it is not only God who can bring about miracles: prophets who are perfect and have attached themselves to the pure forms and understand the movements of the stars can act on them in special circumstances. However, when the future of the Jewish people is at stake, the prophet can influence the movement of the stars in any direction he desires. Commenting on Ibn Ezra's views, Joseph Tov Elem distinguishes between three types of influence: (l) those who influence nature in the lower world by using its laws; (2) those who influence terrestrial events by using celestial laws; (3) those who know the mysteries of the heavenly world and thereby perform miracles in this world that transcend both terrestrial and celestial laws. The first and second types are confined to scientists and astrologers, but the third type pertains to the prophets.

Each country and people, Ibn Ezra contends, is ruled over by a different star: Eretz Israel and the Jewish nation are under the dominion of the planet Saturn which he describes at length:

> Saturn is cold and dry; its nature is very pernicious; it denotes destruction, ruin, death, affliction, weeping, grief, complaint and ancient things. In the human activity it has control of the mind, and its area covers the first zone, which is India. Its group of people embraces the Moors, the Jews, the natives of Barbary, the assembly of all the elders, the husbandmen, the cultivators, the tanners, the cleaners of lavatories, the servants, the outcasts, the thieves, the diggers of wells and ditches, and the undertakers who get the mortuary shrouds.
>
> (*Ibid.*, 110)

In order to protect the Jewish people from such planetary domination, God has given Jewry a number of positive commandments. These decrees are based on three principles:

1 Respecting the conditions that allow the reception of positive influences.
2 Making a sacrifice to evil when it is due to the influence of an astral body, thereby averting a greater evil.
3 Attracting the power of superior beings.

Sacrifices belong to the first category: as a perfect being, God has no need of sacrificial offerings. If they are ordained, this is for an important purpose, the necessity of acting in consonance with the character of the star that rules over the Holy Land. If the nation does not conform to such celestial laws and stops making the required sacrificial offering, the Land will reject its inhabitants. Similarly, those unions which are forbidden in the Torah will bring about the same result. Hence in Mesopotamia Jacob could marry two sisters, and in Egypt Amram was able to marry his aunt, but in Eretz Israel such a liason would be forbidden.

A number of sacrifices are associated with the second principle. The scapegoat that is sent into the desert on Yom Kippur bore the sins of the people – it was destined to appease the wrath of Mars who rules over goats and demons. Further, this second principle is related to the act of circumcision: in accord with the decrees of the stars, each Israelite male must shed his blood. By giving Mars an appropriate substitute, death is avoided.

The third principle, however, is more complex. The attraction of the powers of higher beings is a positive act, yet this should not be done through magic which is specifically forbidden in Scripture. Israel, Ibn Ezra states, has no need to utilize forbidden magical procedures; if they were prohibited, this was because Israel has been given the divine commandments as well as a direct communion with God which are more effective than any artificial means.

Nethanel Ben Al-Fayyumi

Flourishing in the first half of the 12th century, Nethanel ben Al-Fayyumi was a Yemenite scholar and philosopher. It appears that he was the father of Jacob ben Nethanel to whom *Maimonides addressed his *Epistle to Yemen* (*Iggeret Teiman*). Nethanel's *Garden of Intellects* is a compendium of theology; it was published by R. Gottheil in 1896, and was subsequently edited and translated into English by D. Levine in 1908. The seven chapters of this work deal with divine unity, man as a microcosm, obedience to God, repentance, reliance upon God, divine providence, the Messiah, and the afterlife.

The book begins with an invocation to God who is called the Cause of the Cause of Causes. God, Nethanel declares, is

the Absolute Unity, the One in eternity; who emanateth souls, originateth forms, createth and produceth the bodies. Great are his benevolence, honor and might. He is free from limitations, acting at will. His are the celestial sphere, wisdom and power, decreeing and disposing, laudation and eulogy, beneficence and munificence, dominion and perpetuity, majesty and grandeur, creation and empire, uniqueness, and omnipotence. He is the Living One who dieth not, the Eternal by virtue of his eternity; the Permanent because of his Permanence; the Divine creator through his Supreme power, potent to do whatsoever he wishes. Nothing is like unto him; he created all things out of nothing. Unto him we cannot apply definition, attribute spatiality or quality. He has no throne that would imply place nor a footstool that would imply a sitting. He cannot be described as rising up or sitting down, as moving or as motionless, as bearing or as being born, as having characteristics or as in anywise defined. Before him all the idols were humilitated, and all creatures bowed in adoration. He does not enter or go out, descend or ascend. He is far beyond the reach of the human intellect, transcending apprehension, conception, and even conjecture. His essence is indescribable and cannot be grasped by means of the attributes.

(Al-Fayyumi, 1966, 1)

According to Nethanel, it is not possible to know God's true nature. In his view the creative act should not be understood as a cause, since such a cause is bound to its effect and God is not directly attached to the world. In this context Nethanel criticizes Bahya Ibn Pakuda for having identified God with the Cause of Causes: it is the Intellect which is the Cause of Causes which God as Creator has formed from nothing. Continuing his discussion of creation, Nethanel argues that the terms 'wish', 'will', and 'commandment' designate the mysterious creative act of which we can know nothing. As human beings we cannot penetrate the divine mysteries: it is impossible to conceive of God in any manner. Human comprehension cannot penetrate beyond the the first created being, the Intellect.

Describing the character of this first creation, Nethanel states that the Intellect has some of the attributes which have been ascribed to God: it is the source of all and the object of intellectual apprehension. Further, the Intellect is perfect and the source of the Universal Soul. Here Nethanel compares the Intellect to number one in a numerical series and the Universal Soul to number two; the Intellect, he continues, was created outside of time and space, but the Universal Soul emanated in a temporal and spacial context. For Nethanel, the Intellect can also be understood as Torah and Wisdom, while the Universal Soul is perceived as the Garden of Eden. In contrast with those scholars who maintain that ten separate intellects emanate from the Intellect, Nethanel maintains that there are seven, corresponding to the seven spheres: these seven spheres are composed of matter and form and emanate from the Universal Soul. Just as the Intellect cognizes its own essence in forming the Universal Soul, so the Universal Soul seeks to emulate the Intellect and thereby emanates the celestial sphere. From this beginning light and movement are transmitted to what is below just as the sun lightens the moon with its beams. In progression the movement of the spheres causes the four elements to combine and form all beings in the lower world: minerals, vegetables, animals, men and prophets.

In portraying this process of emanation, Nethanel stresses that the the five orders in the lower world are hierarchically arranged:

> Of the non-liquefiable minerals, he made a superior kind, the ruby; and of the liquefiable metals there is a superior kind, gold; which is very closely related to plants since it grows like them. Of the plants he made a noble species, the palm tree, which is very closely related to animals . . . God placed among animals a creature of the same class as man, the ape . . . there must be in the genus man a class resembling the angels. This class consists of the prophets and their heirs . . . Consider . . . how splendid this arrangement is: the last member of each series is connected with the first of the succeeding series.
>
> (*Ibid.*, 50–51)

In addition to the seven spheres, Nethanel contends that there is an eighth which contains the twelve signs of the Zodiac. As an advocate of astrology, he goes on to discuss the significance of various numerical combinations. In presenting his theories about divine emanation, Nethanel stresses that the Bible contains a myriad of scientific and philosophical ideas which can be discovered by the wise. Such esoteric knowledge, he insists, should be revealed only to those who are worthy of receiving such illumination.

Turning to the subject of prophecy, Nethanel adopts a naturalistic approach. In his view, the divine influx which emerges from the Intellect is obscured by its distance from its source. Yet God desires to bestow upon human beings a means of deliverance from the world of generation and corruption. As a consequence he has decreed that a revelation should proceed from the Universal Soul and find expression through the intermediacy of a prophetic figure who is pure and unsullied by the terrestrial world. Through such disclosure, such a person is able to predict future events, perform miracles, confound the wicked and reward the righteous. His prophecy serves as a means of redemption, and those who rebel against him remain imprisoned in the material world.

In offering this interpretation of prophecy, Nethanel contends that the prophet has the duty of insisting on the strict observance of the law as well as the dictates of the heart. Such intellectual duties are common to all people, and therefore every nation has its own prophets. For Nethanel then, prophecy should be understood as a process common throughout history: God eternally causes his goodness and perfection to emanate toward the Universal Soul; the divine influx thereby emanates eternally toward sages who are able to receive it. Because all peoples are able to be saved, each nation receives from its prophets a revelation appropriate to its needs. As far as the Torah is concerned, it was given to Israel for all time: it is perfect and must guide the Jewish nation until the advent of the Messiah. Revelations differ from one nation to another because God knows the particular character of individual peoples and adjusts his disclosure accordingly.

Abraham Bar Hiyya

Abraham Bar Hiyya lived in the latter half of the 11th century and died in about 1136. Living in Barcelona, little is known about his life. Nonetheless, two of his titles possibly reveal something of his existence: the first title *Savasorda* is a corruption of the Arabic meaning 'captain of the bodyguard' – by Bar Hiyya's time this title denoted a functionary with both judicial and civil responsibilities. Possibly Bar Hiyya held such a position in the court where he would have been able to convey his mathematical and astronomical knowledge. The second title *Nasi*, possibly denoted a position within the Spanish Jewish community. In any event, there is one incident known from Bar Hiyya's life: his conflict with Judah ben Barzillai Al-Bargeloni. This occurred at a wedding which Bar Hiyya insisted on postponing because the position of the planets were not propitious; Judah, however, regarded such astrological calculations as without foundation and wished to proceed with the ceremonies.

Unlike his predecessors, Bar Hiyya wrote in Hebrew as opposed to Arabic – such a change reflects the altered conditions of 12th century Jewish life in Christian lands. By this time Arabic had given way to Latin in literate circles; although some Jews knew Latin, they inevitably gravitated to the language of their literary sources. Apart from other works including studies of land-surveying, Bar Hiyya wrote two books on astronomy based on the Ptolemaic system. His philosophical and religious thought is found in two treatises: *Scroll of the Revealer* and *The Meditation of the Sad Soul*.

The *Meditation of the Sad Soul* begins with an affirmation of the validity of the discoveries of science. According to Bar Hiyya, science as well as the knowledge which enables the soul to return to its source cannot be taught by philosophers because they have not received the

Torah. Further, even if they were able to teach scientific subjects, Jews should not learn from them. Nonetheless, after expounding theories reflecting Aristotelianism and Neoplatonism he asserts that they are based on the Torah. There is no inconsistency here, he contends, since science as a discipline is the heritage of the Jewish people – the wise men from all nations have simply derived it from the Torah.

The *Meditation* continues with a discussion of creation as portrayed in the Book of Genesis. As both Jewish and non-Jewish thinkers have observed, before the creative act all creatures were non-being. When God determined to create the universe, their existence in potentiality consisted of matter, form and non-being; when they were actualized, God removed the non-being and made form inhere in matter. Thereby the world came into existence. In this process all existing things emerged from the conjunction of matter and form:

> They say that when (God's) Pure Thought decided to actualize them, he empowered the closed Form to come into existence and to be clothed with its splendour, without contact with the hyle. This Form, which is not connected with the hyle, is the Form of angels, seraphim, souls and all forms of the upper world . . . Subsequently the Form attaches itself to the impure hyle, and from this union were created all kinds of terrestrial bodies.
>
> (Bar Hiyya, 1969, 40)

According to Bar Hiyya, Form penetrates all things from angels to the material world: the ladder of being culminates in human beings who possess reason. The Torah elucidates such a hierarchy. In this scheme of creation, Israel plays a pivotal role – the final purpose of this created order is to give meaning to Israel in the unfolding of God's plan for the redemption of the world: 'Just as God has distinguished man from all other living beings and granted him superiority over them, so he has distinguished one nation and sanctified it for his glory above all mankind.' (*Ibid.*, 52).

In presenting this cosmological scheme, Bar Hiyya distinguishes between the four categories in which form exists:

1 Self-subsistent form that never combines with matter.
2 Form that is attached inseparably to matter
3 Form that is attached temporarily to matter.
4 Form which is attached to a body.

The second category, Bar Hiyya asserts, is not eternal – it has a beginning and will have an end. Its evolution is bound to the soul. The human soul – the fourth category – emerges from the world of pure forms. After residing in the body it must return to the angelic realm (the domain of light). In his estimation there are five worlds of light, corresponding to the three degrees of prophecy:

> The first degree is the resplendent light that appeared to the angels engaged in the divine service, to the prophets and to the most eminent of the children of Israel at the time of the Revelation on Mount Sinai . . . The second degree is the Voice emanating from among the cherubim which was heard by Moses; the angels hear it when they accomplish their missions, all the people of Israel heard it on Mount Sinai . . . The third degree is the light of Wisdom, of Knowledge, of Intelligence and of the Law, and it is the intellection transmitted to the angels and the seraphim; this intelligible light spreads and flows over the just among men . . . The fourth degree is the soul or the breath that God breathes into men, into sages, and into those who are not wise . . . The fifth degree is that of the light that God has reserved for the just in the next world to come.
>
> (*Ibid.*, 22)

The degrees of prophecy and the worlds described here correspond with one another: the luminous world is that of the visual and auditory revelation that was reserved for Moses as well as various prophets; the world of the Voice was reserved for the second class of prophets; and the world of knowledge is an indistinct revelation that is reserved for just gentiles.

Continuing this exposition, Bar Hiyya outlines the role of Israel in the history of the world. In his view, the universe only reached perfection after Adam was created; hence human history will not be complete until Israel has attained its destiny. At this time the Jewish nation will exercise its sovereignty over all peoples. Such an historical evolution, Bar Hiyya explains, corresponds to the hierarchy of the soul. For Bar Hiyya, there are three souls: the two inferior souls have the same destiny as plants and animals; the third soul, however, is rational in character. This higher soul is intelligent and eternal – it is either rewarded or punished in accordance with its merits. This was the pure soul that God breathed into human beings at creation and was subsequently defiled by Adam's sinfulness. As a result, it was plunged into the darkness of the other two souls. For this reason it exists in only one individual in each generation.

Since the time of the flood, the pure soul has commenced its path of liberation from the lower domain of inferior souls. Instead of dwelling in the vegetative soul, it is imprisoned in the animal soul. But on the third day of creation, Jacob appeared who announced the fourth day, produced a family of worthy individuals, and formed a people who were capable of receiving the gift of the Torah. By this means, the world can be brought to a state of perfection.

The history of the soul's quest for liberation corresponds to the history of Israel. This is because the duration of the world – 7,000 years – can be divided by 7: this mirrors the 7 days of creation. Furthermore, all creatures formed during the 7 days of creation symbolize what will take place during the corresponding day of the advent of the Messiah. In each epoch, symbolizing each of these days of creation, there are 7 generations (also symbolizing these days). At the end of the third epoch, God bestowed the Torah upon Israel, and this act heralds the beginning of the fourth epoch. The seventh day, the seventh epoch, and the seventh millennium will hence be the Day of the Messiah. Throughout this work, the preoccupation with the coming of the Messiah predominates – through the interpretation of biblical verses and the determination of astrological data, Bar Hiyya seeks to calculate the advent of the Messianic Age.

Abu Al-Barakat

Abu Al-Barakat (Hibat Allah Ali Ibn Malka Abu al-Barakat al Baghdadi al Baladi) resided in Baghdad in the latter half of the 11th century and the first half of the twelfth. Serving as a doctor at the court of the Caliph al-Mustanjid, he became well-known as a physician. In 1143 he dictated a commentary on the Book of Ecclesiastes in Arabic to Isaac, the son of *Abraham Ibn Ezra; however, at an advanced age he converted to Islam. As a consequence, he was rarely referred to by later Jewish philosophers; in Arabic circles, on the other hand, his writings were frequently cited, particularly by Fakh-al-Din-Razi. In addition to his commentary on Ecclesiastes, Al-Barakat wrote a philosophical work in three volumes as well as studies of Hebrew and Arabic and several works on medicine and pharmacy.

Al-Barakat's philosophical treatise, *The Book of What Has Been Established By Personal Reflection*, commences with a history of philosophy. The ancient philosophers, he argues, conveyed their views orally; consequently their teaching was disseminated only to those students who were capable of comprehending their ideas. During this period there were many scholars, and such knowledge was passed on from one generation to the next. This process of transmission was without error, and nothing was lost. Nonetheless, at a later date when the number of sages decreased and lives were shorter, much of this information disappeared. To remedy this situation, scholars began to write down this knowledge so that it could be transmitted to those individuals who were able to comprehend such teaching. In many of these works, Al-Barakat explains, these authors deliberately used obscure expressions so that only those of advanced learning could understand what was being conveyed, thereby insuring that these sciences would be hidden from those who had no aptitude for such investigation.

As time passed, scholars were compelled to interpret these abstruse explanations so that the ideas of previous sages could be understood. As a result, the number of commentaries increased, and even those who had little ability to grasp the scientific subjects contained in these early works engaged in interpretative efforts. By this means the writings of earlier thinkers were contaminated. Hence, when Al-Barakat sought to devote himself to the philosophical sciences, he discovered that despite his study of ancient thinkers, their ideas were of little significance. Even though his own thought conformed to some notions contained in these works, he reached conclusions of a different nature. As he explains in the introduction to his philosophical treatise:

> Nevertheless my notes became more and more numerous and they have constituted such a considerable sum of scientific knowledge that . . . having been implored again and by persons who deserved a favourable reply, I complied with their request and I composed this book treating of the philosophical sciences which have as their subject that which exists, that is physics and metaphysics. I have called it *Kitab al-Mu'tabar* (*The Book of What Has Been Established By Personal Reflection*), because I have put in it what I knew by my own intelligence, established by personal reflection verified and perfected by meditation; I have transcribed nothing that I have not understood and I have understood and accepted nothing without meditation and personal reflection. In adopting such or other opinions and doctrines, I have not let myself be guided by the desire of finding myself in accord with the great names because of their grandeur or in disagreement with the small because of their insignificance.
>
> (in Pines, 1979, 2–4)

Paralleling the *Book of Healing* by the Islamic thinker Avicenna, Al-Barakat embraces a number of theories found in this work, but subjects others to criticism. Turning to the subject of human psychology, Al-Barakat maintains that human beings believe in a soul which animates the body. Following Avicenna, he argues that the soul is the same as selfhood. Such knowledge – an awareness of self – precedes all knowledge and is independent of sense data. This explains why a person with an amputated leg does not have a diminished sense of selfhood. Such a perception of self is not limited to scholars; it is immediate and certain.

Arguing for the unity of the soul, Al-Barakat draws out several important implications. First, he alleges that human beings are able to see by means of the agency of the eye, yet it is not in fact the eye that sees. As with the other senses, they are no more than instruments whereby the soul of man is able to perceive the physical world. In this process there is no division: it is the person who sees, feels, hears and thinks. Second, Al-Barakat argues that there is a range of instinctive actions that do not belong to consciousness. Because one's conscious attention is limited, internal processes take place without a person's awareness. This theory about unconscious activity helps to explain how memories are able to surface within the conscious mind by means of an association of ideas. Third, Al-Barakat contends that there is no distinction between the soul and the intellect.

In presenting his view of the self, Al-Barakat asserts that the soul has an a priori apperception of time: 'The soul has a similar awareness of time by, and together with, its own self and existence prior to its being aware of any other thing of which it is aware and which it considers in its own mind. (in Pines, 1979, 289). Unlike Aristotle and others, Al-Barakat does not concieve of time as the measurement of movement; instead he asserts that there is only one time which is similar for all beings including God. Similarly, Al-Barakat argues against the Aristotelian concept of place. Distincing himself from Aristotle and his Arabic commentators, he advances the idea of three-dimensional space and accepts the possibility of movement within the void. Space, he believes, is infinite since it is impossible to conceive of a limited space. To explain this notion, Al-Barakat states that if we imagine the totality of spheres and reach the last sphere, we cannot then conceive of a finite limit – something must lie beyond, whether it is a body or the void. Concerning the fall of bodies, he also rejects Aristotle's view that a body moves because it has a mover and continues to move because such a mover continues to act. In this context Al-Barakat accounts for the acceleration of heavy bodies on the basis of the principle of natural inclination contained within them.

On the basis of these theories of physics, Al-Barakat rejects the idea that God is an Unmoved Mover who stands apart from the world. On the contrary, God can be known through the order of the universe. In opposition to earlier Jewish thinkers influenced by the Mu'tazilite kalam, he insists that God's attributes are positive. Through human knowledge, it is possible to attain an understanding of God's nature and activity in the world:

> He is endowed with knowledge, this being proven by the existence of knowledge in the things created by him. He is bountiful, this being proven by his bountifulness with regard to the things created by him. He is powerful, this being proven by his power over the things created by him. He is endowed with various kinds of cognitions, this being proven by the knowledge existing in the things created by him.
>
> (*Ibid.*, 306)

Here Al-Barakat posits a causal relationship between God's attributes and those attributes found in other beings. Yet, in God every quality exists in the universe exists in perfection: these are his positive attributes.

According to Al-Barakat God is perfectly wise; he necessarily exists and causes all things to come into being. Yet because there is an analogy between God's nature and that of human beings, we can speak of him by means of positive attributes. The essence of God, Al-Barakat continues, contains will, power and knowledge just as a triangle has three angles equal to two right angles. Such equality is inherent in the nature of triangularity; similarly, God necessarily possesses these characteristics. Turning to the attribute of knowledge, Al-Barakat insists that in the same manner that human knowledge necessarily includes the knowledge of particularities, so God knows individuals, although possibly not all of them. Like human beings, God directs his attention wherever he wishes: 'He directs his attention towards what he wills and turns away from what he will.' (Ibid., 330)

Here, then, is a fundamentally different conception of the Diety from what is found in Aristotle's writings. For Al-Barakat God knows, is wise and exerts his power in the same fashion as human beings. He is free to act and exercise his will. As a personal God located in time, he 'hears and sees, rewards and punishes, is angry and pleased, directs his attention toward things and turns away from things, as he wills and through what he wills; causes do not dominate him. For it is he that has rule in and according to them. And he renews and changes according to the requirement of wisdom with reference to what he necessitates in accordance with motivating and deterrent factors known and cognised by him in the whole world. (*Ibid.*, 332)

Abraham Ibn Daud

Born in Cordoba, Abraham Ibn Daud lived in Spain from 1110–1180. Initially he received a religious and secular education including Arabic poetry, literature and philosophy. Fleeing Cordoba before the Almohad conquest, he settled in Toledo where he collaborated in translating texts from Arabic into Latin; subsequently these works were further translated into the vernacular in collaboration with other scholars. Among the texts translated in this way was the *Fountain of Life* by *Solomon Ibn Gabirol. Like most philosophers, Ibn Daud was both a physician and astronomer; in addition, he worked as an historian producing *Sefer ha-Kabbalah* (*Book of the Tradition*).

Ibn Daud's most important philosophical work, *the Exalted Faith* (*Emunah Ramah*), was composed in 1160–1; although the original text is not extant, Hebrew translations of the work dating from the fourteenth century were made by Samuel Ibn Motot at the suggestion of Isaac Ibn Sheset. The Exalted Faith had little influence on medieval philosophers who did not know Arabic, and was overshadowed by *Maimonides *Guide for the Perplexed* written some years later.

In the introduction Ibn Daud states that he wrote this work to resolve the difficulties connected with determinism and free will; in his view, this issue can only be dealt with in a broader context. Hence the book is structured in two parts: the first deals with physics which he calls philosophy including proofs for the existence of a Prime Mover; the second is devoted to revealed religion. For Ibn Daud these topics are in fact the same since scientific truths are found in all sacred texts. Philosophical demonstration, he argues, must always be perfected by demonstrating that the Bible alludes to such philosophical proof. In particular, when passages appear to conflict with such demonstration or contradict one another, they need to be interpreted according to the intellect – this is because many verses are directed to the common people and do not reveal their deeper meaning on a superficial reading. The purpose of *The Exalted Faith* is to illustrate that Scripture is in accord with Aristotelian philosophy:

When someone is just beginning his study of the sciences, he is perplexed about what he knows from the point of view of the traditional knowledge because he has not attained in science the degree where he could state the truth in the questions which are not clear. Accordingly, this book will be very useful to him for it will acquaint him with many points of Science which we have built on the principles of religion.

(Ibn Daud, 1982, 2–4)

Like *Moses Maimonides, Ibn Daud composed this treatise because beginners in philosophy were unable to harmonize the Bible with science; as a result they were inclined to reject either biblical teaching or Aristotelianism:

The first (reason) is that the Torah and philosophy are in flagrant contradiction when they attempt to describe the divine essence; for the philosophers, the incorporeal God is in no way capable of alteration; the Torah, on the contrary, narrates God's movements, his feelings . . . Given that philosophy and the Torah are in opposition on this subject, we are in the situation of a man with two masters, one great and the other not small; he cannot please the first without opposing the opinion of the second without opposing the opinion of the second.

(*Ibid.*, 82)

To alleviate such difficulty, Ibn Daud explains that the biblical text should be understood in a rational sense. In the first part of this work, Ibn Daud begins each chapter with an exposition of philosophical ideas; this is followed by supporting scriptural verses. The first chapter commences with a discussion of substance and accident – this is followed by a treatment of substance, infinite length and breadth, movement, the soul, and the spheres. The second part of *The Exalted Faith* continues with an exposition of what Ibn Daud regards as the principles of the Jewish faith. Beginning with the concept of religious commitment, he attempts to answer the question: what is faith? Ibn Daud contends that it is not the faith of popular belief which is of concern. The common people assume that what is not matter does not exist; thus they do not believe in an incorporeal God. When such individuals advance in their understanding, however, they believe in the tradition of the sages – yet there remains the danger that they will not know how to deal with confusion and doubt.

Regarding the faith of the rabbis, it is based on a knowledge of

God's activities – it is to this type of religious conviction that the Torah directs the common people. However, such true belief grounded in a perception of God's acts does not prove that God is incorporeal: he could be either a sphere or a star. The true sages among the philosophers predicate their belief on the demonstration that God is the Prime Mover. At this stage in the argument, Ibn Daud attempts to prove that the Prime Mover exists by demonstrating that such a being is unique and non-material. A second proof of the necessity of a unique and incorporeal God is based on cause and effect. The existence of all beings, Ibn Daud argues, is contingent; a necessary being, however, can cause them to exist, creating them ex nihilo. Eternal beings, like angels, do not come into existence from the state of non-being; rather, their existence is derived from another than themselves, and ultimately from God himself.

After discussing the concept of God's unity, Ibn Daud turns to the divine attributes. In his opinion, the only true attributes are negative in character. This discussion is followed by a consideration of the nature of angels. The existence of angels is certain, he argues, because the human soul is initially in potentia, and then in actu. The transition from one state to the other involves movement: all movement is caused by a mover, and the Active Intellect is the motive power for such change. Another proof concerns the course of the stars: in Ibn Daud's view, such a phenomenon is explicable only through incorporeal intermediaries and a unique God. It is he who produces the material world. Multiplicity does not emanate directly from God since only One can come from One. Instead, it accompanies the First Being issued directly from God – this is what the philosophers call the Intellect and the Torah designates as Angel. In comparison with God, it is imperfect since it receives its being from something other than itself. Duality is therefore at its very root. From this First Intellect emerge three beings: a Second Intellect which is less perfect than the first because it does not arise directly from God but from a being outside the divine realm; the soul of the sphere, and its matter.

Ibn Daud goes on to explain that the soul of the sphere of the fixed stars and the matter of the sphere of the fixed stars emanate from the Second Intellect. Hence from Intellect to Intellect, we reach the Final Intellect, that which presides over the lower world which gives forms to all sublunary beings. It is this which makes our intellect pass from potentiality to actuality and serves as the source of prophecy. Concerning prophetic apprehension, Ibn Daud maintains that there are three types of prophetic states: (1) true dreams; (2) visions that take place in an unconscious state; (3) visions that occur while the prophet is awake and conscious. Describing the highest degree of prophecy, he writes:

> Divine providence on behalf of his creatures is already evident to all those who mediatate, but since these are few in number, the perfect goodness of God makes it still more evident by making it repose on those men who are of perfect conduct and irreproachable morals, so that, as it were, they become intermediaries between God and his creatures. He elevates them to such a point that they have a power comparable to that of the eminent substances which incline towards them in prophecy . . . Only perfect and pure souls can attain such a level. This perfection and this purity are sometimes in a man from the beginning of his formation, and also moral perfection, but study is of great utility, as is the society of virtuous men . . .
>
> (*Ibid.*, 73–4)

In Ibn Daud's view, although prophecy is a natural phenomenon, only Israel has the gift of attaining this highest state of perfection. Hence the biblical text, which is the fruit of prophecy, should not be understood as depicting God in corporeal form. To interpret anthropomorphic expressions in Scripture literally is to commit an act of heresy. In this light, Ibn Daud criticizes his coreligionists who have misinterpreted the biblical text in contrast with those Christians and Muslims who read Scripture correctly:

> The other, non-Jewish, religious communities have not wished to belittle God by attributing to him these vile details unworthy of him, thus, the Christians have translated the verses: God said, God descended, by: the Lord said, the Lord appeared; thus the Moslems have never claimed that God spoke to the prophets or appeared to them . . . while among our coreligionists certain have so little discernment that they are not satisfied with attributing to God change and movement, they go so far as to attribute to him more transformations than to any of his creatures.
>
> (*Ibid.*, 90–1)

Before concluding with a discussion of the divine commandments, Ibn Daud returns to the problem of free will. Free will, he believes, consists in keeping God's commandments – if there were no such choice, the notion of reward and punishment would have no place in Jewish teaching. Citing l Samuel 26:10, Ibn Daud illustrates that there are three major causes of human events: divine, natural and accidental causes. The fourth cause – free will – is exemplified by a description of the flight from Keilah. This event was an episode in the conflict between David and Saul in 1 Samuel 23. From this example, human events are described as determined by divine, natural and accidental causes, but the wise person who hears the divine word can foresee future events and take precautions. Free will thus consists in the liberty to follow God's law and purify one's soul – when this occurs, God's providence watches over those who are faithful to him.

Moses Maimonides

Born in Cordoba, Spain, Moses ben Maimon (Maimonides) was the son of the dayyan (rabbinical judge) of Cordoba. Due to the conquest of Cordoba by the Almohads in 1148, Maimonides left Cordoba with his family; for the next eight or nine years they wandered from town to town in Spain, eventually settling in Fez in North Africa in 1160. During this period Maimonides began a commentary on the Mishnah, wrote short treatises on logic as well as the Jewish calendar, and completed notes for a commentary on several tractates of the Talmud as well as a legal code. In Fez Maimonides studied under Judah ha-Kohen ibn Susan, and continued working on his commentary on the Mishnah in addition to other projects. After the martyrdom of his teacher, Maimonides together with his family fled from Fez to Acre where they stayed for several months. The family then left for Egypt; after a short stay in Alexandria, they took up residence in Fostat (Cairo).

After his father's death, Maimonides was supported by his brother David who imported precious stones – at this stage he devoted himself to writing and acting as a religious leader of the community. However, when his brother drowned in the Indian Ocean on a business trip, Maimonides worked as a doctor eventually becoming one of the physicians to the ruler of Egypt. During this period Maimonides wrote his legal code, the *Mishneh Torah* and his philosophical work, the *Guide for the Perplexed*. In a letter written to the translator of the *Guide*, *Samuel ben Judah ibn Tibbon, Maimonides describes his busy life at this time:

> My duties to the sultan are very heavy. I am obliged to visit him every day, early in the morning . . . I do not return to Misr (Fostat) until the afternoon. Then I am almost dying with hunger . . . I find the antechambers filled with people, both Jews and gentiles, nobles and common people, judges and bailiffs,

friends and foes – a mixed multitude who await the time of my return. I dismount from my animal, wash my hands, go forth to my patients, and entreat them to bear with me while I partake of some slight refreshment, the only meal I take in the twenty-four hours. Then I go forth to attend to my patients, and write prescriptions and directions for their various ailments. Patients go in and out until nightfall, and sometimes even, I solemnly assure you, until two hours or more in the night.

(Encyclopedia Judaica, Jerusalem, 1971, Vol, 11, 758)

In his major philosophical treatise, *The Guide for the Perplexed*, Maimonides draws on the great Muslim expositors of Aristotle such as Avicenna and al-Farabi. In line with Islamic teaching he argues that reason and faith are harmoniously interrelated, yet he criticizes various features of Muslim Mu'tazilite and Asharyite philosophy. The central aim of the *Guide* is to reconcile the Torah with a number of central tenets of Aristotelianism. As Maimonides explains in his introduction to this work, the *Guide* was deliberately written for an intellectual elite. His book was thus intended only for those whose study of logic, mathematics, natural science and metaphysics had led them to a state of perplexity about seeming contradictions between the Torah and human reason.

The first part of the *Guide* begins with a discussion of the anthropomorphic terms in the Hebrew Scriptures. A literal reading of these passages implies that God is a corporeal being, but according to Maimonides this is an error: such descriptions must be understood figuratively. In this connection, he argues – as does * Abraham Ibn Daud in the *Exalted Faith* – that no positive attributes can be predicated of God since the Divine is an absolute unity. Hence when God is depicted positively in the Bible, such ascriptions must refer to his activity. The only true attributes, Maimonides contends, are negative ones – they lead to a knowledge of God because in negation no plurality is involved. Each negative attribute excludes from God's essence some imperfection. Therefore, when one says that God is incorporeal, this means He has no body. Such negation, Maimonides believes, brings one nearer to the knowledge of the Godhead.

Turning from God's nature to prohecy, Maimonides points out that most people believe that God chooses any person he desires and inspires him with the prophetic spirit. Such a view is opposed by the philosophers who contend that prophecy is a human gift requiring ability and study. Rejecting both positions, Maimonides states that prophecy is an inspiration from God which passes through the meditation of the Active Intellect and then to the faculty of imagination. It requires perfection in theoretical wisdom, morality and development of the imagination. On the basis of this conception, Maimonides asserts that human beings can be divided into three classes according to the development of their reasoning capabilities. First, there are those whose rational faculties are highly developed and receive influences from the Active Intellect but whose imagination is defective – these are wise men and philosophers. The second group consists of those where the imagination alone is in good condition, but the intellect is defective: these are the statesmen, lawgivers and politicians. Thirdly there are the prophets, those whose imagination is constitutionally perfect and whose intellect is well developed.

Maimonides insists that God witholds prophetic inspiration from certain individuals, but those whom he has selected teach speculative truth and adherence to the Torah. Unlike the other prophets who only intermittently receive prophecy, Moses prophesied continuously and was the only one to give legislation. The purpose of the body of Mosaic law is to regulate society and provide for spiritual well-being and perfection. As far as ceremonial law is concerned, Maimonides argues that the purpose of a number of ritual commandments was to prevent Israel from participating in pagan cultic practices which could lead to idolatry. Sacrifice, he suggests, was a concession to the popular mentality of the ancient Israelites since the nation could not conceive of worship without sacrificial offerings.

The problem of evil is also a central theological topic in the *Guide*. Maimonides contends that evil does not exist as an independent entity; rather it is a privation of good. What appears evil, such as human immorality, is frequently due to the fault of human beings and can be corrected through good government. Likewise, personal suffering is often the result of vice. Physical calamities – earthquakes, floods and disease – are not the result of human failing but are part of the natural order. To complain that there is more evil than good in the world results from an anthropomorphic conception of humanity's place in the universe – God's final purpose cannot be known. Unlike Aristotelian philosophers, Maimonides conceives of God's providence as concerned with each individual. For him such providential care is proportionate to the degree than a person has activated his intellect. In this regard, Maimonides argues that the ideal of human perfection involves reason and ethical action. To illustrate his view, Maimonides uses a parable about a king's palace. Those who are outside its walls have no doctrinal belief; those within the city but with their backs to the palace hold incorrect positions; others wishing to enter the palace not knowing how to do so are traditionalists who lack philosohical sophistication. But those who have entered the palace have speculated about the fundamental principles of religion. Only the person who has achieved the highest level of intellectual attainment can be near the throne of God.

Such philosophical attainment, however, is not in itself sufficient; to be perfect a person must go beyond communion with God to a higher state. Quoting Jeremiah 9:23–24, Maimonides proclaims:

> Let not the wise man glory in his wisdom, let not the mighty man glory in his might, let not the rich man glory in his riches; but let him who glories glory in this, that he understands and knows me, that I am the Lord who practice steadfast love, justice, and righteousness in the earth; for in these things I delight, says the Lord.

Just as God is merciful, just and righteous, so the perfected individual should emulate God's actions in his daily life. Here then is a synthesis of the Aristotelian emphasis on intellectualism and Jewish insistence on the moral life. Such a philosophical exposition of the Jewish faith not only influenced Jewish writers, but also had an impact on medieval Christian scholars such as Albertas Magnus and Thomas Aquinas.

By the thirteenth century Maimonides' writings – along with the works by other medieval Jewish philosophers – had been translated into Hebrew by Jews living in Southern France. As a result of this scholarly activity, Jews in Spain, Provence and Italy produced a variety of philosophical and scientific writings including commentaries on Maimonides' *Guide*. Though Maimonides was admired as a legal authority, some Jewish scholars were troubled by his views. In particular, they were dismayed that he appeared not to believe in physical resurrection; that he viewed prophecy, providence and immortality as dependent on intellectual attaiment; that he regarded the doctrine of divine incorporality as a fundamental tenet of the Jewish faith; and that he felt that knowledge of God should be based on Aristotelian principles. For these sages, Maimonides' theology was seen as a threat to Judaism and to rabbinic learning. In 1230 some of those opposed to the Maimonidean philosophical system attempted to prevent the study of the *Guide* as well as the philosohical sections of Maimonides legal code, the *Mishneh Torah*. The bitter antagonism between Maimonideans and anti-Maimonideans came to an end when Dominican inquisitors in France burned copies of Maimonides' writings – both sides were appalled by such an action. Yet opposition to Maimonides continued throughout the century. In 1300 anti-Maimonideans issued a ban against studying Greek philosophy before the age of twenty-five, but the conflict subsided when many Jews were expelled from France in 1306.

Chapter 4

13th Century

By the 13th century most of the important philosophical texts had been translated into Hebrew by Jews living in southern France. *Judah Ibn Tibbon who emigrated from Muslim Spain to Provence translated such works as *Ibn Pakudah's *Duties of the Heart*, *Judah Halevi's *The Book of the Khazars*, and *Saadiah Gaon's *Book of Beliefs and Opinions*; his son Samuel translated Maimonides' *Guide for the Perplexed*. Furthermore, the writings of Plato and Aristotle as well as commentaries on Aristotle by such Islamic scholars as Averroes were translated into Hebrew as well. As a consequence of this scholarly activity, Jews in Spain, Provence and Italy produced philosophical and scientific writings including commentaries on Maimonides *Guide*. In this century Jewish philosophy took several different directions. In Islamic countries, Jewish thinkers were deeply influenced by Arabic speculation while making use of *Maimonides' work. In Provence a school of Maimonidean exegesis emerged under the influence of *Samuel Ibn Tibbon. In Spain, an esoteric movement developed which was deeply influenced by aggadic and midrashic sources dealing with the combination of the letters of the Hebrew alphabet. Finally, in Italy Maimonidean exegesis was influenced by Latin scholasticism.

Joseph ben Judah Ibn Aknin

Born in Barcelona in c. 1150, Joseph Ibn Aknin was a philosopher and poet. Either he or his father moved to North Africa probably due to the Almohad persecutions; although he wished to live elsewhere so he could practice Judaism freely, he remained there throughout his life. From his discussion of forced conversion, it is evident that he felt guilty about living as a Crypto-Jew. When Maimonides travelled to

North Africa, he met Ibn Aknin; when Maimonides' left for Egypt, Ibn Aknin composed a couplet dealing with the great philosopher's departure. Little more is known of Ibn Aknin's life, his family or descendents; possibly he earned his livelihood as a physician.

Aknin's works consist of several texts covering a wide range of topics:

1 In *Sefer Hukkim u-Mishpatim*, Ibn Aknin deals with Jewish law; this work is divided into a series of treatises of which the first deals with doctrines and beliefs. Possibly this work was modelled on Maimonides' *Mishneh Torah*, although it was limited to those ordinances which were still observed in Jewish life.

2 Although Ibn Aknin's *Clarification of the Fundamentals of the Faith* is no longer in existence, it is known from a reference in another work that his treatise dealt with human freedom.

3 *Ma'amar al ha-Middot ve-ha-Mishkalot* is a Hebrew translation of an Arabic text. According to the introduction, this tract deals with Mishnaic and Talmudic references to coins, weights, measurements, boundaries and time which are compared with contemporary notions.

4 *Mevod ha-Talmud*, divided into 12 chapters, deals with those principles a person must know if he wishes to engage in Talmudic study.

5 *The Hygiene of Healthy Souls and the Therapy of Ailing Souls* is a moral treatise composed in Arabic. In the introduction, Ibn Aknin presents a discussion of the parts of the soul and its functions; here he explains the nature of the afterlife as well as such topics as speech and silence, confidentiality, piety, food and drink, and the true aim of life. In this presentation he encourages readers to be moderate in their actions; in his view self-indulgence is to be avoided. What each person should seek, he argues, are spiritual and religious virtues. In its composition, each section begins with a statement of the right course to follow, buttressed by references to rabbinic sayings (and in some cases statements from classical and Arabic sources). A later chapter concerns the laws of Abu Yusuf Yaqub al-Mansur, one of the Almohad rulers; the next chapter outlines the qualities of a good instructor, the conditions necessary for scholarship, and the appropriate curriculum. Until the student has reached thirty, Ibn Aknin states, he should be preoccupied with traditional Jewish lore – this should be mastered so that he is able to deal with difficult issues and challenges to the faith. The rest of a

person's life should be devoted to the the study of logic, music, mathematics, mechanics and metaphysics.

6 The *Sefer ha-Musar* – composed in Hebrew – is a commentary on the *Pirkei Avot*; here Ibn Aknin was indebted to Maimonides' commentary which he follows. Of particular note in this work is Ibn Aknin's interest in psychology and ethics. Further, he writes at length about the soul, human responsiblity, miracles, and natural law.

7 Ibn Aknin's *The Divulgence of Mysteries and the Appearance of Lights* is an Arabic commentary on the Song of Songs. In the introduction to this work, Ibn Aknin discusses the emanation of intellects from God; here he refers to the view of Al-Farabi, stating that he was not in any disagreement with him except in one area. Aristotle and his followers, he explains, believe that intellects have their source in God by necessity, whereas Ibn Aknin believes that their formation took place by an act of the divine will. According to Ibn Aknin, the lover in the Song of Songs is the last of the intellects, the Active Intellect; the beloved, on the other hand, is the human soul which is encouraged by the Active Intellect to attain intelligible knowledge and forsake the material world.

In this work Ibn Aknin claims that he was the first writer to provide a philosophical commentary on the entire text. Yet unlike those writers who came after him such as Moses Ibn Tibbon, Caspi, and Gersonides, his own interpretation owes little if anything to Maimonides' *Guide*. For Ibn Aknin, the Song of Songs symbolizes the quest of the soul to unite with the Active Intellect as well as the Active Intellect's love for the soul. In advancing this allegorical interpretation, Ibn Aknin does not seek to reject the literal meaning of Scripture, nor by implication the commandments contained in the Pentateuch.

In the commentary itself Ibn Aknin gives an explanation of each verse: first, he discusses its exoteric sense, providing an exposition of its grammatical forms and simple meaning. He then offers a midrashic interpretation of the text related to the destiny of Israel. Finally, Ibn Aknin draws out the philosophical, psychological and physiological implications of the words themselves. Here and in his other writings Ibn Aknin was typical of those philosophically minded Jews living in an Islamic environment who sought to provide a synthesis of Jewish learning and secular study. Convinced of the validity of the system of Jewish belief and practice, he saw no conflict between secular knowledge and religious faith.

Samuel ben Judah Ibn Tibbon

The son of the translator, Judah Ibn Tibbon, Samuel Ibn Tibbon was born in c. 1160 possibly in Lunel. Subsequently he resided in Arles, Marseilles, Toledo, Barcelona, and Alexandria. It appears that he was a disappointment to his father because he was not sufficiently interested in academic pursuits; to rectify this situation, Judah wrote an admonitory will encouraging Samuel to mend his ways. When he left Lunel, it appears that he took such advice to heart.

Like his father, Samuel translated a variety of important works from Arabic into Hebrew. His first translation was in all likelihood Galen's *Ars Parva* with an Arabic commentary; this was completed in 1199. This was followed by Aristotle's *Meterologica* accompanied by notes probably drawn from Alexander of Ahrodisias commentaries. Subsequently he is reputed to have translated the *Alexander Romance*. Of *Maimonides' writings, he translated the *Guide for the Perplexed*, the *Letter on the Resurrection of the Dead*, and the introductions to the *Commentary on the Mishnah*. In 1213 he compiled a *Glossary of Unusual Words to be found in the Guide*.

In addition to these translations, Samuel composed a Commentary on Ecclesiastes, a treatise on Genesis l:9 (*Let the Waters Be Gathered*), and a *Letter on Providence* addressed to Maimonides. The intention of *Let the Waters Be Gathered* is to address an issue in physics. According to Aristotelianism, the four elements – earth, water, air and fire – occupy their natural positions. Yet Genesis states: 'Let the waters under the heaven be gathered together unto one place, and let the dry land appear.' (Genesis l:9). On the basis of this biblical verse the natural series of the elements is disrupted since earth follows water and is placed before air. What brought about such a transformation of the natural world? For the philosophers this was not a real problem: the earth was always next to air and water existed in the form of clouds. It is this juxtaposition of the four elements and their change from one to another that enables plants, animals and human beings to exist. For Samuel, however, this discussion is unnecessary; the rabbis do not permit any exploration of the beginning or end of the world.

In Samuel's view, the world was not created in time ex nihilo. The reason Moses did not state this explicitly was because the purpose of the Torah is to serve the common people. Scripture does contain true doctrines about creation, but Moses intentionally presented ideas to the masses that they were capable of understanding. In opposition to Maimonides, Samuel asserts that scholars should attempt to explain the philosophical ideas contained in the biblical text. Only a few Jews understand Scripture correctly; this has led to a situation in which fewer members of the community are acquainted with true science than is found among Muslims and Christians. In order to rectify this situation, Jewish sages must be enlightened about their own holy books. Such knowledge which has been suppressed for ages has paradoxically become the preserve of other nations who were able to mock the Jews for their ignorance.

In presenting this programme of reeduction of the Jewish people, Samuel explains why David and Solomon taught about the process of creation more clearly than Moses. Moses himself was aware of such doctrines, but he refrained from passing on such knowledge to the the nation since the masses had no conception of an incorporeal God. Hence in the Book of Genesis no mention is made of the separate Intellects who act as intermediaries between God who is incorporeal and the spheres which have a material existence. Nonetheless, Samuel points out the the last four verses of Psalm 104 as well as two passages in aggadic sources depict the nature of the angelic domain – these texts supplement the presentation of creation contained in Genesis.

After explaining that the rabbinic view of creation contained in aggadic sources is largely uniform, Samuel examines the difference between the views of the philosophers and rabbinic sages. Both the rabbis and philosophers agree that the separate Intellects antedate the world as a cause, yet the philosophers argue that these Intellects are co-eternal with God. In addition, they attribute eternity to the universe that emerges from these Intellects. The rabbis, however, state the the creation of the sublunary world occurred in time and that these Intellects as well as matter existed before the four elements.

According to Samuel, such matter which exists before creation is eternal. Regarding the Intellects, they derive their existence from God. Thus everything flows from God: the Lord is the true cause of both the celestial and the sublunary world which he formed from eternal matter by means of the separate Intellects. On the basis of this interpretation, Samuel maintains that the third verse of Genesis (which describes the creation of light) precedes in the order of creation the first two verses of Genesis (which refer to earth and heaven). Thus before creation itself and prior to God's decree 'Let there be light',the heavens already existed and they underwent no alteration when creation took place. The sublunary world consisting of the four elements, however, were in their natural order (tohu va-vohu) until God transformed them, thereby placing them in their present order.

Light – the world of the Intellects – existed from all eternity. Here creation should be understood as indicting that light (the emanation transmitted by the Intellects) was strengthened, and that the spheres reinforced such terrestrial light. As a consequence, the relations between the elements were modified so that life emerged on earth.

When light struck the abyss, it caused the emergence of mountains and the hollowing of valleys where water was collected. This effect of the stars on the elements continues to take place; it maintains the waters in the seas and oceans, thereby allowing the earth to raise itself above the waters. This permits animals to continue, and there is thus a continual creation that occurs in the universe: the emanation of God through the Intellects and the spheres continually causes life to emerge.

Turning to the issue of prophetic visions, Samuel asserts that Isaiah's vision in the Temple describes the entire creation: every word represents one of the entities of the celestial and terrestrial words as well as their interaction. 'The Lord sitting on a throne' denotes divine existences; the throne is the world of the spheres. Since the spheres are limited by their corporeality, they cannot by themselves be invested with eternal movement. Such movement is bestowed by the separate Intellects which are eternal and incorporeal. In Samuel's view, these eternal beings demonstrate God's existence.

In accordance with rabbinic teaching, both Isaiah's and Ezekiel's visions point to the same terrestrial and celestial beings. Isaiah composed his vision beginning with the highest stage of perfection; Ezekiel began from the lower world, proceeding to the heavens. Both prophets sought to demonstrate how human beings are able to free themselves from the material domain through knowledge of the Divine. Such apprehension provides the basis for the ascent to God. Hence both philosophers and prophets share the same quest to reach the divine realm; they are different only in their roles. The prophet, unlike the philosopher, has a social and political role.

Regarding the concept of divine providence, Samuel contends there are various forms. The first type, general providence, is directed to all living beings, affecting the species rather than individuals – it is identified with divine emanation which bestows existence on all things and comprehends the laws that regulate the sublunary world. This kind of providence is linked to the world of generation and corruption; because human beings are a combination of body and soul they are not able to participate in the second type of providence – true providence – if the soul is not completely purified and the intellective faculty has not been actualized. This discussion is followed by a consideration of Maimonides' conception of miraculous providence. This would consist of the protection given to the sages against bodily ills. Yet, Samuel writes that if God were to alter the laws of nature so as to favour scholars who have attained the degree of the Active Intellect, the regularities in the natural world would cease to exist. Given the unlikeliness of such a situation, Samuel concludes that Maimonides included this notion in his *Guide* to satisfy the common people so that they would not doubt the truth of God's providential care.

In the presentation of Samuel's theories, the Books of Ecclesiastes, Proverbs and the Song of Songs are of crucial significance. In his introduction to the *Commentary on Ecclesiastes*, Samuel declares that he wrote to Maimonides, asking him to explain the meaning of these three Scriptural books. However, because the letter arrived after Maimonides' death, it was left to Samuel to pursue this subject. In his opinion, these three works focus on the problem of the union of the soul and the Active Intellect. Solomon, he argues, composed Ecclesiastes in accordance with the views of the philosophers rather than according to his own ideas. Thus the Book contains conflicting opinions about the doctrine of the soul after the death of the body and its conjunction with the Active Intellect. Samuel goes on to state that the Book of Proverbs deals with matter whereas the Song of Songs celebrates the union of the human intellect with the Active Intellect.

David Kimhi

Born in c. 1160, David Kimhi (known as Radak) was a grammarian and exegete of Narbonne, Provence. The son of Joseph Kimhi and the brother and pupil of Moses Kimhi, he taught in Narbonne and was a public figure in the town. Between 1205–1218, he was involved in the judgment given about several individuals who dishonoured the memory of the Jewish scholar Rashi. In the controversy surrounding *Maimonides of 1232, he went to Toledo to solicit the support of Judah Ibn Alfakhar on behalf of the followers of the great philosopher; he was, however, unable to accomplish this task due to illness.

Kimhi's first treatise was a philological study. The grammatical section of this work came to be known as *Mikhlol*; the lexicon was known as *Sefer ha-Shorashim*. In composing this tract, Kimhi's aim was to provide an alternative to the complex treatises of Jonah Ibn Janah and Judah ben David Hayyuj and the shorter writings of

*Abraham Ibn Ezra and the elder Kimhis. His main contribution to grammatical study was his innovative arrangement of the material and the popularization of his father's and brother's writings. In addition, Kimhi made a number of original points of his own. Despite the significance of this work, Kimhi was regarded as unconventional in his approach to grammar and criticized by such scholars as Joseph Ibn Kaspi, Profiat Duran, David ben Solomon Ibn Yahya, and Abraham de Balmes. Nonetheless, he did have some advocates, and in time his grammatical studies were widely esteemed in both Jewish and Christian circles.

A significant amount of material contained in Kimhi's *Mikhlol* was abridged in the *Et Sofer*, a manual for copyisits of the Bible; this work was produced to help scribes in their work. In this work Kimhi deals with a number of grammatical problems, and his observations are recorded in subsequent commentaries. Of particular importance is his discussion of the readings of the biblical text which developed out of a confusion as to the correct interpretation during the period of the men of the Great Sanhedrin. In order to ascertain the correct reading of the Bible, he embarked on numerous travels in pursuit of old manuscripts.

As far as biblical exegesis is concerned, Kimhi began his studies with a commentary on the Book of Chronicles; this was composed in response to a request by a student's father for a commentary in accord with the plain meaning of the text. This work was followed by commentaries on Genesis, all the prophetic books, and Psalms. In these studies Kimhi employs the approach advocated by Ibn Ezra and the elder Kimhis which stresses the correct philological understanding of the text. In his discussion, Kimhi frequently refers to rabbinic sources in distinguishing between the plain meaning of Scripture as opposed to its homiletical interpretation. Throughout he strives for clarity and comprehensibility.

In addition to these textual and philological studies, Kimhi was preoccupied with philosophical issues. Influenced by the rationalism of Ibn Ezra and Maimonides, he often refers to philosophical and theological matters in his exegesis of the biblical text. In this regard his understanding of prophecy is similar to that of Maimonides: in Kimhi's view the prophet must have attained a high degree of philosophical sophistication. However, unlike Maimonides, Kimhi believes that gentiles, in addition to Jews, are able to engage in prophetic activity. Like Maimonides, he also contends that individual providence is directly related to intellectual attainment, yet he argues that animals may be guided by divine providence in so far as their actions affect human beings. As far as miracles are concerned, Kimhi offers a naturalistic interpretation and attempts to minimize their importance. Regarding the mitzvot, Kimhi similarly relies on the teachings of scholars prior to Maimonides; in his presentation he does not seek to provide an explanation why God commanded particular ordinances. Finally, under Maimonides' influence Kimhi wrote commentaries on creation as well as the first chapter of Ezekiel. In response to these philosophical observations, a variety of scholars including Judah Ibn Alfakhar, Jacob Emden and David ben Solomon Ibn Abi Zimra mounted severe criticism. Yet, despite such a conservative reaction, Immanuel ben Solomon of Rome regarded Kimhi as lacking a sufficiently rigorous rational approach.

In addition to the philosophical dimensions of his commentaries, Kimhi was concerned to defend Judaism from criticism. Hence throughout his works, he is anxious to demonstrate the inadequacy of the christological interpretations of Scripture. Frequently he attacks the allegorical mode of Christian interpretation, and also seeks to expose Christian corruptions of the text as well as the irrationality of Christian exegesis. Moreover, he attempts to refute Christian doctrine, emphasizing the religious superiority of the Jewish people. Although conscious of the vulnerability of the Jewish nation in exile, he stresses that God's exercises a special providence for the Jews; in this context, he points to the future redemption of the Jewish people in the messianic age.

Abraham Ben Moses Maimonides

Born in 1186, Abraham ben Moses Maimonides was the only son of Maimonides. Under his father's guidance, he studied biblical and rabbinic sources as well as philosophy and medicine. After Maimonides' death in 1204, Abraham was appointed nagid (leader) of the Egyptian Jewish community; he held this office until his death in 1237. Once his appointment was announced, a controversy raged concerning the use of his name in public prayer as was the custom with the exilarchs in Babylonia. Those opposed to this practice boycotted synagogues and held services in one another's homes; such a situation resulted in a considerable loss of income for the community. As a result, the leaders of Egyptian Jewry decreed that all references to the nagid in worship be abolished; simultaneously they declared that all those who cut themselves off from synagogues should be excommunicated.

In this teaching, Abraham held Islamic mystics in high esteem. Under their influence, he attempted to revive a number of practices which had fallen into disuse (such as prostration and the spreading of arms). In addition, he attempted to introduce customs that had no Jewish precedent including washing the feet before prayer, sitting cross-legged, and standing in rows. Although a number of authorities approved of such changes to Jewish worship, they were opposed by various sectors of the Egyptian community. In protest, the Nathanel and Sar Shalom families, descendants of Moses ha-Levi who was head of the Fostat academy in the 12th century, presented a petition to the Sultan. When Abraham became aware of this action, he wrote to the sultan explaining that he had not wished to impose these innovations on any member of the community.

In the midst of this conflict, Abraham became embroiled in a virulent debate about his father's writings. In 1213 Daniel ben Saadiah, a Babylonian scholar, sent Abraham strictures on Maimonides halakhic works (the *Mishneh Torah* and the *Sefer ha-Mitzvot*). Replying to these charges, Abraham wrote two works of defence: *Birkat Avraham* and *Ma'aseh Nissim*. Subsequently when his father's studies were attacked in Spain, he refrained from becoming involved in this dispute; however, when he heard that Maimonides' books were burned in Montpellier in 1235, he composed a tract, *Milhamot Adonai*, criticising this action which was addressed to the scholars of Provence.

Regarded as an authority on Jewish law, Abraham received numerous queries regarding halakhic issues from scholars throughout the Jewish world. His responsa, written largely in Arabic, were models of clarity and brevity. Acting as nagid, he issued a series of important ordinances which gained acceptance in other communities such as Acre, the most important settlement of Jews in Eretz Israel. In his capacity as a physician, he served as a doctor in a hospital established by Saladin; there he became acquainted with Ibn Abi Usaybi'a who included a brief biography of Abraham in his *History of Doctors*. Overwhelmed by his communal and medical responsibilities, Abraham often complained that such burdens prevented him from completing his literary studies.

Abraham's major philosophical work, *Comprehensive Guide for the Servants of God*, is an encyclopedic study of the Jewish faith. The first three books of this treatise deal with the commandments; the fourth book focuses on the intention of a person who seeks to keep the law. In Abraham's view, these ordinances should be carried out for the love of God. Although the fear of God leads to the keeping of the law, it is the love of God which gives rise to a burning intensity to carry out the mitzvot (commandments). According to Abraham, eternal life can only be attained by the knowledge and fulfilment of the mitzvot when one is motivated by such loving dedication.

In propounding this view of Jewish pietism, Abraham argues that communion with God does not consist in the knowledge of the external world; rather, it is the result of inner solitude. Beginning with a discussion of Sufi mysticism, he writes:

> Also do the Sufis of Islam practice solitude in dark places and isolate themselves in them until the sensitive part of the soul becomes atrophied so that it is not even able to see the light. This, however, requires strong inner illumination wherewith the soul would be preoccupied so as not be pained over the external darkness. Now this path is the last of the elevated paths and it is contiguous with the (mystic) reunion (with God), external solitude thereof being a journey, and the internal (solitude) being in its beginning a journey and at its end a reunion, 'and there are examples for all of them'. Note: These elevated paths are associated with each other, as for example, humility is associated with gentleness, and mercy with generosity, and contentedness with abstinence and so forth. Now the course that unites one (with God) consists of travelling through all of them and traversing the (various) stages of every path and reaching its end, or to traverse most of its stages until one approaches its end. Second Note: These paths also have an order and some of them precede the others in order. Third Note: What thou must know and grasp is that the useful course that leads to true union (with God) generally has it as its condition that it be (pursued) under the direction of a person who communes (with God).
>
> (in Rosenblatt, 1938, II, 419– 23)

In advocating such a pietistic way of life, Abraham deviated from the teaching of his father. For Maimonides, knowledge of God is the goal of human existence. Due to his mystical inclination, however, Abraham views the soul's union with God as the goal of life. Regarding the body as a prison of the soul, he advocates a life of asceticism in which material pursuits should be kept to a minimum. A true servant of God, he maintains, should not even raise a large family because of the demands it would inevitably cause. Deeply influenced by the traditions of the Sufis, he regarded these Islamic mystics as the spiritual disciples of Israel's prophets, and advocated the Sufi method of training for spiritual enlightenment and human perfection.

Jacob Ben Abba Mari Anatoli

Flourishing in the early part of 13th century, Jacob Ben Abba Mari Anatoli was a homilist and translator. He married the daughter of *Samuel Ibn Tibbon to whom he taught mathematics. Following the suggestion of friends living in Narbonne and Béziers, he translated Arabic works on astronomy and logic into Hebrew; however, before he finished them he set off for Naples where he was employed as a physician. There he became an associate of Michael Scott who had translated the writings of Aristotle and Averroes into Latin. Anatoli himself translated a series of important works: Averroes' *Intermediate Commentary* on the first five books of Aristotle's Logic; the *Almagest* of Ptolemy; the astronomical text of Al-Farghani; and Averroes' *Compendium of the Almagest.*

In addition to his work as a translator, Analtoli engaged in preaching activities. Througout his discourses, he employs both allegorical and philosophical exegesis. Frequently he follows Maimonides, and his endorsement of his ideas evoked a hostile response. In all likelihood this was one of the major reasons why he left Naples for France. Anatoli's homilies are collected in his *An Incentive to Scholars* which is arranged according to the weekly scriptural readings. In this work Anatoli argues that the observance of the mitzvot should be based on an understanding of their rationale as well as a correct interpretation of the biblical text and the liturgy. In this collection he attacks the superficial reading of Scripture, and seeks to illustrate the ethical significance of the biblical narrative as well as its underlying truth which is inherent in the language of Scripture. His sermons therefore are philosophical in character, yet they also contain practical advice.

Among the Jews of Italy Anatoli was responsible for disseminating philosophical knowledge; his *An Incentive to Scholars* was widely discussed and parts of this work are quoted in the writings of Zerahiah ben Isaac Gracian and Immanuel of Rome. Because of the popularity of Anatoli's writing, Solomon ben Abraham specifically mentioned *An Incentive to Scholars* when he issued his ban against philosophy; in his opinion, Anatoli's work was dangerous and should be proscribed. The work itself consists of a series of philosophical sermons, each beginning with a verse from Proverbs. The sermons constitute a commentary on the verse rather than a full exegesis of the entire Torah portion. The central themes running through this study are the moral concepts of Proverbs and the struggle against the evil instinct and matter.

Of particular significance in considering Anatoli's importance in the history of Jewish thought is his relationship with Christian exegetes. In his writings, Anatoli quotes a number of exegeses of biblical verses given by Michael Scott similar to the explanations he himself offers. In addition, he refers to the interpretations of Scripture given by Emperor Frederick. Such openness was based on his affirmation that the the truth or falsity of an argument does not depend on the religious persuasion of the person who puts it forward:

> In (the possession of) this Divine image, all the peoples are equal, for we do not say that only Israel possesses soul, as those foolish gentiles do, who say that Israel possesses no soul; for this only reflects their arrogance and folly. In truth, they are all possessed of (the Divine) image, for such was the will of God . . . A member of any of the peoples who engages in the study appropriate for him is greater than any of the sons of our people, who does not engage in that (study) appropriate for him. As R. Meir said: 'Whence know we that even a non-Jew who engages in the Torah is like the High Priest? For it is said, "Ye shall therefore keep My statues and Mine ordinances,) which if a man do, he shall live by them" (Lev. 18:5). "Priest", "Levite" or "Israelite" were not said, but "man". Thus we learn that even a non-Jew who engages in the Torah is like a High Priest' (*Baba Kamma*, 38a). Now, the Talmud understands this passage with reference to (the non-Jew's) seven commandments; the same applies to the study of any wisdom necessary for establishing the essence (that is, theoretical truth) of these (seven) mitzvot or the essence of the mitzvot of the Torah.
>
> (in Gordon, 1974, 329)

Despite such a scientific orientation to his investigations, Anatoli is the only Jew known to have performed experiments in alchemy. Although such practices were commonly referred to in Christian and Islamic sources, there is very little information in medieval Hebrew writings on this subject. Michael Scott, however, mentions Anatoli in this regard: when providing a formula for bleaching tin in his *Alchemy*, he states that he was frequently successful in this procedure which had been taught to him by 'Rabbi Jacob the Jew'.

101

Moses Ben Samuel Ibn Tibbon

The nephew of Jacob Anatoli, Moses Ibn Tibbon continued the work of translation of his family; between 1244–1274 he translated a variety of texts in Montpellier where he resided. These translations include: Averroes' *The Great Commentaries, The Middle Commentaries,* and *The Short Commentaries;* Al-Farabi's *Book of Principles;* Themistius' *Commentary on Book Lamba of Aristotle's Metaphysics;* and Al-Batalyosi's *Book of Intellectual Circles.* In addition, he produced translations of numerous studies of mathematics, astronomy and medicine.

Moses' original studies consist chiefly of commentaries including a study of the Song of Songs (this completed the vast project of commenting on the works of King Solomon which was initiated by his father, *Samuel Ibn Tibbon); a commentary on *Abraham Ibn Ezra's writings; and a study of the number of the commandments in *Ibn Gabirol and *Maimonides. In these works Moses' opinions parallel those of his father except concerning miracles, providence and creation. Moses' interest in Neoplatonism is illustrated in his examination of Ibn Ezra's *Commentary* as well as his translation of the *Book of Intellectual Circles* by Al-Batalyosi.

According to Moses, there is a divine providence apart from the providence which is provided by the laws of nature and that which accompanies the emanation of the Intellect. When human beings attain perfection, they become attached to the Active Intellect and are able to comprehend the laws of the divine influence over angels, the spheres and the stars. Having attained such knowledge concerning the laws which regulate the universe, the sage can equip himself and those close to him against misfortunes and prepare himself and others to benefit from advantageous circumstances. For Moses, this constitutes the working of providence.

In expouding this theory, the influence of *Abraham Ibn Ezra is evident: as Ibn Ezra explained, astrological influences on human affairs are of crucial importance. Yet, astrology is simply one element in this comprehensive system – it constitutes only a part of the knowledge which is bestowed upon the sage when he is conjoined to the Active Intellect. Despite such a conviction about the nature of divine providence, Moses does not state explicitly whether human beings are able to influence the future outcome of events or astral laws themselves except through prayer or observance of the law.

As far as miracles are concerned, they are always the handiwork of

God. In Moses' view, all of nature is subject to law and is regulated by the movement of the stars; thus miracles cannot take place as a result of natural processes. According to Maimonides God made an alliance at the moment of creation with certain things; as a result at any particular moment of history they would deviate from their natural course. Such changes, he believes, demonstrates the operation of the divine will. For Moses Ibn Tibbon, another type of miracle exists: there are other things whose nature is not determined. They generally act in a certain way – this is called a 'law'; but exceptions are possible. For example, a mouse is normally born from another mouse; but infrequently a mouse is born from dust. Such spontaneous generation is an example of a natural miracle.

Turning to Moses' exegetical activity, he is anxious to provide a rational explanation for even the most unusual parts of Scripture. As he explains in relation to Talmudic aggadot (rabbinic teachings):

> I have realized that the Gentiles have invented stratagems against us and have scrutinized our own traditions; they laugh at us and at our Ancient Holy Ones who composed the Talmud, because of the aggadot that seem to defy the intelligence and are impossible in nature, and nevertheless most of them have a meaning for him who comprehends their content. This has happened because our coreligionists, wise in their own eyes, have understood them in their literal sense as they have done for numerous scriptural allegories and allusions, for they have not distinguished the things (regulated) by nature from those made in a miraculous manner; they have not understood (what separates) the impossible from the possible, what must necessarily be affirmed concerning the Creator and what must be absolutely denied (of him). They did not know that the ancient sages in all nations, had the habit of speaking of the sciences by allegory, parable and symbol.
>
> (in Sirat, 1995, 230)

It is therefore necessary when reading such passages to distinguish the exoteric from the esoteric sense. This approach should also be used when seeking to determine the meaning of Scripture. The esoteric meaning of the Song of Songs, for example, is the love of the human intellect for the Active Intellect. The poetic character of this book is designed to evoke feelings of love, but it is a mistake to conceive of the Song of Songs as a love poem between a young man and his beloved. Using such a method, Moses sought to uncover the true meaning of both Scriptural and talmudic texts, finding in them hidden significance of an esoteric character.

Gershom ben Solomon of Arles

Flourishing in the latter half of the 13th century, Gershom ben Solomon of Arles was a Provencal scholar who produced *Sh'ar ha-Shamayim* (The Gate of Heaven), a work which was widely read in the Middle Ages. In 1547 it was published in Venice in an incomplete form. This work is a summary of the natural sciences, astronomy and theology divided into three parts.

In the beginning of the book, Gershom explains his intention:

I, Gershom son of Solomon – I have written this book, I have called it 'The Gate of Heaven' and I have divided it according to the hierarchy of the beings, and made to precede it an exposition on the four elements. The first generated and corruptible being is constituted by the vapours and their different species. Then comes the mineral and its different species, then the vegetable species. Then I shall speak of the nature of animals not endowed with reason and finally of the nature of the species man, which is the ultimate composition. The second part (deals with) astronomy. I have written the essential part of it after the writings of Al-Farghani. I have joined to it some (elements borrowed) from the book of the *Almagest* and from other books. At the end, I have transcribed many things due to the wise Avicenna as well as some borrowed from the book of the wise Averroes and from the book *De Coelo et Mundo*. The third part (deals with) divine science and the soul. There I have innovated nothing but I have borrowed from the information on matters of divine science from the book of the soul composed by the Master, Light of the Exile, our Master, Moses ben Maimon . . . At the end of this part I have added a treatise by the learned Averroes dealing with metaphysics.

(Gershom ben Solomon, 1968, 5)

Throughout this text Gershom cites Greek, Latin, Arabic and Jewish authors including Homer, Plato, Pythagoras, Aristotle, Galen, Hippocrates, Al-Farabi, Avicenna, and Averroes. Apparantly Gershom obtained his knowledge of these authors largely through translations of scientific and philosophical studies rather than through the original texts. In addition to these early sources, Gershom reported what he had heard through reports from both Jewish and Christian thinkers. One of the most important features of this book is the information given about these various authors.

The three parts of this work are unequal in length: the first section, comprising nearly five-sixth's of the text, contains ten treatises on the four elements, inanimate objects, plants, animals; fowls; bees, ants and spiders; fish; human beings; parts of the body; and sleeping and waking. The second part deals with astronomy, whereas the third part is concerned with metaphysics. Here Gershom discusses the nature of the soul and its faculties. This section of the book also contains a transcription of a short treatise by Averroes on the *Possiblity of Conjunction with the Active Intellect* which was translated by *Samuel Ibn Tibbon.

Shem Tov Ben Joseph Falaquera

Born in c. 1225, Shem Tov Ben Joseph Falaquera was a philosophical author and translator. Born in Spain, he appears to have lived in the border provinces of Spain and France. Knowledgable about Islamic and Greek philosophy, he produced a wide variety of works. During his youth he engaged in poetic activity, but subsequently declared that he wished to devote himself to less frivolous pursuits. As a philosopher, he did not propound any original theories – his writings frequently consist of quotations from Arab sources which he translated into Hebrew. The Neoplatonic texts he translated and cited include the *Book of the Five Substances* by Pseudo-Empedocles; in addition, he composed five works on ethics, a treatise dealing with psychology, and another tract that depicts the degrees of intellectual perfection. His *Letters on Discussion* seeks to differentiate between the realms of religion and science, and his *Guide to the Guide* is an exposition of various passages in *Maimonides' *Guide for the Perplexed*.

Falquera's most important philosophical study, *The Opinions of the Philosophers*, depicts his own intellectual position. In his view, it is everywhere accepted that true happiness consists in the knowledge of the Creator; it is therefore necessary to strive to reach him by thought. Moreover, the sages concur in declaring that such knowledge is gained through an apprehension of the divine acts and their intellectual representation. What is separate from matter, he argues, can only be the object of human comprehension.

Hence, human beings are given two distinct paths: the prophetic and the scientific. Whoever receives the influx of the intellect and prophesies will attain truth without study; others, however, can only engage in scientific study – this consists in attempting to gain an understanding of all which exists. There is simply no proof of God's existence other than what exists before our own eyes. Yet to be able to derive from material reality the proof for God's existence, we must represent it to ourselves intellectually according to both its nature and form. This, he believes, can only be accomplished by reading works composed by non-Jewish philosophers; if Jews had written philosophical treatises in previous ages, they have been lost. In the quest to attain true knowledge, everything that is demonstrated and is in accordance with faith should be accepted from whatever source. Quoting from Aristotle, Falaquera insists on the universality of philosophy and science: truth is truth no matter who proclaims it.

In this exercise both education and habits of thought acquired during one's youth play an important role. At times what is in fact true may appear false because it is unfamiliar. Yet, as Prophyrius states, one should neither accept nor reject such information: instead, foreign notions should be carefully examined. Hence all theories that have been propounded or will be formulated in the future should be studied with care. Those that correspond best to reality should be accepted as most probable. Continuing this discussion, Falaquera states that the philosopher should be seen as possessing two human perfections: the perfection of morality and of intellect. By definition, a lover of wisdom is a virtuous man who gains knowledge of what is true. In the Jewish tradition, such an individual is designated a hasid (pious person). In this light, an ignorant individual can be virtuous, but never pious because he would be devoid of understanding.

One of the main aims of *The Opinions of the Philosophers* is to draw together various philosophical ideas, enabling one to choose between truth and error. According to Falaquera, one should not believe everything that philosophers have previously declared. Paralleling Maimonides, he points out that in physics theories are supported by proof, but in metaphysics a wide range of issues inevitably remain unresolved. A second intention of this treatise is to provide a Hebrew translation of philosophical doctrines. Here Falaquera follows Al-Farabi, Averroes and Maimonides in tracing the development of philosophical ideas. Regarding the physical sciences, Falaquera provides a summary of the *Middle Commentaries* of Averroes which he occasionally elaborates with the aid of citations drawn from the *Short Commentaries* and the *Great Commentaries*.

106

Throughout he limits himself to transmitting the views of these writers.

In his other works Falaquera discusses many of the themes found in this philosophical study including the relationship between prophecy and science. Drawing on Neoplatonism and the writings of Avicenna, he states in his *Guide to the Guide* that a prophet comprehends all things by the grace of God; for this reason, his knowledge is perfect and is no different from that of the philosopher. In Falaquera's view, the prophet is able to attain such illumination through intuition rather than demonstration. Further, the prophet is different from the philosopher because divine providence is attached to him.

Regarding the concept of providence, Falaquera addresses the question whether God alters the laws of nature in favour of the prophet. In response Falaquera differentiates between two types of miracles:

1 Miracles that change the order of nature – these are performed by the action of the prophet and have nothing to do with individual providence.
2 Miracles that God brings about to preserve the just from calamity.

According to Falaquera, this latter type of providence which is in accord with the laws of nature (such as saving a person from drowning) is connected with the conjunction between the sage's intellect and the Active Intellect. As Falaquera explains, this is not a philosophical concept since the sage is not always protected because of his wisdom; it is rather a matter of statistical probability. Another central issue concerning the notion of personal providence is the question what one should believe if philosophical truth differs from religious belief. For Falaquera, this should not be regarded as an overwhelmingly problem: the concept of individual providence cannot be demonstrated, yet it does not contradict the findings of science.

In general Falaquera was content to juxtapose philosophical ideas even if they appear not to be in agreement – rather than offering a solution to seeming inconsistencies, he regards the philosophical tradition as internally coherent. This, however, is not the case with regard to the doctrine of creation. In a letter written to defend the work of Maimonides, he offers two explanations as to why Maimonides wrote the *Guide*. The first was Maimonides' wish to demonstrate that philosophical reasoning is inapplicable to this subject; the second was Maimonides' desire to illustrate that Scripture must be read figuratively so as to avoid ascribing anthropomorphic characteristics to God. According to Falaquera, Maimonides insists that the world was created, and his explanation of the existence of miracles is based on this assumption. Further, the doctrine of creation serves as the basis for belief in divine revelation. As a consequence, Falaquera rejects the proof of the existence of God by an appeal to the concept of a Prime Mover because such a proof would entail the acceptance of eternal movement and the eternity of the world. Instead, in the *Guide to the Guide*, Falaquera expounds two other proofs of God's existence: the argument based on eternal movement, and the argument based on the contingency of all existing things. As Maimonides himself points out, the first proof is contrary to Judaism, but the second constitutes the only truly philosophical proof for God's existence.

Isaac Albalag

Living in the second half of the thirteenth century in either Provence or Catalonia, Isaac Albalag was a translator and philosopher. In his philosophical treatise, *Righting of Doctrines*, he offers a commentary on the Islamic philosopher Al-Ghazali's *Intentions of the Philosophers*. As the title of Albalag's work illustrates, *Righting of Doctrines* is a critical discussion of Al-Ghazali's text; in addition, he is also censorious about the views of *Maimonides, Avicenna and Al-Farabi. According to Albalag, faith and philosophy have different aims and both are necessary:

> Four beliefs are common foundations to all the revealed religions, and they are built on them. Philosophy also admits them and tries to establish them, with this difference that the revealed religion teaches them according to a method adapted to popular intelligence, that is, by way of tales, while philosophy teaches them by the demonstrative method which is suitable only to the elite. These are the four beliefs: the existence of reward and punishment; the soul's survival after the death of the body; the existence of a rewarding, punishing Lord who is God; the existence, finally of a Providence which watches over men's ways to give to each according to his acts . . . The Torah aims at the felicity of the simple people, their estrangement from evil and their instruction in truth, as far as their spirit is capable of it

... On the other hand, philosophy does not purpose the instruction or the happiness of the vulgar, but only the felicity of the perfect.

(Albalag, 1973, 2–3)

Like the Islamic philosopher Averroes in his *Decisive Treatise*, Albalag seeks to hide truths from the Jewish masses which would prove too difficult for them to assimilate. In Albalag's view, the Torah contains doctrines which could potentially be harmful to those whose understanding is deficient, yet for the initiated these truths are of fundamental importance:

It is certain that if the expounding of the truth had some usefulness for the vulgar, or if this truth was not untimely for the realization of the aim (the material facility) designed for them, the Torah would not have hidden it and would not have refused a benefit to those entitled to it. Besides, there is no true philosophical thesis which the Torah has not mentioned by some allusion to nature to arouse the attention of the wise, while the ignorant do not notice it.

(*Ibid.*, 3–4)

Here Albalag distinguishes between two mysteries contained in the Torah: philosophical doctrine and prophetic doctrine. The former, he argues, is obtained through demonstration and is supported by the Bible. In such cases, rational argument is required first:

It is not incumbent on the seeker after truth to establish it according to what he understands of the scriptural texts themselves, without first having recourse to rational demonstration. On the contrary, the truth is established first by means of rational demonstration, and afterwards one searches for corroborative authority in the Scriptures.

(*Ibid.*, 37)

As Albalag explains, this is the method he employs whenever he wishes to corrorobate a theory contained in Scripture and rabbinic sources: After establishing a theory through rational demonstration, he examines the biblical text – if it provides support for the theory then he interprets the Scriptural text in accordance with it. On the other hand, if the text does not conform to what has been demonstrated, he admits that its meaning escapes him. 'I say,' he writes, 'that I do not comprehend it and that its intention eludes me;

this is not a philosophical mystery, but one of the prophetic mysteries revealed only to those on whom God has bestowed a spirit of superior knowledge.' (*Ibid.*)

Philosophical truth, he continues, can only be understood by philosophers whereas prophetic truth is reserved for prophets. Yet there is a fundamental difference between these two types of comprehension: sages are able to understand philosophical doctrines through rational consideration using the scriptural text as a starting point. As a consequence, they are have right to interpret Scripture using this method. Prophets, however, are the only ones able to understand prophetic truths and it is only through their mediation that such truths can be transmitted to others. Hence in understanding such prophetic notions, the sage is in no respect superior to ordinary persons – prophetic doctrines are hidden truths which can only be understood through prophetic insight.

But what if a philosophical doctrine is contradicted by Scripture? In such a situation, there would be two truths: the truths of science and those of religion. The correct method to employ when this conflict arises is as follows:

> One should learn truth only from demonstration. Afterwards, one should consult the Torah, and, if its words may be interpreted in conformity with the demonstrated doctrine, we shall admit this in our belief both in virtue of demonstration and in virtue of faith. If no scriptural text can be found to support the demonstrated doctrine, we shall believe this in virtue of speculation alone. Finally, if a scriptural text is found to contradict this doctrine, we shall similarly believe the literal sense of the text in the manner of miracle, being aware that the doctrine of the scriptural text in question looks strange to us only because it is one of those divine doctrines reserved for the prophets to understand, and depending on a supernatural power. It is in this way that you shall find my rational opinion contrary in many points to my faith, for I know by demonstration that such a thing is true by way of nature and I know at the same time by the words of the prophets that the contrary is true by way of miracle.
>
> (*Ibid.*, 43–4)

This approach is illustrated by the contradiction between the philosophical notion of the eternity of the world and the religious belief in creation. Although Albalag accepts the literal meaning of the

110

text – that God created the universe – he also interprets the first verse of Genesis as indicating that God as First Cause and Prime Mover preserves the world. To support this view, he appeals to the kabbalistic idea that the archetype of the visible world is contained in Wisdom – it is through Wisdom that God eternally creates the universe. Even though Maimonides did not want to reveal this hidden truth in the *Guide*, Albalag does not hesitate to do so for the following reasons:

1 Maimonides wanted to maintain the literal sense of the Torah and demonstrate the falseness of the philosopher's doctrine with the help of speculation, something that absolutely cannot be done. As for myself, I recognize the literal sense of the Torah by the way of simple faith, without proof, and the truth of the philosophers by the way of nature and human speculation.

2 The present work is not of a religious character as his was. It is not intended for the common people, and, if an ignorant man accidentally starts to read it, having understood nothing from the beginning, he will grow tired of it, will abandon the effort and will not even reach this point. Thus if he has understood all that precedes this, he has left the ranks of the vulgar and has raised himself to the level of those with whom one speaks of these questions. He will understand from then on, that I only acquiesce in the doctrine of the philosophers because speculative research does not permit me to deny it and this is why I acquiesce in it by the way of human knowledge, not that of faith.

3 In the period of the Master the theory of the eternity of the world was altogether alien to the minds of the common people, so much so that the simple believers imagined that if anyone accepted it he so to speak denied the whole of the Torah. In our time this question is widely known among them and is diffused in their circles to such an extent that most of them are not loath to accept the belief in the eternity of the world such as Epicurus professed it, that is, a universe eternal in itself and without cause. They think that it is this eternity that the philosophers demonstrate; while in fact the philosophers reject such a suggestion with horror. Thus the ignorant of our time find themselves denying both the Torah and philosophy.

(Ibid., 51)

Albalag thus holds that philosophical doctrines and religious beliefs can both be true even if they appear to be in conflict: the first can be true by way of nature, and the second by means of miracles.

Levi Ben Abraham Ben Hayyim of Villefrance of Conflent

Born in c. 1245, the French philosopher Levi Ben Abraham's writings became the focus of the anti-philosophical conflict which occurred among Jews living in Provence and Catalonia at the beginning of the 14th century. Under attack by the opponents of philosophy, he left his hometown of Villefrance de Conflent and wandered from town to town; settling in Montpellier in 1276, he moved to Arles in 1295, and in 1393 to Perpignan where he lived in the house of Samuel of Escalita. However, influenced by the criticisms of philosophy levelled by Solomon ben Abraham Adret, Samuel was persuaded that the death of his daughter was a divine punishment for housing Levi – as a result he expelled him from his home. In 1305, Solomon ben Adret composed a letter from Barcelona to the Spanish communities in France and Germany outlining his objections to philosophical inquiry. Objecting to the interpretations of philosophers like Levi, he writes:

> For they say that Abraham and Sarah represent matter and form, and that the twelve tribes of Israel are the twelve constellations. Has a nation ever heard such an evil thing since the world was divided into territories? Or has such a thing ever been heard that men should reduce everything to chaos? The blasphemers of God further say that the holy vessels which were sanctified, the Urim and Thumim, are the instrument known as astrolabe, which men make for themselves . . . A man who does such things reduces the entire Bible to useless allegories; indeed they trifle with and pervert all the commandments in order to make the yoke of their burden lighter unto themselves . . . some of them say that all that is written from the section of Bereshit (Genesis) to the giving of the Law is nothing more than an allegory. May such men become a proverb and a by-word, and may them have no stay and no staff. Indeed they show that they have no faith in the plain meaning of the commandments . . . The chief reason of all this is that they are infatuated with alien sciences . . . and pay homage to the Greek books.
>
> (Kobler, 1952, 256–7)

Levi' writings consist of two major works. The first, *Battei ha-Nefesh ve ha-Lahashim* (Chests of Perfume and Amulets), is an encyclopedia of medieval science and philosophy, composed in rhymed prose; this work was written in Montpellier in 1276. Containing of ten chapters, it treats such topics as ethics, logic, kabbalistic doctrines, the soul, prophecy, mathematics, astronomy, astrology, physics and metaphysics. A second work, *Livyat Hen* (Ornament of Grace) is another encyclopedic text consisting of various scientific treatises. Divided into six sections, it existed in both a long and short version. The first five parts are devoted to science and philosophy whereas the six treats the topic of faith.

In the *Ornament of Grace*, Levi delineates the relationship between religion and philosophy:

> It has already been explained that our Torah is entirely philosophical (literally, intellectual as opposed to practical, knowledge), that its commandments cannot be accomplished and its secrets known except through the theoretical sciences; it is thanks to these theoretical sciences that false beliefs are repulsed and the foundations of the (true) belief are strengthened for they are not all clearly explained in our books; very much on the contrary, certain verses contradict each other and numerous midrashim are opposed one to another. On what can we rely if not on the balances of the intellect? Science shall be the instrument of the examination of belief and through it we shall know the richness of the revealed text; we shall reject what is futile and deceitful and we shall not be like the fool who believes no matter.

(in Sirat, 1995, 245)

For Levi, science consists of the world view propounded by *Maimonides and Averroes. In expounding the biblical text, he proposes a variety of allegorical interpretations; nevertheless, at the beginning of each chapter, Levi emphasizes that his interpretation of the text in no way undermines the literal meaning. Thus, for example, in explaining the process of creation, Sarah and Abraham are viewed not only as historical personages but as designating matter and form, and the twelve tribes of Israel are portrayed as symbolically representing the twelve signs of the zodiac; in addition, the four kings who battled against the five kings as well Abraham are presented as the four elements and the five senses. Moreover, the Urim and the Thumim on the High Priests breastplate symbolize among other things the astrolabe. Such interpretations constitute the type of philosophical exegesis which infuriated such traditionalists as Solomon ben Adret.

These allegorical explanations of Scripture were not innovative – they were present in the works of a number of Levi's predecessors such as *Moses and *Samuel Ibn Tibbon. However, in these studies they were applied to rabbinic midrash as well as the poetical parts of Scripture which had traditionally been the subject of allegorical interpretation. Yet for Levi, this method of exegesis was extended to the Torah itself. In propounding his views, Levi adopts an elitist stance. Unlike the ignorant who are attached to matter and religion, he perceives his intellect as joined to the Active Intellect. In this context, Levi expresses a distaste for women – they are associated with matter, seduction and destruction.

The distinction between intellectuals and the ignorant serves as a framework for Levi's analysis of the commandments which he believes are of two types: (l) commandments that can be justified by reason; and (2) commandments which reason cannot explain. The former have their source in philosophy; the latter serve as no more than a prepartion for the first type. Because not all people are capable of becoming philosophers, such commandments pave the way to philosophical discovery. Such an interpretation constitutes the logical conclusion to the Maimonidean tradition: in Levi's writing Scritpure is reduced to allegorization and philosophical abstraction. It is not surprising, therefore, that he became a target for those who protested against the pernicious influence of philosophical reflection.

Judah Ben Solomon Ha-Cohen Ibn Malkah

Born in Toledo in c. 1215 to a illustrious family of astrologers, Judah Ben Solomon Ha-Cohen Ibn Malkah corresponded with Michael Scott, the philosopher attached to the court of Emperor Frederick II. In 1245 he moved to Lombardy, becoming part of the court. There he translated his encyclopedic study, *Exposition of Science*, from Arabic into Hebrew. The work itself is concerned with three topics: (1) physical science dealing with the world of generation and corruption; (2) mathematical and astronomical science concerning the world of the spheres; and (3) divine science regarding the spiritual world. The first part of this work commences with a study of logic, the instrument of scientific investigation. After discussing Aristotle's physics and metaphysics, Judah explores the nature of divine science. The second part concludes with a further treatise on divine science containing an examination of the letters of the Hebrew alphabet; this is followed by a third treatise consisting of various rabbinic expositions connected with theology.

The exposition of Aristotelian logic, physics and metaphysics of the first section of this work are based on Averroes' *Middle Commentaries* of these treatises. Yet, unlike Averroes' *Short Commentaries*, Judah does not discuss Aristotle's ideas in detail; instead he outlines the central ideas of these writings. In addition to Averroes' commentaries, Judah utilized other authors including Al-Farabi and Avicenna. Preceding Judah's discussion of the science of astronomy, Judah provides an account of Euclid's *Geometry* as well as Theodosius' and Menelaus' works on spherical figures. In his view, astrology is just as much a science as astronomy and geometry.

Nonetheless, Judah questions the status of physics and Aristotelian metaphysics; in his view, these disciplines do not provide the same sort of certitude:

> The kinds of demonstration adduced in physics are the opposite of those adduced in the mathematical sciences; in the latter, one goes from the anterior to the posterior, while in physics one goes from the posterior to the anterior, and as the things known by the mathematical sciences are also known by the physical sciences, the demonstrations of the mathematical sciences are absolute, while those of physics are not known completely.
>
> (in Sirat, 1995, 251)

According to Judah, physics is inferior to the mathematical sciences because its premises are not based on primary evidence and it is incapable of a perfect demonstration; in addition, a number of its facts are not explained even by its proofs. As a consequence, it is not possible to adjudicate between competing theories. Because of these reservations, Judah does not entirely reject Aristotelian physics but he expresses doubts about its underlying principles. Some of them, he admits, are self-evident but others require further demonstration. The central difficulty with the Aristotelian system is that it is not based on experimentation.

In Judah's view, human knowledge is inevitably limited and must be supplemented by revelation. The kabbalistic mystical tradition, he declares, is the source of true and perfect understanding – this oral tradition goes back to Moses who passed it on to Israel. Such knowledge concerns the spiritual world and that of the spheres. Kabbalah, or the divine science, is fundamentally different from the science of the inferior worlds which is imperfectly known through the books of the gentiles. In this regard, Judah writes citing Judah ha-Cohen ben Solomon ha-Cohen of Toledo:

> When you reflect and preoccupy your thought with these sciences in order to acquire the knowledge of everything which exists from the beginning to the end, you will see in the end that you will know only a very few things concerning the two worlds perceived by the senses: the world of the spheres and that of generation and corruption. As for the spiritual world, even if you know by heart the thirteen books of Aristotle on divine science, you will not get from them more than the knowledge of the Prime Mover, Rock, One, Living, who is neither body nor force in a body, and that there is for each sphere a separate Intellect; that is all you will learn concerning this (spiritual) world, if you occupy your spirit with these treatises.
>
> (*Ibid.* 253)

However, divine science has been revealed by God to the Jewish nation. For this reason Judah refrains from quoting any non-Jewish philosopher when discussing the divine science; instead he refers to the writings of Jewish exegetes. In his commentary on the creation account, the Book of Psalms, and the Book of Proverbs, he expounds his understanding of this subject. God, he states, is absolutely unknowable – thus the more a person advances in his understanding of the Godhead, the more he realises that the negative attributes provide a basis for comprehending the Divine. In his view, it is only because of the divine emanations that one can describe God in a positive way. These emanations serve as the basis for the language of prayer in which God is depicted as possessing various characteristics.

In the commentary on creation, Judah asserts that the two inferior worlds were created ex nihilo: matter and form were the first things which God made. Matter, which was fashioned from nothingness, is divided into the heavens and the earth. Form itself is light which gives matter life; it is an emanation of the Intellect that moves all created beings and makes them emerge from nothingness into being. In explaining this process, Judah differentiates between the three Hebrew terms (beriah, yezirah, and asyah) which are used to signify creation. Beriah, he writes, denotes the coming into being of a thing out of nothingness. For Judah, nothingness is real and absolute. Unlike Aristotle, he asserts that before creation there was no First Matter. According to Judah, the Lord created matter and form, and from their union everything that exits was produced.

After matter and form, the nine Intellects that govern the spheres were created – these are symbolized by the first nine letters of the Hebrew alphabet; the world of the spheres which follow are symbolized by the next nine letters; and the sublunary world by the next letters in the Hebrew alphabet plus the final forms of the letters. In this scheme, the letter yod represents the supreme sphere; the letter kaf is the sphere of the fixed stars; lamed is Saturn; mem Jupiter; nun Mars; samekh Venus; ayn the Sun; pe Mercury; and zade the Moon. The inferior world consists of: qof, the primary matter of this lower world; resh, the four qualities (heat, cold, humidity, dryness); shin, fire; taw, air; final kaf, water; final mem, earth; final nun, metals; final pe, plants; final zade, animals.

Divine science thus seeks to understand the nature of God and his relation to the world. It consists of the knowledge of the names of the Intellects and the beings which are superior to them, the relationships between the superior beings and the spheres as well as the connection between the spheres and the beings of the lower world. and the disposition of the stars. According to Judah, everything that takes place in history is dependent on the spheres. One planet rules over each day of the week as well as the months of the year, and the periods of different empires are regulated by the revolutions of the planets. In propounding such theories, Judah was insistent that mystical tradition of the Kabbalah provides a secure foundation for theological and cosmological speculation.

Isaac Ben Abraham Ibn Latif

From 1210–80 Isaac Ben Abraham Ibn Latif appears to have lived in Toledo. The first and most important of his works was published in 1238; a shorter version, *The Gate of Heaven*, was completed about two years later. Other writings consist of *The Treasures of the King*, *The Forms of the World*, and *Bouquet of Myrrh*, a collection of aphorisms, philosophical responsa, and commentaries on the Book of Ecclesiastes, the Book of Job and the *Sefer Yetsirah*. Knowledgable about Arab philosophy, Ibn Latif nonetheless wrote in Hebrew and drew on Jewish Neoplatonic philosophy, especially the work of *Solomon Ibn Gabirol.

In his view, the universe is divided into three worlds: the world of the Intellects, the world of the spheres, and the world of generation and corruption. God is ultimately unknowable and cannot be comprehended by the intelligence or defined by language. Rather he is infinite and all attributes constitute a limitation on his nature. Through the exercise of the divine will God has created the cosmos. In *The Gate of Heaven*, he criticises Aristotle's notion of the eternity of the world. According to Ibn Latif, it is inconceivable that the Infinite can be linked to the finite domain. If the world had emanated from the divine source, it would also be infinite in in number and extent.

Such criticism of Aristotelian notions is applied to Aristotle's conception of science. For Maimonides, Aristotle's scientific ideas are true – this is disputed by Ibn Latif. In his view, Aristotleian notions are nothing more than hypotheses and in no way empirically demonstrated. In a similar vein Ibn Latif attacks the astronomer Ptolemy: there is no way to know whether the heavenly bodies move in circular fashion. Indeed, it is not even possible to determine if the sky is composed of the stars and the spheres. Further, we cannot ascertain their number or whether their movement is voluntary or involuntary. It is nothing more than speculation to claim that their movement is eternal.

Turning to the nature of logic, Ibn Latif argues that it is based on three modes: perception. syllogism, and demonstration. The perceptions of the senses, he explains, are represented to the soul; these are compared to the images which have already been perceived. By this means human beings are able to comprehend the essence of things. The second mode of logic, syllogism, is of three types. The first deals with the relationship between matter and form and the transformation from potentiality to actuality. The second deals with what exists in actuality. Finally, the third is concerned with the relationship between the spheres and the Intellects. This type of syllogism concerns the whole of creation and through such a discipline it is possible to attain religious and intellectual knowledge which would otherwise be hidden.

According to Ibn Latif, Jewish mysticism as found in kabbalistic teaching provides true knowledge about the creation of the universe and the role of the Divine Will according to the modes of perception which are afforded by syllogism and demonstration. Yet this secret doctrine is not concerned with combinations of the Hebrew letters in the process of creation as found in kabbalistic texts. For Latif, those who aim to explain the formation of the cosmos through the permutations of the letters of the Hebrew alphabet are utterly misguided: in his view the secret of the Will in the process of creation is totally abstract; yet the letters of the alphabet and their combinations belong to the realm of images. Although human beings need such imagery in their speculation, the letters disappear as one rises toward what is separate from matter. In Ibn Latif's view, the aim of intellection should be to attain a comprehension of what is totally simple and pure, unencumbered by any imagistic form.

For Ibn Latif, Scripture and rabbinic midrash contain such secret knowledge of the nature of God and his activity. In his view, God who is absolute perfection and unknowable is linked by means of the ten sefirot (divine emanations) to the corporeal world. God, he argues, is an absolute unity who is revealed through the ten words by which he created the universe. The first of the series of numbers is the first sefirah (divine emanation) which symbolizes fire; the second is Air and the third, Water. Fire is here understood as matter and form which are eternal in their aspect. Air is the first of the two intelligible entites in their separated dimension, like two lines that converge towards a point. At this stage in the process of creation, all entities exist in potentiality. With the third serfirah, Water, the appearance of the hidden substance carries the form of corporeality; it cuts short the two lines that were continuing to infinity. This is the third dimension of space; in relation to Fire it is like the light of the moon in relation to the sun.

Continuing this exposition, Ibn Latif identifies the fourth sefirah as First Matter; it is the light of the sun which emanates from the spiritual light, causing the light of the stars and planets to appear. The next sefirah is Form, designated by the name of the Sphere of Intellect. The sixth sefirah is the form of the ninth sphere – this encompasses all other spheres. Finally, the four other sefirot constitute the other forms of the spheres. Despite their diversity, all these sefirot are united into a whole. Human beings, Ibn Latif argues, are capable of attaining some comprehension of the sefirot, and can in theory even arrive at the level of the Will, the Divine Name. The human soul is like a spark of the Name that has penetrated matter and can ascend to its source. When all the captive sparks have returned to their origin, the corporeal world will vanish. Here then is a philosophical system blending numerous features of Greek metaphysics with kabbalistic notions derived from the *Sefer Yetsirah* and elsewhere.

Judah Ben Nissim Ibn Malkah

In all likelihood Judah Ben Nissim Ibn Malkah lived in Morocco during the latter half of the 13th century. His main work, *The Consolation of the Exiled*, is a discussion between a master and his disciple concerning the nature and destiny of the soul. According to Ibn Malkah, each soul is exiled in the material world; eventually it must die to the corporeal world so as to revive in the world of the Intellect. This is the way of knowledge, rather than the pursuit of divine illumination since God is unknowable.

Drawing on the kabbalistic tradition, Ibn Malkah argues that the first emanation from the Godhead, Intellect, is denoted by the Tetragram; this is the most subtle of all substances, the light of the world, the first knowable cause which is perfect in itself. Within the hierarchy of Intellects, the human soul is the third degree – it longs for the Intellect and the Song of Songs illustrates this yearning. In this context, biblical texts, midrashic sources, and the liturgy provide the basis for an understanding of the cosmos. Further, the twenty-seven letters of the Hebrew alphabet symbolize all of creation: the letters alef to tet symbolize the Intellects, yod to ayn the spheres, and kof to the final letter the beings in the lower world. In propounding this scheme Ibn Malkah connects the notion of male and female characters to the superior entities. Although Ibn Malkah does not clarify whether he believes in the Neoplatonic doctrine of creation or the concept of creatio ex nihilo, he does express the opinion that matter and form are the source from which emanate the world of the Intellects, the spheres, and the lower realm.

Ibn Malkah's explanation of the workings of the universe was deeply influenced by astrological theories. Throughout this writing, he maintains that the wise are capable of influencing their own destiny and that of others through a knowledge astrological and physical laws. Regarding the nature of prayer, he states that a pure soul can function as an astral force; when it yearns for its original place, its prayers to the astral forces are answered. Even though it cannot abolish death, it can overcome various ills. Communal prayers, he continues, can be even more efficacious than those of individuals – such collective prayer set the astral forces and souls in motion.

Explaining the nature of the stellar realm, Ibn Malkah contends that a star can be dominant for several generations; as a consequence those who live during the period of the star's influence believe that its dominion is unalterable. They are not able to see that its domination is limited in time. Because of this ancient peoples who practised a cult appropriate for a particular star prospered for a certain period and then disappeared. A sage, however, who knows the star dominant in his own time and place can regulate its influences. At the end of the star's domination, another sage will appear who is able to recognize the situation, and thereby take steps to prepare others for the change which is to take place.

Addressing the question whether miracles can disrupt the natural order of events, Ibn Malkah maintains that what the masses perceive as a miracle is simply an event brought about by a stage utilizing the influence of astral bodies. In this context, various religious practices – including divination and miracles – are restricted to the sage. Nonetheless, magic can be practised by the vulgar, especially women, where neither purity of the soul, prayer, nor sacrifice occurs. Yet, according to Ibn Malkah even here astral forces can be manifest. Hence sorcerers are able to exercise influence even though they do not understand the causes of their abilities.

Regarding politics, Ibn Malkah contends that there are several types of government. The reign of a perfect philosopher is characterized by its subordination to astral influence. Here, there are several determinations having their own peculiar ranges: the most general extends to the entire universe whereas others govern only a smaller area. While it may occur that through the effect of the astral determination, such a philosopher is able to meet many well-disposed persons, the converse is also possible – he might occasionally find it necessary to punish others by death. Some philosophers will carry out this action out of a concern for the general good; others, however, will prefer to escape from society rather than carry out such a decree. Yet, two conditions must be fulfilled if the sage is able to function effectively:

1 The sage must explain in a way suitable to his listeners, that it is necessary to respect God whose wisdom is incompatible with evil actions.
2 The sage must obtain a leader's assistance in carrying out his task.

An inferior type of regime is that of the naturalist philosopher; such an individual sees nothing more than the movement of the sky whereby the life of form and matter originates. Because of the limitations of his knowledge, he does not perceive the influence of astral bodies, and thereby believes in freedom of the will. Nor does he accept that the soul will survive death. Government undertaken by such a person will permit the fulfilment of the natural desires.

In *The Consolation of the Exiled*, Ibn Malkah views the domination of religion as a victory of the ignorant. Here he encourages the sage to conform to the belief of the masses only as a prudent action. For Ibn Malkah, such a policy is simply a preparatory step in the pursuit of truth. With reference to Jewish law, Ibn Malkah stresses the importance of secrecy. Israel is superior to all other nations in its orientation toward universal determination. Yet despite the subtelty of this system, Ibn Malkah's philosophical doctrines had little influence on subsequent Jewish thought. In the next century he was cited only by Isaac of Acre and Samuel Ibn Motot, and in the fifteenth century by Johanan Alemanno.

Abraham Ben Samuel Abulafia

Born in 1240 in Saragossa, Abraham Ben Samuel Abulafia grew up at Tudela in Navarre. His father died when Abulafia was eighteen, and he subsequently travelled to Palestine where he searched for the mystical river Sambatyon where the ten tribes were believed to reside. Returning by way of Greece, he spent some time in Capua where he studied *Maimonides' *Guide for the Perplexed* under the direction of Hillel ben Samuel of Verona. In addition he was introduced to the Kabbalah by Baruch Togarmi who wrote a commentary on the *Sefer Yetsirah*. In 1271 he studied Maimonides' work in Barcelona, became convinced that he had attained prophetic inspiration, and proclaimed his mystical doctrine to a small circle of followers. In 1273 he wandered through Italy, Sicily, and Greece, and also wrote a number of mystical essays combining kabbalistic ideas and Maimonides' philosophy. In 1277 he lived in Patras in Greece where he wrote a series of mystical tracts; three years later he attracted a large circle of disciples in Capua.

In 1280 Abulafia went to Rome in an effort to persuade Pope Nicholas III to improve the condition of the Jewish people. On his arrival, the Pope sentenced him to death by burning. However, because of the Pope's death, the decree was not carried out, and after a month in prison Abulafia was released and went to Sicily. In Messinia he wrote *Or Ha-Sekhel* about the mysteries of God's name, and the autobiographical text *Ozar Eden Ganuz*. Here he announced the onset of the messianic era in 1290; many were persuaded by this prediction and prepared to emigrate to Palestine. Nonetheless, his teachings aroused great hostility, and his opponents approached the scholar Solomon Ben Abraham Adret of Barcelona, accusing Abulafia of claiming to be the Messiah. In response Adret called him a scoundrel: Abulafia was forced to flee to the island of Comino where he wrote polemical treatises in which he defended himself and his views.

Abulafia's mystical ideas were based on the doctrine of the ten sefirot (divine emanations), and utilized the methods of zeruf (combinations of letters), gematria (numerical value of Hebrew words), and notarikon (letters of a word as abbreviations of sentences). Believing prophetic kabbalah enabled human beings to have prophetic powers and commune with the Deity, he argued that human reason can thereby become subject to the rule of God's universal reason. This process he called the 'Way of Divine Name'. Convinced that he had such knowledge of the mystery of the alphabet and numbers, he was certain that he could attain the heights of revelation. By understanding the mystery of letters, vowels, numerals, and God's name, it became possible for him to exercise miraculous powers. According to Abulafia, Israel suffers in exile, because it has forgotten God's true name; only by means of such knowledge (which Abulafia possessed) will the redemption take place.

Explaining the technique of combining the letters of the alphabet as a means of realizing human aspirations toward prophecy, Abulafia writes in his *The Book of Life of the World to Come*:

> Make ready to direct the heart to God alone. Cleanse the body and choose a lonely house where no one shall hear your voice. Sit there in your closet and do not reveal your secret to any person. If you can, do it by day in the house, but it is best if you complete it during the night . . . Now begin to combine a few of many letters, to permute and to combine them until your heart is warm. Then be mindful of their movements and of that you can bring forth by moving them. And when you feel that your heart is already warm and when you see that by combinations of letters you can grasp new things, which by human tradition or by yourself you would not be able to know, and when you are thus prepared to receive the influx of divine power which flows into you, then turn all true thoughts to imagine his exalted angels in your heart as if they were human beings sitting or standing about you.
>
> (in Cohn-Sherbok, 1995, 108–9)

After mastering the technique of letter manipulation, the next step in Abulafia's system involved the pronunciation of God's name. This method is presented in *Or Ha-Sekhal*. The system contained in this work involved the combination of the four letters of God's name (Yod, Hey, Vav, Hey) with the letter Aleph pronounced with the five vowels:

When you begin to pronounce the Aleph without any vowel, it is expressing the mystery of unity. You must therefore draw it out in one breath and no more. Do not interrupt this breath in any manner whatsoever until you have completed the pronunciation of the Aleph. Draw out this breath so long as you extend a single breath. At the same time, chant the Aleph, or whatever other letter you are pronouncing while depicting the first form of the vowel point. The first vowel is the Holem above the letter. When you being to pronounce it, direct your face towards the east, not looking up or down. You should be sitting, wearing clean, pure white robes over all your clothing, or else wearing your prayer shawl over your head and crowned with tefillin.

(*Ibid.*, 110)

An anonymous follower of Abulafia, composed *The Gates of Justice* in which he explains that his master taught him this method of letter manipulation:

When I had done this for a little while, behold, the letters took on in my eyes the shape of great mountains; strong trembling seized me and I could summon no strength, my hair stood on end, and it was as if I were not in this world. At once I fell down, for I no longer felt the least strength in any of my limbs. And behold, something resembling speech emerged from my heart and came to my lips and forced them to move . . . When I got up in the morning I told my teacher about it. He said to me, 'And who was it that allowed you to touch the name. Did I not tell you to permute only letters?' He spoke on, 'What happened to you represents indeed a high stage among prophetic degrees.'

(*Ibid.*, 112)

In providing an account of the path that leads to prophecy, Abulafia explains that prophecy should be understood as the emanation of the Active Intellect. This emanation begins in God, overflowing to the intellect and imagination of the prophet. This Active Intellect is identified with Metatron, the angel who possesses knowledge of esoteric truth. This divine influence passes into the human soul in two ways: if the influx only reaches the intellect, knowledge and science are produced; however, if it embraces both intellect and imagination, it becomes the divine 'Word'. The central feature of Abulafia's system is that it is a blend of rationalism and mysticism. In providing an account of prophetic experience, he utilizes doctrines drawn from Greek philosophical speculation combined with theories about letter manipulation derived from kabbalistic sources.

Zerahiah Ben Shealtiel Gracian of Barcelona

An eminent commentator on *Maimonides, Zerahiah Ben Shealtiel Gracian was deeply influenced by the Maimonidean tradition which was brought to Italy by Jacob Anatoli. Anatoli's pupil Moses Ben Solomon of Salerno wrote a *Commentary on the Guide for the Perplexed*. This work illustrates the close collaboration between Jewish and Christian philosophers of this period – repeatedly Moses refers to the Latin translation of the *Guide*, providing the vulgar Latin equivalents of various Hebrew terms. In addition to this work, Moses composed a Hebrew-Italian glossary based on *Samuel Ibn Tibon's *Glossary of Difficult Terms in the Guide*.

Living in this Italian environment, Zerahiah became an official commentator of Maimonides. Born into a Barcelona family, he emigrated to Rome where he expounded Maimonidean philosophy and attracted a circle of pupils. In addition to translating books on medicine by Galen, Avicenna and Maimonides, he translated from Arabic Aristotle's *De Anima*, Themistius' *Commentary on the De Coelo*, Al-Farabi's *Book on the Substance of the Soul*, the *Middle Commentaries* of Averroes on the *Physics*, the *Metaphysics* and the *Parva Naturalia* and *The Book of Causes* by Pseudo-Aristotle. Of his own works, not all his treatises have been preserved; his major work – a commentary on Maimonides' *Guide* – exists only in part. This, however, is supplemented by letters to Judah ben Solomon and his controversy with Hillel of Verona. Other important studies include his commentaries on the Book of Proverbs and the Book of Job.

Drawing on *Moses Ibn Tibbon's distinction between statistical laws and extraordinary facts, Zerahiah contends that certain kinds of unusual phenomena exist, such as giants. To buttress this argument, Zerahiah contends that archaeology has revealed the existence of such curiosities. In Rome, for example, he discovered an enormous tooth which could only have come from a giant. Moreover, the existence of a gigantic skeleton was reported in a village near Rome. Such claims, however, do not signify an abandonment of philosophical argument in favour of a return to religious belief. Rather, following Averroes, Zerahiah distinguishes philosophy from religion. Whoever combines both, he states, understands neither. In this light Zerahiah contends that Maimonides' thought can only be comprehended by reading his philosophical works.

Zerahiah's adherence to Maimonidean thought is illustrated by Zerahiah's correspondence with Hillel of Verona. Aligning himself with *Saadiah Gaon, Hillel understands Jacob's struggle with the angel in the Book of Genesis as an historical event; similarly, Hillel viewed the account of Balaam's ass speaking as literally true. Zerahiah, however, interprets both passages on the basis of Maimonides' teaching in the *Guide*: these events took place in a vision without any reference to external reality. Such stories, he argues, are simply allegories intended to convey truths of a different order.

Hillel Ben Samuel of Verona

A physician and talmudist, Hillel Ben Samuel was born into a distinguished family of rabbinic sages. In 1254 he lived in Naples, and then settled in Capua. He translated a number of treatises on medicine by Hippocrates, Galen as well as Bruno of Lungoburgo who composed his *Chirurgia Magna* in 1254. In addition to these works, Hillel was known for his participation in the counter-attack of the philosophers against the anti-philosophers at the end of the 13th century. Two of his letters to his friend Issac ben Mordecai reveal his attitude concerning this affair. In all likelihood it was due to his influence that Solomon Ben Abraham of Montpellier who issued the ban against the philosophers was excommunicated by the rabbis of Babylonia, Israel and Italy. Yet despite Hillel's defence of *Maimonides, he was keen to uphold the literal interpretation of the Scriptural text. Unlike his contemporary *Zehariah Ben Shealtiel Gracian, he did not accept the allegorical understanding of biblical passages.

Hillel's major work, *The Retributions of the Soul*, is an amalgam of texts drawn from various writers; it is composed of three short tractates concerning the soul. The first part consists of several fragments of the Latin version of Avicenna's book on the soul, *Liber Sextus Naturalium*; to this are added various sections from the *Liber de Anima* composed by the 12th century Christian scholar and translator Dominicus Gundiaslinus. Aware that Avicenna's explanation would no longer be regarded as acceptable to his contempories, Hillel added a treatise by Averroes entitled *Three Articles on the Intellect*. Finally, Hillel appended to these works the translation of the first chapter of the *Tractatus de Unitate Intellectus contra Averroistas* written in 1270 by Thomas Aquinas.

Unlike the first two treatises, the third is presented as the work of Hillel himself; it is a commentary designed to update both older and contemporary works. Here Hillel refashions the writings he had read and translated either paraphrasing the texts or summarzing them. In his view, Aquinas demonstrated the errors of Averroes's conclusions concerning the end of the individual soul when it departs from the body – both the soul and the eternity of its intellectual part could, he believes, be demonstrated using Aristotelian philosophical categories. Like Aquinas, Hillel subscribed to the belief in the immortality of the soul. On this basis, he seeks to reinterpret the doctrine of reward and punishment in spiritual terms. The final part of Hillel's book deals with miscellaneous topics including knowledge and free will, the connection between Adam's fall and mortality, and the fall of the angels.

Judah Ben Moses Ben Daniel Romano

Born in c. 1280, Judah Ben Moses Daniel Romano was a student of *Zerahiah Gracian; in all likelihood he succeeded him as a teacher of *Maimonides' philosophical system. Serving as a translator at the court of Robert of Anjou, he produced numerous translations including *The Book of Causes* of Pseudo-Aristotle, *De Substantia Coeli* by Averroes, a treatise on the *One and the Unity* by Dominicus Gundissalinus, several studies by Aegidius of Rome, as well as works by Alexander of Hales, Angelo of Camerino, and Thomas Aquinas. These translations were made very soon after the appearance of these treatises. In addition to working as a translator, Judah composed a Judeo-Italian glossary of Maimonides' *Mishneh Torah*, a commentary on the Book of Genesis, *Chapters on Prophecy*, exegeses on biblical passages, a commentary on the Kiddush and the Kedushah, and a commentary on the first four books of Maimonides' *Book of Knowledge*.

Influenced by Latin scholasticism, Judah argues in line with Maimonides that there are no conclusive scientific proofs that the universe was created or that it is eternal. Yet philosophically the notion that the world is eternal is so beset with difficulties that one must assume that it was created. Turning to the subject of the Intellect, Judah argues that Adam was created pure – as a result, he inclined toward the Intellect. However, Eve actualized man's tendency toward materiality. By allowing himself to be tempted by Eve, Adam ceased to be under the domination of the Intellect, and both he and Eve were expelled from the Garden of Eden. Of their children, Cain was totally material, whereas Abel was half-material; only Enoch was able to attain authentic intellection.

Concerning the question whether human beings can achieve union with the Active Intellect, Judah maintains that this is a possibility for certain individuals. Regarding the nature of the Deity, he contends that God cannot be known as he is in himself, but as far as the separate Intellects are concerned we can know of their existence although not their essence or the differences between them. On the other hand, the Active Intellect can be known in its essence and existence – through such knowledge human beings are able to attain a conjunction with it.

According to Judah, such a union with the Active Intellect requires a particular conception of biblical exegesis. The exegete must first reach a degree of abstract thought – this can be achieved through meditating on philosophical issues, even those of a scholastic character. Both the prophet and the philosopher are able to attain this level of thought by engaging in scientific study. Although the prophets are able to pass on to a higher degree of intellection through the prophetic science of sciences, such study is a necessary first step on this path of intellection. When the philosopher has attained a sufficient degree of intellectual insight, he is able to fathom the deeper meaning of Scripture and thereby offer an esoteric interpretation of the biblical text which may be totally different from its literal meaning.

Immanuel Ben Solomon of Rome

Born in c. 1261, Immanuel Ben Solomon of Rome was both a poet and a philosopher. His poetry deals with love, friendship as well as wine whereas his philosohical studies explore the contrast between the material and the spiritual world. In addition to these works, Immanuel composed biblical commentaries on nearly all the books of the Bible, but only those on Proverbs, Psalms, Lamentations, Esther, Ruth and the Song of Songs have been published. In addition to these studies, he composed a work on logic of which only the introduction has appeared. In his biblical studies, Immanuel first explains the literal meaning of the text, and then proceeds to its philosophical implications. Throughout he repeatedly cites the writings of *Abraham Ibn Ezra, *Maimonides, *Jacob Anatoli, *Judah Ben Solomon Ha-Cohen Ibn Malkah, and *Judah Romano. The theme of intellectual love, is a dominant topic and its explication appears to be the main purpose of these studies of Scripture.

Chapter 5

14th Century

The fourteenth century was a time of intense philosophical activity: in Provence, Spain and the Byzantine empire Jewish thinkers engaged in prodigious speculative endeavours. Throughout this century a number of topics were of particular significance. First, there was a preoccupation with astrological investigation often accompanied by an interest in Neoplatonic theory. In this context, the writings of *Abraham Ibn Ezra served as the basis for further study. Hence, according to Judah Ibn Mosconi writing in 1362 at least thirty commentaries on Ibn Ezra's writing had been composed. The first of these was composed by Abishai of Sagori in 1170; the second by *Moses Ibn Tibbon in the 13th century, and all the rest were written in the 14th century. In addition, the works of *Moses Maimonides and Averroes continued to be regarded as the foundation for philosophical reflection. The philosophical texts of *Gersonides composed at the beginning of the 14th century also came to be viewed as of seminal importance; his theories dominated philosophical thought during the rest of the century. During the latter half of the century Latin translations of medical books from Latin into Hebrew came into prominence and translations of books of logic began to appear. Finally, kabbalah continued to exert an influence on a variety of Jewish thinkers as it had done in the previous century.

Yedayah Ha-Penini

Born in c. 1270 Yedayah Ha-Penini was born in Beziers and lived in Perpignan and Montpellier. In all likelihood he worked as a physician. In his youth he composed a long poem, each line of which begins with the Hebrew letter Mem. He subsequently wrote a treatise in defence of women, and a moral work entitled *Examination of the World* which was widely disseminated. Another composition of importance was his *Letter of Apology*, defending the study of philosophy; this tract, addressed to Solomon Ben Adret, was in all likelihood composed before the decree expelling the Jews from France in 1306. In this text Yedayah states that he is unaware of the exegesis that Levi Ben Abraham was criticised of writing:

> You have been told that someone has explained Abraham as representing matter, Sarah as representing form and the tribes as representing the planets; but I can assure you that this is by no means the case. All that one does in the schools is to explain as allegories the aggadic (rabbinic teaching) passages of the Talmud, which cannot be taken literally, and in this we follow the steps of our great master (*Moses Maimonides) . . . as for the crime of which we are accused, that instead of the Talmud we study foreign sciences, that is, the books of Aristotle and his commentators, we declare that the study of logic, physics and metaphysics is useful to fortify religion; thus these studies furnish us with proofs of the existence of God, of prophecy, of free will, of creation ex nihilo, and so on . . . the rabbis in Spain, in Babylonia and in Andalusia, by their knowledge of Arabic, were able to make use of philosophical books; they were able to demonstrate the unity of God and to repel anthropomorphism.
>
> (in Sirat, 1995, 274)

After surveying the history of Jewish philosophy, Yedayah stresses that Maimonides' quest was to reconcile philosophy with the Jewish tradition. In his view, Maimonides in his *Guide* provides a true interpretation of the nature of prophecy and correctly explains how the anthropomorphic depictions of the Deity in Scripture should be understood. Anxious to defend Maimonides' approach from criticism, he writes:

> We have seen letters coming from all parts of the world, attacking him . . . the poet En Vidas says in fact of his contemporaries in Spain that they know the Measure of the Creator, but they do not proclaim it for fear of being considered unbelievers. Nahmanides also says in his *Apologetic Letter* that Maimonides is he who has contributed most to the overthrow of anthropomorphic ideas.
>
> (*Ibid.*, 275)

In light of Maimonides' contribution, Yedayah pleads with Solomon Ben Adret to retract his decision to excommunicate those who study Maimonides' works. This should be done because Maimonides writings will be read regardless of such a threat: 'It is certain that if the Prophet Joshua were to come to tell the Provencals of the present generation not to study the books of Maimonides, he would hardly succeed; for they have the firm intention of sacrificing their fortunes and even their lives to defend the books of Maimonides . . . Why then continue the struggle?' (*Ibid.*, 275)

In the same letter Yedayah goes on to explicate how rabbinic texts should be understood. Here he discusses the human intellect and its relation to the Active Intellect. In this context divine providence is seen as the natural law that God created to regulate the cosmos. As far as astrological influences are concerned, Yedayah cautions that preoccupation with this science can hinder one from action. Like other philosophers of his age, he emphasizes that the philosophical quest is reserved for an intellectual elite rather than the masses. Indeed, he insists, if it such knowledge is misconstrued, it can do actual harm.

Yedayah's writings were widely discussed by both Jewish and Christian thinkers. One of his works – a manuscript containing five treatises which is located in the Bibliotheque Nationale – deals with the nature of the intellect. The first two of these treatises explore the nature of the intellect, beginning with a summary of a study by Al-Farabi; this is followed by a number of opinions about the hylic intellect. The following two treatises explore the concept of opposition and contrariness in movement with reference to Averroes' *Great Commentary on the De Coelo*.

Of particular importance in this discussion was Yedayah's appeal to Aristotle's ideas about physics and logic, the distinction between space located under the sphere of the moon, and the idea that number resides only in the soul or the intellect. These notions are in line with Aristotle's writings as well as Averroes' commentaries, and it is possible that Yedayah's views were shaped through discussions with Christian thinkers. Of note in this regard are Yedayah's opinions concerning the concept of species. In his *Treatise on the Particular and Individual Forms*, he states that every species possesses a form which distinguishes it from other species. Nonetheless within a species, individuals are different. Dogs, for example, come in different shapes and sizes and possess a wide range of dispositions. What causes such differentiation then is not a difference in form, but the existence of various particular features. Within this context, however, Yedayah affirms that different forms exist – such a view sets him at odds with the Judeo-Arabic intellectual tradition where form was understood as general. This is so by definition. Such a departure from the traditional understanding was in all likelihood due to the influence of the theories of Duns Scotus even though he does not refer to him by name.

Nissim Ben Moses of Marseilles

In the first half of the 14th century, Nissim Ben Moses composed a commentary on the Torah entitled *Book of Miracles* – this work was designed for religiously sophisticated individuals over the age of 40. In the introduction, Nissim outlines the central principles of biblical exegesis. In his view, science and Torah both have a divine origin, but they have different functions:

> Your great principle should be the following: try whenever you can to adjust the texts to what the intellect positively indicates, even if the explanation be far-fetched; if you cannot (make them agree with reason) place (these verses) in the class of the promises that no religion can do without. In fact, religion is a general law which is given to the few, the philosophers, and to the common people, the ignorant, and also to women and children. However, the law applies to all without distinction.
>
> (in Sirat, 1995, 277)

In this work, Nissim differentiates between philosophy and faith. Knowledge, he argues, leads to supreme happiness which is understood as union with the Intellect. The intention of religion, on the other hand, is to act as a corrective to the errors of human composition. Its role is to perfect human corporeality and create harmony between individuals. Philosophy serves as the basis for enlightening the spirit; faith, however, is the source for health and peace. In his view, a philosopher is able to obtain knowledge, thereby freeing himself from the constraints of material existence. A prophet, on the other hand, does not strive to attain philosophical truth – his role is to caution communities about the dangers that threaten them due to his awareness of astral laws. True wisdom, he argues, thus consists in adapting one's actions to the influence of the stars.

Within this astrological context providence should be understood as (1) divine commandments designed to guide individuals in righteous paths; and (2) the gift of prophecy bestowed upon those capable of warning the community of impending dangers. For Nissim, there is no fundamental difference between the prophet and the sage who is knowledgeable about astral laws: both are near to God. For both individuals, the imaginative faculty provides an awareness of future events. Nonetheless, Nissim insists that certain religious rites can enable one to gain prophetic insight. For example, animal sacrifice or concentrating on stones such as those on the High Priest's breastplate can awaken the imagination and lead it to a comprehension of future events.

Miracles, too, can enable the prophet to gain knowledge of the future. Such extraordinary events are of two kinds: those performed through prophetic intervention, and those that occur without the influence of a prophet. The first category includes events which take place in the presence of God and the prophet, as well as those incidents which involve other people. Those events involving only God and a prophet take place either in visions or in a waking state. In such cases the sensations felt by a prophet are caused by the action of the imaginative faculty and the internal senses without any recourse to the external world.

Miracles involving other people are of two kinds: the announcement of future occurances, or efficacious action. In both cases, the knowledge of divine secrets hidden in God's works and creatures is of fundamental importance. Yet, regarding efficacious action one must also have an awareness of those actions which are indispensable to the miraculous act. For example, in Exodus 15: 23f where Moses sweetened the waters of Marah, the wood he cast into the water served as the means whereby the water was changed.

In his work, the distinction Nissim makes between science (or philosophy) and prophecy compels him to focus on the value of the Scriptural text. In his opinion, whatever is the product of philosophical reflection should be eliminated from the Bible. In so far as the books of Scripture are concerned, Nissim is anxious to distinguish between the Torah and the Neviim (Prophetic Booksl) and Ketuvim (Writings). If the law contained in the Pentateuch were understood allegorically like some prophetic passages, the Jewish people would not feel compelled to observe all the commandments. For Nissim, however, the law is perfect and must be observed. Yet, he points out that only true philosophers perceive the truth of the Mosaic law. As far as the masses are concerned, a more authoritarian system was needed to impose these ordinances on an ignorant public. Because coercion was practically impossible, Moses instituted threats and promises to compel the ignorant to obey the law.

Turning to *Maimonides principles of the Jewish faith, Nissim outlines Maimonides' views and then assesses them philosophically. In his opinion, eight of these principles can be demonstrated by the intellect: (l) God's existence; (2) divine unity; (3) God is not a body (4) God alone is to be worshipped; (5) omniscience; (6) prophecy; (7) the divine commandments are unchangeable; (8) the coming of the Messiah. There other principles, however, are grounded on faith: (l) resurrection; (2) creation; (3) the superiority of Moses' prophecy.

Regarding these three latter principles, Nissim states that the concept of the resurrection of the dead is not a product of intellectual reflection – rather it was designed for the masses who need the promise of eternal salvation to lead righteous lives. Temporal creation, he continues, is not proved by philosophical demonstration, but its practical efficacy is obvious: belief in the origin of the universe is necessary since if there were no temporal creation, there would be no possibility of miracles. Here he asserts that Moses hearing the commandments and passing them on to the Jewish people is a miraculous occurance; without this supernatural basis, the masses would not faithfully observe the Torah. Hence, the Jewish legal system rests on an unproven religious assumption without which the Jewish community would be led astray. Similarly, the superiority of Moses' prophecy is of paramount importance in insuring that Judaism continues.

The final two principles are a compound of the first two types: (1) reward and punishment; and (2) the divine origin of the Torah. In Nissim's view, these doctrines can be demonstrated through reason and also constitute part of the Jewish religious system. Reward and punishment, he contends, can be proved philosophically when this doctrine is understood as relating to souls who have the capacity to obtain knowledge about future events in an another life. Yet, when one interprets the biblical and rabbinic promises in their literal and corporeal sense, they relate to a future existence and thereby become a matter of faith. Similarly, the belief in Torah MiSinai (Torah from Sinai) is true from a scientific point of view because Moses gave only one divine law which prepares the intellect for philosophical reflection. But if one construes the divine origin as a voice from heaven, it becomes a matter of religious belief.

Abner of Burgos

Born in c. 1270, Abner of Burgos was a an apostate and anti-Jewish polemicist. In 1295 he served as a physician in Burgos; at this time a false Messiah appeared in Avila and some of those who witnessed his miraculous deeds came to Abner for medical assistance. Their accounts had a profound effect on Abner and undermined his faith. Unable to account for the suffering of those Jews who lived in exile, he turned to the Christian religion. After struggling with this problem for twenty five years, he eventually converted to Christianity at about the age of 50 and took on the name Alfonso of Valladolid. After his conversion, he sent his disciple *Issac Pulgar a copy of a tract in which he formulated his messianic theories. In response Pulgar circulated a work in which he put forth his own view. Subsequently Abner published a series of works in Hebrew directed to the Jewish community; in addition, he engaged in various Jewish scholars including Moses ben Joshua of Narbonne. In 1334 he attempted to persuade the scholars of Toledo that they had made a mistake in determining the date of Passover.

In his writing Abner attempted to justify his conversion to Christianity. As a philosopher and advocate of astrology, he attacked his correligionists. Describing Abner's views, Moses of Narbonne states:

> There was a scholar, an older contemporary of mine, one of the singular men of his time, who composed a treatise on determinism, in which he stated that 'the possible' does not exist, but only 'the inevitable', since everything is predestined . . . Now this man, called Abner, possessed great knowledge, so that I do not believe that he was himself in error, but that his intent was to mislead others. For he had come upon hard times, and he realized that he could expect not assistance, only opposition, from his correligionists, who, being strangers to philosophy themselves, hated those who cultivated it – so he turned apostate . . . For he was not one of those pious men whose faith remains unimpared even by extreme material want . . . Later, when he saw that what he had done was wrong even according to philosophy – for even a philosopher should not discard the Torah in which he was nurtured – he tried to absolve himself of guilt by preaching an all-embracing determinism, claiming that everything was preordained.
>
> (in Baer, 1961, Vol. I, 332)

Advocating an absolute determinism, Abner argued that human actions are the necessary result of causes. Although human beings choose between alternatives, these actions are not free since they depend on necessary laws. Here he points out that if human actions were freely chosen, then God could not know what decisions would be made until the last moment since they would be unforeseeable even for those who chose them. If this were the case, then God would not be omniscient. God, however, knows all things and therefore human actions cannot be free even though human beings believe they are not constrained to act in a particular fashion. Yet despite such a rigid view, Abner contends that the divine commandments remain in force and that reward and punishment are the necessary consequences of human action.

Not only does Abner advance such a deterministic philosophy, he provides an explanation of the will that justified forced baptisms and the tortures of the Inquisition. In his *Offering of Jealousy* which was composed in response to a polemical letter from Isaac Pulgar, he states that the will is the immediate cause of the act itself. The fact that this will is the result of an unchanging decree or is dependent on another cause is of no importance. Although one can argue that a fixed will is in fact not a will at all, an intention which gives rise to certain acts is an attitude that exists in the soul due to multiple causes that are linked to the movements of the spheres. If such a will leads to action, the will is perfect even if it is under an external constraint. Hence a person who is obliged to will something while being tortured is no less willing, consenting, and freely choosing.

Such views were refuted by a series of philosophers of the same period. In Moses of Narbonne's *Treatise on Free Will*, he summarizes the views of Abner and other determinists. These writers, he argues, maintain that all things are fixed and determined and that effort and zeal are indispensable since they are the intermediary causes which are necessary for those things which necessarily come into existence. In Narboni's view, it is illogical to assume that all things are determined; such a conception is also refuted by experience. Moreover, such a deterministic conception is flawed since zeal and effort must be irrelevant if all things are fixed in advance. Regarding the human intellect, Narboni argues that free will has been given to human beings as is evident from experience. Humans gain knowledge by perceiving what exists; God, however, knows all things without recourse to experience.

Similarly attempting to defend the doctrine of free will, another Jewish thinker of this period Joseph Caspi argues that God's knowledge of future events in no way undermines their contingency:

This is what Rabbi Akiva the perfect sage said . . . 'All is forseen and liberty is given to man' (*Pirkei Avot*, III, 17). Let us take an example: God revealed to Jeremiah that Jerusalem would be destroyed by Nebuchadnezzar if Zedekiah did not surrender to Nebuchadnezzar; if he surrendered to him, the town would not be destroyed; he also revealed to him that Zedekiah would freely choose to rebel against Nebuchadnezzar. It is as if he had said to him: know that Zedekiah the accursed will choose the evil way. Our sages are practised in conjecture and supposition; they forsee that a man accursed in his actions and in all that he touches will take a bad decision tomorrow or the day after tomorrow, whether in an affair of marriage or in some other affair concerning common things – business or a journey. Now, if we are seldom mistaken in our anticipations, how much more certainly can God, who presides over intellectual prediction as over established knowledge, direct his knowledge towards the decision that we shall take in one or other specific situation.

(in Sirat, 1995, 314)

Levi Ben Gershom

Born in 1288, Levi Ben Gershom (Gersonides) resided in Bagnols-sur-Cèze in Languedoc, Avignon and Orange. Like *Maimonides, he was a philosopher, halakhist and man of science. Of his scientific works, the *Treatise of Astronomy* is the most important – in this study he criticizes various aspects of Ptolemy's astronomical theories: relying on his own astronomical observations, he refers to ten eclipses of the sun and moon as well as nearly a hundred other astronomical occurances which he witnessed. In addition, he deals with the method of constructing and using the Baculus Jacob which enables one to measure the angular distance between stars and planets.

Between 1325–1338 Gersonides composed biblical commentaries in which differing methods are deployed according to the nature of the books being treated. Added to these commentaries, Gersonides wrote philosophical studies on Averroes' *Short Commentaries* and *Middle Commentaries* as well as poems, a confession, a parody for the Purim festival, two responsa, and a commentary on the Talmudic treatise *Berakhot*. Gersonides' most famous philosophical work, *Wars of the Lord*, took twelve years to complete and was finished in 1329.

In the introduction Gersonides outlines the topics to be treated in this investigation:

1 Whether a person that has only partly achieved perfection can enter into the afterlife.
2 Whether a person can know the future either through dreams, divination, or prophecy.
3 Whether God knows existing things.
4 Whether there is divine providence for existing things.
5 How the movers of the spheres operate.
6 Whether the world is eternal or created.

Concerning the doctrine of God, Gersonides rejects the view of Aristotelian philosophers that it is possible to derive the existence of a Prime Mover from the motions that exist in the universe. Instead, Gersonides offers a proof of God's existence based on the orderly processes that take place in the world. According to this proof (the argument by design), the regularity of the processes of generation in the sub-lunar world imply that they are caused by an intelligence, the Active Intellect, which rules over this domain. The Active Intellect endows matter with its different forms and is conscious of the order it generates; its activities are mediated by natural heat which is found in the seeds of plants and the sperm of animals. In turn this natural heat is produced by the motions of the celestial spheres. Because these motions contribute to the perfection of the earthly realm, they must also be produced by inteligences which are the cause of them, namely the intelligences of the celestial spheres. Hence, the celestial and terrestrial worlds constitute an ordered whole requiring the existence of a supreme being which knows this order.

Critical of Maimonides' notion of the negative attributes, Gersonides argues that it is possible to ascribe positive attributes to God; these attributes, he believes, do not undermine God's unity. Accepting that multiplicity exists when objects are composed of form and matter, he maintains that all those attributes which are predicated of a non-material being are derived from the subject: these predicates are simply an explanation of its nature. In Gersonides' view, human beings are capable of attaining a positive knowledge of God based on his action of which the essential activity is thought. All the attributes which human beings recognize in themselves are just so many attributes of God, and since the attributes which are shared by human beings and God have the nature of cause and effect – it is a mistake to regard them as homonyms (terms which are different except for their names).

According to Gersonides, God eternally perceives the general laws of the universe, namely those laws which order the movements of heavenly bodies and through them sublunar beings. Thus God is aware of what awaits all persons as members of collectivities, yet as specific individuals each person is able to exercise freedom of the will. When such free choices are made, human beings are able to liberate themselves from the constraints of determinism They cease to be subject to the universal laws known by God, and their acts are therefore totally undetermined and unknown to the Deity. In presenting this explanation of divine knowledge and human freedom, Gersonides contends that God's knowledge does not undergo any modification: it remains true regardless of individual choices since each agent is no longer included in the necessary and universal propositions which are thought by God. For Gersonides, God's knowledge embraces all events of this world with the exception of freely chosen actions that cannot be foreseen. By means of this theory Gersonides believes he is able to resolve the seeming contradiction between God's omniscience and freedom of the will.

As far as providence is concerned, Gersonides argues that this manifestation of divine direction increases in relation to a person's moral and intellectual perfection. Through the activities of the stars which are predetermined, God insures a maximum of good to human beings. Hence premonitions, dreams and prophecies as well as the exercise of free will rescue individuals from the harmful effects of determinism. Yet, it is impossible to deny the existence of evil since the righteous occasionally do suffer; nonetheless Gersonides maintains that the true human good is the immortality of the soul which is bestowed in proportion to an individual's moral excellence and intellectual perfection.

In contrast with Maimonides who held that creation cannot be demonstrated philosophically, Gersonides attempts to prove that the world came into being. Thus he maintains that everything which is produced by a final cause, ordained for a certain end, and serving as a substratum for accidents cannot exist eternally. Because the universe fulfils all these conditions, it follows that it must have a beginning in time. In his opinion, many of Aristotle's arguments used to prove the eternity of the world actually beg the question – they are based on the presupposition that the physical laws operating in the world can be applied to its beginning. This assumption, however, is without substance; even though there are some similarities between the events taking place in the world and creation, the origin of the universe is unique. Terrestrial motions take place in time, whereas creation occurred in an instant. Yet, since nothing can be created out of nothing, the world has a formless substratum – it does not have existence in the technical sense since existence is derived from form.

Regarding Geronsides' conception of human nature, God arranged the universe in such a way that human beings are the most perfect of all creatures in the sublunar world. Hence revelations of various types protect them from danger: through their imaginations – which are under celestial influences – they are able to envisage the problems that can befall them. Possessing a practical intellect, man is able to learn the mans of self-preservation; through the speculative intellect, he is able to perceive truth and attain immortality. The material or potential intellect is not a substance, but a simple disposition whose substratum is the imagination. On the basis of sensations, the human intellect is able to form abstract concepts, yet true knowledge should be conceived as the comprehension of intelligibles. Having understood what is intelligible and eternal, the human intellect becomes immortal.

Gersonides' philosophical system also deals with the concept of Israel's chosenness. Providence, he argues, extends particularly to the Jewish people. In his view, prophecy should be conceived as a form of revelation which is superior to all other types of divine disclosure. The prophet must necessarily be a distinguished philosopher who is able to comprehend the general laws governing the sublunar world as they are manifest in the agent intellect. Through his imagination, he is able to apply this knowledge to individual or communal events; such knowledge enables him to proclaim whatever is to befall both individuals and groups as a result of the operation of the laws of nature. Further, he is capable of foreseeing a miraculous occurance which violates the laws of nature. According to Gersonides, a miracle takes place at a specific time and place when the Active Intellect suspends natural laws. Though such extraordinary occurances are not consonant with natural law, they nonetheless follow patterns of their own. However, since miracles are produced by the Active Intellect which can only act in the sublunar realm, no miracles take place in the translunar world. Commenting on Moses' prophetic role, Gersonides maintains that through his intermediacy, God gave Israel the Torah which enables the Jewish people to attain moral and intellectual perfection: in this way they are able to attain immortality.

Finally, Gersonides outlines an eschatological unfolding of human history in which two Messiahs – the Messiah ben Joseph and the

Messiah ben David – play a fundamental role. As Gersonides explains, the Messiah ben David will be greater than Moses since he is able to accomplish a greater miracle than Moses was able to achieve – the resurrection of the dead, an event which will result in the transformation of earthly existence. In propounding this view, Gersonides predicted that the Messiah would arrive in 1358.

Isaac Pulgar

Very little is known of Isaac Pulgar except that he was the major critic of Abner of Burgos. In his most important work, *The Support of the Faith*, Pulgar mentions other of his writings including commentaries on Genesis, Ecclesiastes and Psalms, a study of ethics, and a tract critical of astronomy. It appears that shortly after Abner's conversion to Christianity, Abner sent Pulgar a treatise he had composed expounding his messianic views. In a response to Abner, Pulgar attempts to demonstrate the superiority of Judaism on rational grounds. In his view, human beings do not have the leisure nor the inclination to gain an awareness of ultimate truth. For this reason the Torah was given to Israel to distinguish it from all other nations. Those who observe the divine commandments are able to inherit eternal life. Pulgar then goes on to explain that the Messiah is destined to redeem his people. After Pulgar circulated this response (*Epistle of Blasphemies*) throughout Spain, Abner replied to it in a tract entitled *Refutation of the Blasphmerer*.

In *The Support of the Faith*, Pulgar attempts to counter Abner's arguments and provide a justification for Jewish rationalism. Divided into five parts, this work describes five kinds of critics of the true religion as conceived by Pulgar: the ignorant, the sceptic, the astrologer, the kabbalist, and the non-believer. In the first part of this work, Pulgar seeks to demonstrate the superiority of Judaism. Utilizing the traditional definition of theoretical reason and that of practical reason, Pulgar states that the Torah enables human beings to develop on three levels: (1) on the moral level by teaching virtue; (2) on the level of social instinct by providing him with just laws; and (3) on the intellectual level by granting human beings true knowledge for the survival of their souls. This third level is a bridge between theoretical science and political necessity as well as between philosophical truth and ethical and social concerns.

One of the chapters of this study is devoted to the conception of the king-statesman. Such an individual is perfect in his bodily constitution, possessing a sound understanding; he must also have a good memory, an intuitive grasp of what is hidden, fluent speech, an ability to teach, love of truth, and hatred of falsehood. Such an individual is remote from bodily pleasures and critical of everything which is mundane. He will naturally love justice, hate evil, and possess a decisive character. For Pulgar, Moses represents such an ideal type:

> We are obliged to believe that all these eminent qualities were in Moses because his soul was withdrawn, detached from its matter and despising it. (The soul of Moses) changed the laws of nature and performed the well-known miracles in the same way as the separate forms change matter at their will. Moses prophesied whenever he wished to do so . . . and all this because he was always conjoined to the spiritual (beings) and had become divine, perfect.
>
> (Pulgar, 1906, 15)

Following a description of the true life which involves the death of the body and all material pleasures, Pulgar turns to the subject of miracles. In his view, the regularity of nature is the best evidence for belief in God. Yet, miracles are necessary for the ignorant masses as Moses discovered:

> If Moses had thought that their intellects were perfect, he would have explained to them that in fulfilling the commandments which are for the good of man, and avoiding the things prohibited, which are bad for him, they would be granted eternal life, which is the world to come, and this was a better reason to believe in God and in Moses, his servant.
>
> (*Ibid.*, 20)

The end of this section discusses messianic prophecies in the light of Abner's criticism of the faith.

The second part of this work presents a dialogue between a young philosopher and an old man who symbolizes religion. In this debate the old man presents traditional arguments in favour of religion. The philosopher, however, argues along different lines. In his view, the commandments were given for their own sake – God does not in any way benefit if they observed. The reward of keeping these obligations resides in the good that results from following them. The philosopher then proceeds to criticise the belief in the magical power of the Hebrew letters. For the philosopher, there is a fundamental difference between religion and science: the philosopher and the prophet are able

142

to attain divine truth, yet by using his intellect, the philosopher is able to understand the causal link between the invisible Intellects and the visible world. The prophet, on the other hand, is unaware of such interconnections because the divine overflow reaches only his imaginative faculty. For this reason, the sage is superior to the prophet.

The person chosen to judge between philosophy and religion is the King of Israel. He decrees that both claims can be reconciled. The divine overflow, he states, is one but comes in two different ways:

> The first is the way of the perfect theoretical science, the second is God's perfect religion; we need the first to imprint in the soul the beginnings of the intelligibles which are part of the existing beings and also of the separate forms; we need the second to guide our actions to the right path, to direct our activity towards good and beautiful works.
>
> (Ibid., 41)

Science and religion, he continues, are both necessary:

> A philosopher without religion is like a man standing in the desert without any society: he will not be able to live and subsist alone, without help. A religious man without science, who studies the Torah for its own sake only, is like a beast without a herdsman. He will not know where his pasture is. Thus they (Torah and philosophy) must be narrowly conjoined and tied together.
>
> (*Ibid.*, 43–4)

According to the King, the real danger is presented by those who, having learned some logic, apply to religion the principles of science. Instead of being in conflict, the King asserts that there is a perfect harmony between religion and science.

The next part of Pulgar's work is directed against Abner and the astrologers. Here he provides a description of the astrologer who is able to impress the masses. Echoing Maimonides' condemnation of astrology, he asserts that the planets do not exercise any control over the physical world. Moreover, he criticises a deterministic understanding of events; in his view, all events are contingent. The human and divine will, he states, are linked together:

> Certainly, I am far from believing that it is by my own zeal and my own will alone that I obtain anything, whatever it may be,

but, as I have told you, my will is linked to that of my Creator and both unite at the same instant so that my will is part of his, and thus I am drawn by him; when he wishes and desires to act, then I too wish it. In all this, we are concerned only with voluntary acts and not natural or accidental events, for as regard these I have no liberty. As for what you have said, that my will is determined without my being aware of it, that all my acts are necessarily fixed and decided in advance without my thought, my reflection or my counsel taking a real part in their production, this is contrary to all our visible experience and destroys the nature of (the contingent) as it has been placed in it.

(*Ibid.*, 57–8)

In Pulgar's view, God knows the future things which will be freely chosen by human beings since he chooses them at the same time that they do. But he does not communicate to the prophets his eternal knowledge of this will; what he conveys instead is a probable knowledge of the world which allows the prophet to judge for himself the greater or lesser possibility of an event occurring:

Thanks to the Active Intellect which overflows into the imaginative faculty of the prophet or the seer, or thanks to the light which this Intellect makes to shine over it, the prophet or seer sees and attains the different degrees of the existing things; he encompasses with his intellect and knows the existence of the causes of the things that are susceptible of happening, or, on the basis of these causes, to come into existence when these causes approach each other and the active (power) is strengthened in order to act or the passive (one) is ready to be acted, and also when the impediments and the obstacles disperse and disappear . . . When (the prophet) apprehends this, he announces it; however, because of the nature of contingency that exists eternally in everything . . . this prophecy and this aptitude to know will not make necessary or obligatory the existence of a thing as long as the moment that the necessary and obligatory will of God has willed has not yet arrived.

(*Ibid.*, 55–7)

After this account, the fourth part of the book discusses the absurdity of magical beliefs and stories; the fifth part contains a dialogue between the dead and the living about the immortality of the soul.

Joseph Caspi

Born in 1279 at l'Argentière or Largentière, Joseph Caspi lived at Tarascon, and was a frequent traveller. In order to increase his knowledge, he went to Arles, Aragon, Catalonia, Majorca, Egypt and Fez. Of his three children, the eldest son, Abba Mari, settled in Barcelona; his daughter lived in Perpeignan; and the younger son, Solomon, lived in Tarascon. It appears that Caspi composed thirty works, consisting largely of commentaries on the Bible, *Maimonides *Guide for the Perplexed*, and the *Mysteries* of *Ibn Ezra's *Commmentaries*. In addition, he wrote a number of studies of Hebrew grammar.

Capsi's range of intellectual interests is reflected in the moral testimony composed for his son Solomon in which he outlines what he believes to be the ideal programme of study for a young man:

> Today thou art twelve years of age. For another two years be a diligent student of the Scriptures and the Talmud. When thou art fourteen, fix regular hours for continuing thy previous studies, and give also a good part of thy time to mathematics; first Ibn Ezra's Arithmetic, then Euclid, and the Astronomical Tables of Al-Fergani and (Abraham b. Hiyya). Besides, appoint set times for reading moral books, which will introduce thee to all good qualities – viz. the Books of Proverbs and Ecclesiastes, the Mishnaic tractate *Fathers*, with the Commentary of Maimonides and his preface thereto, and the same authors Introductory chapters to the *Code*. Also read Aristotle's *Ethics*, of which I have made a digest. There is also available among the *Collection of the Maxims of the Philosophers*. This course should occupy thee for two years. Then, when thou art sixteen appoint times for the Scriptures, for the writings of Alfasi, Moses of Coucy, and the *Code* of the perfect teacher (Maimonides). Also give much time to Logic . . . In this way thou shouldst pass another two years, by which time thou wilt be eighteen years old. Then review all thy former work, and study natural science.
>
> (in Abrahams, 1926, 144–5)

Although Caspi insists on the importance of philosophical and scientific study, he was not as concerned about ritual law. Even though his son Solomon was encouraged to gain an understanding of the Talmud and its commentaries as well as *Maimonides' *Mishneh Torah*, Caspi recounts the limitations of his own knowledge of rabbinic sources:

145

I will confess to thee, my son! that though in my youth I learned
a great portion of the Talmud, I did not acquire (for my sins) a
knowledge of the posekim (scholars in the law). Now that I am
old and grey, I have often to consult rabbis younger than myself.
Why should I be ashamed of this? Can one man be skilled in
every craft?

(*Ibid.*, 151)

Despite the fact that Caspi was not learned in the complexities of
Jewish law, he was insistent that knowledge of Hebrew was of
fundamental importance. In this regard he relates:

Once a bishop honoured in our country, who was versed in the
Holy Scriptures, asked me: Why do you demand that kings,
popes and bishops respect and render homage to your Scrolls of
the Torah when they enter a city as we do with the Cross? . . .
My answer was: My lord, certainly our books are superior and
more saintly than yours because these books were first made in
our tongue and our writing. And this is for two causes: (One):
the writing our books are written in is the Script of God and it is
in this tongue (Hebrew) that they were given.

(in Sirat, *op. cit.*, 326)

For Caspi, not only was logic of crucial significance for the scholar, so
too was an understanding of history. Scripture, he states, describes
real persons who must be placed in their geographical and historical
context. In this light Scripture should be interpreted literally rather
than by means of allegory. Further, the events described in the Bible
should be understood as historical occurances. The revelation on
Mount Sinai, for example, took place as depicted in the Torah – it was
not a prophetic vision as Maimonides believed. Such a belief led Capsi
to locate the biblical narrative into a historical and cultural context.

Caspi's emphasis on history caused him to interpret a number of
biblical expressions in the light of current practices which he believed
reflected the practices of ancient times. Hence, after travelling to
Egypt, he wrote:

The people of our country cannot understand when God says to
Moses: Put off thy shoes (= shal; Exodus 3:5) and (in Ruth 4:7)
concerning Boaz, A man plucked off his shoe (= shalaf), and
regarding the levirate (Deuteronomy 25:9) (she) shall loose his
shoe (= halats). In fact, in these countries (Egypt) people are in
the habit of wearing leather sandals which are not attached to

146

the foot, and when one wishes to remove them, it is enough to move the foot about a little to make the sandal fall off by itself; the verb shal has the same sense in Deuteronomy 19:5: The head slippeth from the helve . . . On the other hand, when one pulls the shoe with the hand one will use the verb shalf as in the expression: Draw the dagger out (cf. Judges 3:22). But if the shoe is attached and tied to the foot with straps, one will use the word halts as in Leviticus 14:40. They take away the stones, and also in the ceremony of the levirate, as our sages have explained.

(in Sirat, *op. cit.*, 329)

In the light of such an emphasis on history, Capsi argues that the prophets' function was to forsee future events. In this regard he envisages the eventual return of the Jewish nation to its ancestral home. The Jews were driven into exile, he states, because they had forsaken God's ways – there is no need to attribute this tragedy to the conjunction of astral events. Rather, he continues, history is composed of conquests and victories. As far as the Jewish people are concerned, they were once captive in Egypt, and later obtained deliverance through the mediation of Moses. After the destruction of the Temple, King Cyrus of Persia permitted them to return to Jerusalem. Similarly, eventually a historical personage – perhaps the Sultan of Egypt or the King of France – will allow them to return to Zion.

Despite Capsi's erudition and originality, he was attacked by a variety of scholars; subsequently Kalonymus ben Kalonymus ben Meir collected the criticisms of several adversaries of Salon in Provence including Moses of Beaucaire and Sen Astruc of Noves. Adding his objections to Caspi's writings, he censures him for lacking respect for the biblical text. In addition, he maintains that Caspi's historical explanation of biblical terminology is not scientific since there is no way to prove that the practices of the peoples of the East have not changed since ancient times.

Shemariah Ben Elijah the Cretan

Born in 1275 probably in Rome, Shemariah Ben Elijah is known as Ikriti (the Cretan) since his family settled in Crete when he was a child. Knowledgeable of Greek, Italian and Latin, Shemariah was the first medieval Jew to translate Greek literature from the original (rather than from Arabic or Hebrew). Until the age of 30, the only Hebrew source he knew was the Bible; only at a later stage did he study the Talmud and philosophy. In 1328 he dedicated a long commentary on the Song of Songs to his patron King Robert of Anjou; in this work he compared the king to King Solomon. According to a poem by Moses ben Samuel of Roquemaure (who later converted to Christianity taking the name Jean of Avignon), Shemariah proclaimed himself the Messiah in 1352 and announced that the day of deliverance would occur in 1358. Shemariah was the author of a number of biblical and talmudic commentaries as well as a short commentary on the Song of Songs and the *Epistle on Creation*.

In his writings, Shemariah advocates a type of philosophical mysticism. Repeatedly he speaks of the union between the soul and the Active Intellect. From the conjunction, the human soul is able to experience sublime pleasure. In this light Shemariah argues that the joy of rabbinic scholars is incomplete since they are occupied solely with the study of the Talmud. Yet, if both philosophical enlightenment and study of the law are combined, then it is possible to attain the highest degree of happiness: this is the state of supreme bliss in which the contemplation of the intelligibles and knowledge of the Torah are combined. When such activity takes place, Shemariah believes that God rejoices. Referring to his own intellectual pursuits, he writes:

> God knows my thoughts and the commentaries that I have engendered in this book (*Book of Fear*) and in my other books. He speaks them in my name. Not only do I affirm that God knows them and speaks them in my name, but I add that he praises them and takes joy and pleasure in them for they were made in his service and his glory.
>
> (in Sirat, 1955, 331)

Discussing the relation of the soul to the material world, Shemariah contends that the separation of the soul from the body should not be seen as a punishment or the result of the Fall. Rather, the human soul was sent to earth as a representative of the Divine. Without its presence (and thereby God's presence as well), the world of both celestial and terrestrial bodies would collapse. God, he asserts, is life and without him nothing exists. Yet this mission is not accomplished by all souls – some are lost in the desert of the body. Others, however, give God with great joy and attach themselves to him. According to Shemariah, one of the reasons why God is pleased by his writing is because he demonstrated that the world was created in time.

In the *Epistle on the Creation*, Shemariah enumerates a number of arguments in favour of creation ex nihilo. Here he states that if God had not formed the cosmos ex nihilo, then part of God must have been transformed into what is now the universe. Countering such a claim, philosophers maintain that to ask how and why the world exists makes no more sense than to ask how and why God exists. Yet, it is a mistake to equate these two questions since the concept of existence does not have the same meaning with regard to God as it does in relation to the world. The statement that God exists, he argues, is the same as the claim that he does not exist; this is so because God's existence does not enter into the category of being: he is neither a body nor a bodily force, and he lacks both quality and limit. Hence it is impossible to compare God and the world. Further, since the infinite and the finite cannot be compared, the problem cannot be solved by arguing that the Intellect emanates from God. Nor does the size of the material world affect the issue – no matter how large the comos is, it will always be finite in nature: it cannot emerge from the infinite except by divine fiat.

Moses ben Joshua Narboni

Born in Perpignan Moses Narboni (Maitre Vidal Belsom) originated from a family originally living in Narbonne. After a traditional Jewish education combined with the study of philosophy and medicine, he became a doctor, composing a work on medicine (*The Road to Life*) in which he describes various prescriptions and cures. In 1344, he moved from Perpignan and settled in several Spanish towns including Cervera, Barcelona, Toledo and Burgos. In 1355 he commenced his *Commentary on the Guide for the Perplexed*; this work was finished at Soria in 1362 after which he died.

A writer of encyclopedic knowledge, Narboni's works consist of studies of Maimonides, commentaries on the treatises of Averroes, a commentary on Al-Ghazali's *Opinions of the Philosophers* and Ibn Tufayl's *Hayy Ibn Yaqzan*, and a commentary on Lamentations. In addition, three short works – *Epistle on the Measure of the Divine Stature*; *Treatise on Free Will*; *The Chapters of Moses* – contain his philosophical views. In the first of these treatises, Narboni deals with the problem of God's knowledge of his creatures and their knowledge of him. Based on *Abraham Ibn Ezra's commentary on Exodus as well as biblical and rabbinic sources, he argues that God is 'the truly existent who knoweth all; (that) his knowledge and he are identical, and (that) in him, blessed be he, intellect, intelligent, and intelligible are one and the same thing.' (in Altmann, 1967, 271)

Narboni goes on to assert that the ultimate knowledge we have concerning God consists in our knowing in which way he is the first principle:

> For thereby we know as much of the truth concerning him as is in our nature to know: that is, (by knowing) that he is the first principle insofar as he is (the unity of) intellect, intelligent, and intelligible, which is perceived in a variety of ways, while he thinks the forms in the most glorious existence possible.
>
> (*Ibid.*, 276)

Further, he contends that one cannot speak of creation in time: if the world is identical with divine thought, it can have no beginning nor end. God is the cause of the universe in a way more profound than if he had formed in in time; he continually gives the cosmos its existence. The flow of forms is derived from him, and it is these forces which constitute the world.

In The *Chapters of Moses*, Narboni elaborates the doctrine of the eternity of the world, emphasizing the difficulties of revealing this doctrine to the vulgar:

> Those who know the verities are few indeed; true belief and perfect knowledge are only attained by some elite beings . . . God emanates existence and maintains existence, thus the emanation of existence and the perpetuation of existence are called 'light.' However, the vulgar people are convinced that the doctrine that the sages are agreed upon (that is, the eternity of the world) is contrary to the traditional teaching and to the prophetic teachings, that it violates the law and the divine will.
>
> (in Sirat, *op. cit.*, 337)

In the second chapter of this work, Narboni deals with the conjunction of the human intellect and the Active Intellect. When this occurs, human beings are capable of exercising power over the forms of material objects and can thereby bring about miracles:

> Our sages have designated God by the name of Intellect; he is the First Intellect and his intellection of the existents is the cause of their existence; the intellect being, in this way, the cause of the existents and the prophet greatly resembling the Active Intellect (the tenth Intellect), the soul of the prophet tends to completely encompass all the exiting beings and their secrets; thus, when it is necessary, the prophets produce (intelligible) representations

of existing beings so that they concord with the aim that they propose to themselves; sometimes, these representations differ from what these beings are in reality, and, according to the predominance of the Intellect over the imagination, the force of miracles differs among the prophets.

(*Ibid.*, 338)

In considering the correspondences between the upper and lower worlds, Narboni relates the divine commandments to astral laws. Here he stresses that astrology should be confined to the observation of those commands which aid human beings in combating evil:

For every man who is born, something necessarily causes all the accidents and the hazards (of his life), and the man versed in the sciences of the prediction of the future knows them in advance; similarly the people, as a whole, came into existence when the stars were under a certain disposition, and, according to this horoscope, a certain number of events must mark its existence. Abraham was a great prophet and versed in astrology, according to the verse: And he brought him forth abroad (Genesis 15:5), which says: Go out, away from your astrology. Thus Abraham knew all the events that would happen to his people even before it was established in its first engendering. He saw that our fate was to be constantly slain and that much blood would be split among our people and he did all that was in his power to avoid this misfortune a little, causing it to be that no man among us would not have his blood spilt during the first eight days of his life (a reference to circumcision).

(*Ibid.*, 340)

Finally, in the last section of *The Chapters of Moses*, Narboni discusses the issue of divine providence. Agreeing with *Moses Ibn Tibbon, he contends that God exercises providence on behalf of the individual in relation to the degree to which he is conjoined with the Active Intellect.

Chapter 6

15th Century

In the middle of the Fourteenth century the Black Death was attributed to the Jews; in the popular mind the Jewish population was perceived as intent on destroying the Christian community by poisoning wells. As a consequence, attacks on Jewry became a frequent occurance. These events were coupled with a growing desire to convert the Jewish community to the Christian faith. In Spain and Provence, Jews were compelled to listen to sermons preached by Christians intent on convincing their hearers that the Jesus was the Messiah. For these sermonizers, Isaiah 53 clearly foretells Jesus' Messiahship; in response a number of Jewish sages engaged in Scriptural exegesis to counter this claim. Paralleling these developments, Jewish scholars also sought to demonstrate that the Jewish community has not been rejected because of its unwillingness to accept Jesus as Saviour.

In such a milieu the previous equilibrium between Jews and Christians was shattered by the riots of 1391 which devastated the Jewish communities of Andalusia and Castile as well as Navarre and the Balearic Islands. In order to escape death and slavery a number of Jews converted to Catholicism, and synagogues were transformed into churches. Such apostasy continued throughout the next century until the expulsion of Jews from Spain in 1492. In the minds of the faithful, Aristotelian philosophy was seen as undermining Jewish commitment and paving the way for the rejection of the tradition.

Preeminent among those who levelled this charge was Shem Tov Ibn Shem Tov whose *Sefer ha-Emunot* is a diatribe against philosophical speculation. In his view, Jewish philosophy is more dangerous than Greek thought since it was propounded in the name of venerable scholars such as *Abraham Ibn Ezra, *Gersonides, and *Maimonides. While accepting the importance of scientific investigation, Shem Tov argues that it is inapplicable to matters of religious belief. How, he asks, can one remain loyal to the Jewish heritage if one has abandoned belief in final judgement, that only an intellect acquired through philosophical and scientific study survives death, that the commandments serve as a preparation for such study, or that the Torah was devised for the ignorant? For Shem Tov what is required is a return to the literal interpretation of kabbalistic sources.

While such figures as Shem Tov envighed against the pernicious influence of Jewish philosophical enquiry, a number of converts such as Solomon Ha-Levi of Burgos (Pablo de Santa Maria) sought to draw their coreligionists to their newly found faith. Following his conversion, Solomon wrote to the chief rabbi of Navarre, Joseph Orabuena, explaining that he had reached the conclusion that Jesus was the long-awaited Messiah predicted by Scripture. By contrast, another figure of this period Joseph Lorki sought to demonstrate the truth of Judaism even though he too subsequently became a Christian. During this period, Jews living in Mediterranean countries also were anxious to defend the Jewish faith on the basis of metaphysical and scientific enquiry. In Yemen, too, philosophical activity took place, focusing on the allegorical exegesis of Scripture. In Italy as well Jewish thinkers influenced by the Renaissance engaged in theological speculation even though their reflections were frequently less systematic in character than earlier medieval thought.

Joshua Lorki

The son of Joseph Abenvives of Lorca, near Murcia in Spain, Joshua Lorki appears to have studied in Alcaniz under Solomon ha-Levi (Pablo de Santa Maria) who converted to Christianity. Responding to the views of his teacher, Lorki composed a manual of therapeutics in which he extolled the Jewish faith. Alarmed by Solomon's apostasy, Lorki speculates why such disloyalty occurred. Perhaps it was due to worldly ambition or the longing for riches and pleasure, or alternatively Solomon was misled by philosophical exploration. On the other hand, such a break with his Jewish past might have occurred because Solomon became convinced that God would not come to the aid of his people in their time of need. Such explanations could theoretically account for his teacher's change of heart. Yet, he offers another interpretation which he believes more probable: Solomon's experience of revelations concerning the true meaning of prophecies contained in Scripture convinced him that Jesus was the long-awaited Messiah.

It is not surprising however that such an alteration in religious commitment came about, he notes. Solomon could read Latin, and he had seen numerous Christian theological tracts in his house. Further, he states that he had seen a letter addressed to Joseph Orabuena in which Solomon explains that he had become convinced of Jesus' Messiahship. Hence, it was not worldly ambition that led his friend to embrace the Christian faith; rather he had become convinced that Jesus had fulfilled the biblical prophecies about the coming of the Messiah.

Lorki, however, was convinced that this was an utter mistake. After outlining a number of objections to this belief, he goes on to remark that even if Jesus were born of a virgin, performed miracles during his lifetime, and had been resurrected, this would not persuade him of his divinity. These events would simply be miraculous occurances which it is within God's power to accomplish. Commenting on the impossiblity of the doctrine of the Incarnation, Lorki writes:

How can one believe that a Messiah of flesh and blood, who eats and drinks, who lives and dies, is the true God, cause of causes, whose emanation of power moves the spheres, and of whose overflowing existence are formed the separate Intellects who are not body nor power in a body and whose dwelling is not among mortals. How can their existence be continuous and perpetual if he is corporeal? That (terrestrial) matter should persist eternally in actu is one of those impossible things of which the sages said that the impossible has a stable nature. In truth the intellect cannot conceive this opinion, and no doubt on this subject can arise in the mind.

(Lorki, 1849, 45)

Continuing this discussion, Lorki asserts that if it is the duty of each person to compare the truth-claims of his religion with those of other faiths, then noone would remain faithful to his own tradition. Rather, every believer would be beset by doubt and confusion. Further, they would no longer be able to accept any religious claims as true unless they could be upheld by reason. Faith would disappear. This is the situation regarding Solomon of Burgos who had left the Jewish fold to embrace Christianity. Having accepted Christianity, he is now in the position of having to judge between it and other traditions. There is, Lorki believes, no end to such a religious quest.

If, on the other hand, it is not appropriate to adjudicate between religions in this fashion, no value judgements can be made about rival traditions. If a person does not compare the claims of his faith with those of another, he is compelled to accept the truth-claims of his own faith without question. If he worships God in the manner prescribed by his faith, then he will attain salvation and happiness. This must be so, otherwise God would be unjust to punish individuals for taking the wrong religious route because of their upbringing. On this basis, Solomon had been misguided in abandoning Judaism for another religion.

Lorki then poses a final question. If Christians who live at the furthermost corner of England have not heard about the Israelites or Muslims, and Muslims live too far away to know Jews and Christians, does it seem plausible that God would punish any of these groups because of their ignorance? Surely one or more of these belief systems is false, yet it does not seem correct that God would punish believers because of their ignorance. How could the innocent be condemned to everlasting torment because they were victims of circumstance? In conclusion, Lorki declares that reason cannot be the basis for determining one's religious allegiance. Yet despite such philosophical reasoning, Lorki eventually converted to Christianity and composed two polemics against Judaism. In addition, he participated in the Disputation of Tortosa of 1413–114 under the name of Gerónimo de Santa Fé. During this disputation, Lorki was disdainful of his coreligionists; as a result the Jews referred to him as Megaddef (the blasphemer). Following this encounter, Lorki travelled widely attempting to convert Jews to the Christian faith.

Isaac Ben Moses Levi

Living at the end of the 14th century and the beginning of the 15th century, Isaac Ben Moses Levi (Maestro Profiat Duran or Efodi) came from Catalonia where he suffered the persecutions of 1391 and converted to Christianity. He then decided to settle in Palestine in order to live openly as a Jew. However, when his friend David Bonet Bonjorn who was to accompany him on his journey told him that he wished to remain loyal to the Christian faith, Isaac changed his mind and lived as a Christian in Perpignan; there he assumed the name Honoratus de Bonafide, serving as an astrologer to John I of Aragon. During this period Isaac composed anti-Christian polemics and corresponded with his students Meir Crescas and Shealtiel Gracian. Later in 1403 he returned to the Jewish faith.

Isaac's literary works cover such fields as medicine, grammar, philosophy, mathematics, astronomy and astrology; in addition, he produced theological writings informed by a knowledge of Christian sources as well as a letter 'Do not be as your fathers' which is critical of Christianity. Addressed to David Bonet Bonjorn, this letter was placed on the Index and continued to remain on the list of forbidden works until modern times. Here he sarcastically comments on a number of central Christian tenets:

> Faith is for thee a girdle round the loins, and Reason with all her lies in unable to entice thee and divert thy paths. Therefore I made up my mind to show thee clearly the ways of faith which thou hast chosen as thy compass in the light of the Messiah. Be not like unto thy fathers, who believed in one God from whose unity they removed any plurality. They have erred indeed, when they said, 'Hear Israel, the Lord is One!', when they understood this unity in the purest sense without the inclusion of species, kind or number. Not so thou! Thou shalt believe that one can become three and that three united make one . . . Be not like unto thy fathers, who conceived by deep meditations the eternal Ruler beyond change and body, as expressed in the words 'I change not', and one who explained in this sense even those passages which, when interpreted unskilfully, perplex simple souls. Not so thou! Heaven forbid that thou shouldst deny his corporeal embodiment, but believe rather that one of his three persons became flesh, when he wanted to shed blood for the atonement of mankind . . . Be not like unto thy fathers, who were continuously engaged in sciences of all kinds, in mathematics, metaphysics and logic, and tried to penetrate to the foundations of truth. Not so thou! Far be it from thee to recognize the first fundamental rule of reasoning in logic. For this would entice thee to deny thy faith by saying: God is Father; the Son, too, is God truly: the Son is therefore the Father. Brother, stick to this belief.
>
> (in Kobler, 1952, 277–9)

Isaac's philosophical views are dispersed throughout his writings. None the less, the introduction to his grammar, *Making of the Ephod*, contains an outline of his opinions. According to Isaac, the Torah is inerrant and provides the basis for human happiness. Regarding the mitzvot he states, in opposition to the view of others, that observance alone is not the key issue. Rather, he contends that the Torah has two parts – the first is knowledge which leads to eternal happiness, and the second consists of action which makes for felicity in this world. Nonetheless, he writes, some degree of earthly happiness can be obtained through knowledge; similarly, the fulfilment of the mitzvot can bring some of the bliss that awaits the sages in the world to come. In fact, he continues, these two parts cannot be separated since only the knowledge of God's law enables one to carry out the divine commandments even though the fulfilment of the legal precepts is not the purpose of such knowledge.

Concerning rabbinic scholarship, Issac points out that the Talmudists reject both the physical and metaphysical sciences because of their alleged Greek origins, and some are even opposed to the study of Scripture. For these traditionalists, only study of the Talmud is permissible. As far as Jewish philosophers are concerned, they seek to reconcile Aristotelian ideas and the Torah. In Issac's view, however, the Torah should not only provide the preliminary course in the acquisition of knowledge, but true knowledge is derived from the Jewish people – science and Judaism are thus inextricably bound together.

Continuing this discussion, Issac argues that religious acts are intended to attract God's emanation as well as saints and angels. Perfect worship consists in observing God's commands in Israel; there the mitzvot are dictated by angels who preside over the land. Regarding the kabbalah, Isaac contends that although such mystical doctrines cannot be conclusively demonstrated, the Torah and the prophetic writings are more in accordance with kabbalistic doctrines than philosophical theories. Nonetheless, since kabbalists vehemently disagree with one another, the danger of error is great.

In conclusion, Issac advocates the study of Torah – it is, he believes, the only way to attain true happiness. In this regard, he points out that because the Torah is composed of divine names, the study of biblical sources – like prayer – enables one to participate in the efficacy of God's Hebrew appelations. Charting the history of the Jewish people, Isaac notes that when the Temple was standing God was among his chosen nation; its devastation took place when the ancient Israelites abandoned the study of the Bible. At present, however, the reading of Scripture and the observance of biblical law fulfil the task of the Temple: the study of Scripture attracts divine providence and ensures the survival of the Jews.

In interpreting Scripture, Issac argues that the Temple should be understood as symbolizing various features of the cosmos: the world of the intellect and the world of the armies of the God of Israel are the

Holy of Holies and the Ark of the Covenant; the celestial world is the Table of Offerings and the Lamp; the world of bodies is the Temple precinct. In his opinion, the Temple understood in this way is designed to enable human beings to attain intelligible, eternal happiness. Further, the Torah is also able to lead humanity to a conjunction with the Divine. Hence Israel must be careful to preserve the words of the Torah which serve as the basis for such spiritual elevation.

In advancing this view, Issac emphasizes that God has preserved his chosen people for 1200 years despite repeated persecution because of their dedication to the Torah. This is illustrated, he believes, by contemporary events: the Jewish communities of France and Spain neglected the study of the Torah; as a result they were subject to discrimination and exile. The Jews of Aragon, however, were saved because they prayed day and night, constantly reciting the Psalms. It is not sufficient to engage in Talmudic study, he claims; instead he proposes that one third of one's time should be devoted to the study of Scripture; another third to the Mishnah; and the final third to gemarah. With regard to scientific investigation, everything that does not conflict with the Torah should be studied.

Hasdai Crescas

Born in 1340, Hasdai Crescas was a Spanish theologian and statesman; he originated from Barcelona where he was a merchant and communal leader. In 1367 he was imprisoned along with his teacher Nissim Gerondi, and Isaac ben Sheshet for desecrating the Host, but was later released. In 1370 he participated in a competition with the Hebrew poets of Barcelona and Gerona. Subsequently he served as a delegate of the Catalonian Jewish community who sought for a renewal and extension of Jewish privileges with the King of Aragon. In 1387 with the ascension of John I, Crescas became associated with the court of Aragon and accorded the title of familiaris, de casa del senyor rey (member of the royal household). In this same year he was empowered by royal decree to exercise judicial powers to issue an edict of excommunication in accordance with Jewish law.

Subsequently Crescas moved to Saragossa where he served as a rabbi in the place of Isaac ben Sheshet who had settled in Valencia. In 1390 John I allowed Crescas to prosecute informers against Jews and enact punishments on them. Later the Queen appointed Crescas as judge of all cases dealing with informers in the Jewish communities throughout the kingdom of Aragon. During this period one of

Crescas' sons died as a martyr in Barcelona during an anti-Jewish riot. In Saragossa Crescas himself was safe from such attack, and he collected funds from the Aragon Jewish community to pay for such protection. In a letter of this period, he described the nature of such massacres on the Jewish community. In 1393 Crescas together with two representatives of the Saragossa and Calatayud communites was authorized by the crown to choose Jews from the communities of the kingdom to resettle in Barcelona and Valencia; in addition he was given authority to raise contributions for the reconstruction of the Jewish quarters in these cities. In 1401 Crescas spent several weeks in Pamplona, possibly to discuss with King Charles III problems regarding the Jewish population.

Given such a busy existence, Crescas had little time to engage in Jewish scholarship. None the less as part of his quest to combat Christian propagandizing literature, he wrote his 'Refutation of the Principles of the Christians' in Catalan in 1397–8. In addition, he composed another Catalan work opposing Christianity and influenced *Profiat Duran to write his polemic against the Christian faith. His own refutation consists of a critique of the central tenets of Christianity: original sin, redemption, the Trinity, the incarnation, the virgin birth, transubstantiation, baptism, Jesus' messiahship, the New Testament, and demonology. Crescas' most important literary work is *Or Adonai* (Light of the Lord), an anti-Aristotelian tract.

In this work Crescas attempts to refute Aristotelianism by criticizing a number of doctrines found in the writings of Aristotle and *Maimonides. In opposition to these thinkers Crescas argues that there is an infinite void outside the universe – hence there may be many worlds. By positing the existence of the infinite, Crescas also calls into question the Aristotelian concept of an unmoved mover which was based upon the impossiblity of a regress to infinity. Similarly, Crescas argues that Maimonides' proofs of the existence, unity and incorporeality of God are invalid because they are based on the concept of finitude. In addition, Crescas disagrees with Maimonides' opinion that no positive attributes can be applied to God. According to Crescas we cannot avoid making a comparison with human beings when we apply the terms 'cause' and 'attribute of action' to God. Maimonides was simply mistaken in thinking that such ascriptions do not imply a relationship between God and human beings.

Regarding divine providence, Crescas holds that God acts either directly or through intermediate agents such as angels and prophets. Providence itself is essentially of two types: general providence which governs the order of nature, and special providence which is concerned with the Jewish nation as well as the lives of individuals. In this respect Crescas rejects the intellectualism of Jewish philosophers such as Maimonides. Intellectual perfection, he insists, is not the criterion of divine providence nor the basis for reward and punishment. In his discussion of prophecy, Crescas also adopts an anti-intellectual position. Unlike Maimonides, Crescas accepts the traditonal understanding of the prophet as a person chosen by God because of his moral virtues rather than intellectual attainment. In advocating such views, Crescas was anxious to present a rational defence of the Jewish faith on non-Aristotelian grounds. Throughout his treatment of the central beliefs of the Jewish tradition, Crescas presents a view of Judaism based on the spiritual and emotional sides of man's nature rather than his intellectual and speculative capacities. In this respect he shares the same view as *Judah Halevi who was equally critical of a rational presentation of Judaism.

Another feature of Crescas' theology concerns the fundamental principles of the Jewish faith. In his *Commentary on the Mishnah*, Maimonides outlines what he believes to be the thirteen central principles of Judaism:

1 Belief in the existence of God.
2 Belief in God's unity.
3 Belief in God's incorporeality.
4 Belief in God's eternity.
5 Belief that God alone is to be worshipped.
6 Belief in prophecy.
7 Belief in Moses as the greatest of the prophets.
8 Belief that the Torah was given by God to Moses.
9 Belief that the Torah is immutable.
10 Belief that God knows the thoughts and deeds of human beings.
11 Belief that God rewards and punishes.
12 Belief in the advent of the Messiah.
13 Belief in the resurrection of the dead.

In Maimonides' view, it is necesssary for every Jew to accept these beliefs; otherwise he is a transgressor in Israel: 'When . . . a man breaks away from any of these fundamental principles of belief, then of him it is said that "he has gone out of the general body of Israel", and "he denies the root truth of Judaism". And he is then termed "heretic" and "unbeliever"'. (in Jacobs, 1988, 15)

Critical of this formulation, Crescas proposed an alternative system in *Or Adonai*. According to Crescas, the central belief of Judaism – that God exists, is One and incorporeal – is in a seperate category from other beliefs. In addition to this fundamental principle of Judaism there are three categories of beliefs:

1 Fundamentals without which the Jewish religion is unimaginable:
   1 God's knowledge of his creatures.
   2 God's providence.
   3 God's power.
   4 Prophecy.
   5 Human freewill.
   6 The belief that the Torah leads to man's true hope and ultimate bliss.

2 True opinions – these are divided into opinions which are independent of any precept and belief, and those which are dependent on particular precepts and beliefs:
   1 Opinions independent of precept and belief:
      1 Creation.
      2 The immortality of the soul.
      3 Reward and punishment.
      4 Resurrection.
      5 The immutability of the Torah.
      6 Moses.
      7 The belief that the High Priest had the oracle of Urim and Thummim.
      8 The Messiah.
   2 Opinions dependent on precept and belief:
      1 Beliefs implied in prayer and the blessings of the priests.
      2 Beliefs implied in repentance.
      3 Beliefs implied in the Day of Atonement and other Jewish festivals.

In Crescas' view, anyone who denies any of the fundamental beliefs or any of the true opinions is an unbeliever, yet the only difference between these two categories is that the Jewish faith is inconceivable without the fundamental beliefs whereas it is imaginable with the true opinions. These two categories are further supplemented by probablities; these are opinions which are based on Jewish teaching which Crescas deduces as being valid. Yet, because these conclusions are neither obvious nor simple, they are not mandatory on Jewish believers:

1 Probablities (many of which are expressed as questions):

   1 Is the world eternal?
   2 Are there many worlds?
   3 Are the spheres living creatures?
   4 Have the stars an influence over human destiny?
   5 Is there any efficacy to charms and amulets?
   6 Do demons exist?
   7 Is the doctrine of metempsychosis true?
   8 Is the soul of an infant immortal?
   9 Paradise and Hell.
   10 Are the mystical doctrines of Maaseh Bereshit (works of creation), and Maaseh Merkavah (works of the heavenly chariot) to be identified with physics and metaphysics?
   11 The nature of comprehension.
   12 The First Cause.
   13 Can the true nature of God be understood?

All of these topics are discussed in traditional Jewish sources, but Crescas is aware that they remain open questions; thus one who does not accept the views of the sages as expressed in rabbinic literature is not to be regarded as an unbeliever.

After the time of Crescas the philosophical approach to religion lost its appeal for most Jewish thinkers in Spain. Though some writers were still attracted to the Maimonidean system, Aristotelianism ceased to be the dominant philosophy in the Jewish world. Instead of philosophizing about Judaism a number of subsequent Jewish writers directed their attention to defining the basic doctrines of the Jewish faith. Such Spanish thinkers as *Simeon ben Zemah Duran, *Joseph Albo, and *Isaac Arama devoted their writings to critiques of Maimonides' formulation of the thirteen principles of the Jewish religion.

Simeon Ben Zemah Duran

Born in 1361 in Majorca, Simeon Ben Zemah Duran departed for Algiers after the 1391 massacres where he became Chief Rabbi in 1408. Conversant in Latin and Arabic, he worked as a physician. In addition to his contributions to Jewish law, he composed a number of philosophical studies. His two major works consist of *Ohev Mishpat* (Lover of Justice) which deals with providence, and *Magen Avot* (Shield of the Fathers) concerning the central principles of the Jewish faith. The fourth chapter of the second part of *Magen Avot* – a polemic against Christians and Muslims – was published separately as *Keshet u-Magen* (The Arrow and the Shield).

Throughout his philosophical writings Duran cites Jewish as well as Greek and Arab thinkers. Yet despite such a philosophical orientation, he asserts that truth can only be discovered through revelation. Even though human beings were created with reasoning capabilities, divine aid is necessary. In the past, he argues, philosophers propounded erroneous views because they lacked such divine succour. The Jewish people, however, have received God's word and therefore do not need philosophy except in order to defend their faith against criticism.

Duran, however, was not an opponent of reason, and he places philosophical topics into three categories:

1 Those beliefs which can be demonstrated by correctly directed reasoning: these are self evident truths which must be accepted by all except those who are ignorant of the laws of logic or who exhibit had faith. The existence of God and his unity are examples of such self-evident doctrines.

2 Beliefs which reason cannot demonstrate, such as the creation of the universe. Since proof is established on the basis of premises and causes, it is not possible to demonstrate that such a doctrine is true; here the premises and causes are God himself who is unknowable. Thus, only God can know the truth about this issue.

3 Topics where human beings assert one thing which appears to be contradicted by experience. For example, philosophy suggests that God is not concerned with the world whereas experience suggests that divine providence is manifest everywhere.

According to Duran, the Torah makes assertions about these various topics without recourse to argument. Scripture is not a work of philosophy, and the proof which the Torah affords is the Torah itself. Nonetheless, in considering the third type of doctrines it is easier to fall into error than in the first two types (as in the case of divine providence which is treated at length in the book of Job). These remarks serve as an introduction to Duran's discussion of providence in this biblical book. For Duran the Book of Job should be regarded as Torah; in his view, it is not possible to distinguish between the different Scriptural books: they all present God's true revelation.

A similar point is made about the commandments contained in Scripture; they are all of equal importance and none can be abandoned. For Duran, to set aside any of the ideas contained in the Hebrew Bible constitutes the abandonment of the entire Torah. Thus, the principles of the Jewish faith are as numerous as the number of commandments or the number of verses in Scripture. Because of this conviction, he was critical of Maimonides' attempt to isolate the central doctrines of Judaism. Rejecting Maimonides' formulation of the thirteen principles of the Jewish faith, he nonetheless argues that there are three fundamental revealed beliefs of the Jewish tradition:

1 The existence of God
2 The divine origin of the Torah
3 Reward and punishment

These beliefs, Duran contends, are explicitly stated in the Mishnah which refers to three persons who are denied a share in the world to come – one who states that the Torah is not from heaven; one who denies resurrection; and the epiqoros. For Duran the denial of these three central beliefs implicitly involves a denial of other basic beliefs:

The foundation of faith is to believe in God, blessed be he, that he is one, that he is eternal, that he is incorporeal and that it is fitting to worship him alone. All these are included in the term epiqoros. Next, one must believe in the predictions of the prophets and of Moses, in the Torah and that it is eternal. These are included in the term 'Torah from Heaven'. Next, one must believe in reward and punishment and their offshoots, which is included in the term 'the resurrection of the dead'.

(in Jacobs, 1988, 20)

Hoter Ben Solomon

Also known as Mansour Ibn Suleiman al-Dhamari, Hoter Ben Solomon wrote a variety of works including a commentary on the Torah, a super-commentary on *Maimonides' commentary on the Mishnah, two collections of *Questions and Answers* dealing with philosophical issues, and a *Commentary on Maimondies' Thirteen Principles*. In composing these studies Hoter utilized traditional

Jewish sources as well as the writings of *Saadiah Gaon, the poems of *Judah Halevi and *Abraham Ibn Ezra, and treatises produced by various Yemenite Jewish scholars. In addition, Hoter frequently cites Arabic philosophical texts and literature.

The three major influences on Hoter's philosophy were Maimonides' writings, Neoplatonic thought as represented by the *Encyclopedia of the Sincere Brothers*, and Aristotelianism. In this regard Hoter's cosmological theories consist of a fusion between Aristotelian speculation and Neoplatonic ideas. In his view the Intellect emanated from God ex nihilo. This contained all the ideas, and from this source the command 'Be' went forth. The universe then came into being: the Ten Intelligences emanated from the Intellect – the last was the Active Intellect. From this emanated the Universal Soul. From this proceeded three further emanations: the First Prime Matter, Nature, and souls. The Universal Soul in-formed the First Prime Matter with various forms of species; this generated the various types of celestial matter and also gave bodies souls which are particular to them. From the last in this sequence – the Lunar Sphere – the Second Prime Matter came forth. This was in-formed by Nature so as to generate the four elements. These four elements were then combined and in-formed by Nature to generate compounded beings. These beings received particular souls directly from the Universal Soul and human beings received intellects directly from the Active Intellect. (Blumenthal, 1974, 21–2)

In advancing this theory, Hoter explains that the ideas that give form to matter have an extra-mental existence; however, those produced by intellectual analysis have only a mental existence. Meditating on a passage of Maimonides' *Guide for the Perplexed*, Hoter outlines his theory of perception. In his opinion, in every object there is a an idea of the object and its form – this is referred to by Hoter as a 'trace of the intellect'. This trace is then preceived by the innermost vision of the soul; the intellect which contains within itself all the forms then represents this 'trace' (or idea) in corporeal form to the soul. At the same time the senses perceive the physical form of the object; this is passed on to the imaginative faculty of the soul which in turn abstracts that perception and passes it on to the rational soul. The rational soul then coordinates the two perceptions which it contains – one from the intellect and the other from the senses. This is accomplished by corporealizing it further into natural characteristics. These natural characteristics are identified with the abstracted results of the senses. This entire process is initiated when the rational soul, which is incomplete by nature and only acquires perfection, seeks perfection from the intellect which being complete in itself would not otherwise be stirred into action. (*Ibid.*, 29)

According to Hoter, the rational soul is one of the forms of the intellect: it perceives according to this process of perception and has no knowledge except in potentiality. However, by the re-acquisition of the perfection that it possessed before it was exiled into the world, the rational soul can rejoin the domain of the Intellects and come nearer to the Active Intellect. By this means it is clad in splendour, becoming virtuous, pure and refined. This is the path to conjunction with the Intellect. For Hoter, Moses represents the culmination of this process. When his soul attained perfection and the link with the Active Intellect was achieved, his soul was joined to the Universal Soul and his intellect conjoined with the Active Intellect. Then the perfections and brilliant lights that are called Torah emanated over him.

Turning to the topic of the afterlife, Hoter contends that the difference between the rational soul and the intellect continues after death. The human intellect identifies itself with the Intellect; perfect rational souls become angels and join the world of the souls of the spheres and eventually the Universal Soul. It appears that Hoter identifies the Garden of Eden with the Universal Soul, a world of continuity, existence without end, and divine presence. The souls of those without knowledge, however, rejoin the world of animal soul whereas the souls of those who have knowledge but used it for immoral ends are punished eternally.

Joseph Albo

Born in 1380, Joseph Albo was a Spanish philosopher and preacher who played a prominent role in the Disputation of Tortosa and San Mateo in 1413–14 as a representative of the Jewish community of Daroca, a province of Saragossa. Albo's most important work, *Book of Principles* (*Sefer ha-Ikkarim*) is a treatise on the central principles of the Jewish faith. Written as a response to the decline of religious commitment among his coreligionists, the *Book of Principles* was designed to restore confidence in Judaism by providing a rational presentation of the Jewish faith. Drawing on the Islamic philosophical tradition, Latin Christian scholasticism, and the writings of his teacher, *Hasdai Crescas, Albo offers a presentation of the central beliefs of Judaism.

In this work, Albo argues that an unbeliever should be defined as one who knows the Torah lays down a principle but denies its truth. Such rebellion against the teaching of the tradition constitutes unbelief. But, a person who upholds the law of Moses and believes in the cardinal principles of the faith

> when he undertakes to investigate these matters with his reason and scrutinizes the texts, is misled by his speculation and interprets a given principle otherwise then it is taken to mean at first sight; or denies the principle because he thinks that it does not represent a sound theory which the Torah obliges us to believe; or erroneously denies that a given belief is a fundamental principle, which however he believes as he believes the other dogmas of the Torah which are not fundamental principles; or entertains a certain notion in relation to one of the miracles of the Torah because he thinks that he is not thereby denying any of the doctrines which is obligatory upon us to believe by the authority of the Torah – a person of this sort is not an unbeliever; his sin is due to error and requires atonement.
>
> (Jacobs, 1988, 21)

The *Sefer ha-Ikkarim* begins in Part I with a critique of earlier attempts by philosophers (primarily *Maimonides and Crescas) to formulate the underlying principles of the Jewish faith. In Albo's view, Maimonides failed to offer any specific criterion by which such selection could be made; further, he questions whether Crescas' list of six criteria actually furnishes a basis for determining the general principles of divine law. In contrast with these writers, Albo was anxious to explain the principles without which it is possible to conceive of a divine law. Albo then goes on to formulate three essential principles of divine law: (1) the existence of God; (2) divine revelation; and (3) reward and punishment. Previously these three fundamental beliefs had been proposed by *Simeon ben Zemah Duran – arguably, both Duran and Albo adopted this system from Averroes where they are specified as examples of the principles of revealed law.

In explaining the nature of these three fundamental principles of the faith, Albo points out that the three benedictions incorporated in the Additional Service for New Year – Kingdoms, Memorials, and Trumpets – represent these beliefs. According to Albo, these three blessings were ordained in order to direct one's attention to the basic beliefs of the Jewish religion at the beginning of the year (the traditional period of divine judgment) so that by properly believing in these principles together with the dogmas derived from them it would be possible to win a favourable verdict in the divine judgment.

Averroes' influence on Albo is reflected in the distinction Albo draws between a person who denies these three principles of the faith, and the individual who, holding to erroneous interpretations of Scripture, denies other articles of Judaism. Hence the sage Hillel who maintained that Jews can expect no Messianic deliverance in the future was guilty of not believing in the coming of the Messiah, yet he was not a heretic. This is because the belief in the Messiah is not a fundamental principle of the Jewish religion, but one of the six dogmas which should be conceived as branches issuing from the principles. In all likehoood, the relegation of belief in the Messiah to this secondary position was designed to refute Christianity which had made belief in the Messiah a fundamental tenet of the faith. In this connection, at the Tortosa Disputation Albo delcared that even if it could be proved that the Messiah had already come, he would not consider himself less faithful a Jew.

Albo concludes his discussion of the principles of Judaism by contending that there are eight derivative principles which branch out from the three major principles of the faith. Together with the belief in the existence of God, divine revelation, and reward and punishment, these derivative beliefs constitute the indispensible elements of the divine law. Four of these derivative principles pertain to the existence of God:

1 Divine Unity
2 Divine Incorporeality
3 God's independence from time
4 Divine perfection

Three other derivative principles are related to revelation:

1 God's knowledge as embracing the terrestrial world
2 Prophecy
3 The authenticity of divine messengers proclaiming the law

Finally, the eighth derivative principle is concerned with the notion of reward and punishment:

1 Providence

In addition to these central beliefs, Albo states that there are six dogmas which everyone who professes the law of Moses is obliged to accept – anyone who denies them is a heretic who has no share in the

World-to-Come. However, they are not referred to as principles of the faith since, in Albo's opinion the only beliefs entitled to be designed as fundamental principles are those without which the Jewish faith is inconceivable:

1 Creatio ex nihilo
2 The superiority of Moses' prophecy
3 The immutability of the Torah
4 Human perfection can be attained by fulfilling even one of the commandments of the Torah
5 Resurrection of the dead
6 The Messiah.

In formulating this list of the central beliefs of Judaism, Albo was preoccupied with the concept of divine law. Previously Jewish, Christian and Muslim philosophers had drawn a distinction between conventional and divine law; Albo, however, argues that there are three major types of law: (1) natural law; (2) conventional law; and (3) divine law. In Albo's view, the superiority of divine law over natural and conventional law derives from its aim to guide human beings to the attainment of true felicity. While natural law is designed to order society and conventional law seeks to improve the social order, divine law regulates conduct and belief. As a consequence, it is perfect, restoring the soul. In presenting this thesis, Albo interprets Psalm 19 as illustrating the supremacy of divine law over conventional and natural laws.

After its appearance, Albo's *Sefer ha-Ikkarim* attained considerable popularity within the Jewish community. It appeared in a large number of printed editions after the editio princeps by Joshua Solomon Soncino in 1485. In the next century it was commented upon by Jacob Koppelmann of Brest and in the 17th century by Gedaliah ben Solomon Lipschuetz of Lublin. In 1884 a German translation by W. Schlesinger with a scholarly introduction by L. Schlesinger appeared in Frankfort, and a critical edition of the text accompanied by an English translation and notes was published by I. Hussik in 1929–30. Within Christian circles, a number of theologians including Hugo Grotius and Richard Simon regarded the work with favour; other theologians viewed Albo's writing as a powerful defense of Judaism and thereby a potential threat to Christian teaching.

Joseph Ben Shem Tov Ibn Shem Tov

Born in 1400, Joseph Ben Shem Tov Ibn Shem Tov served first at the court of John II of Castile and then under Henry IV of Castile. Due to his position at court he was able to participate in discussions with Christian theologians. However, it seems that he was disgraced in about 1456 and wandered from place to place preaching on the Sabbath. In 1460 he died as a martyr.

From 1400–60, Joseph wrote a number of philosophical studies including a commentary on Aristotle's *Nicomachaean Ethics*, two commentaries on Averroes' *Possibility of Conjunction with the Active Intellect*, a commentary on Averroes' *Paraphrase* of Alexander of Aphrodisias' *Treatise on the Intellect*, and a commentary on the Lamentations of Jeremiah. In addition, he translated into Hebrew and commented on *Hasdai Crescas' *Refutation of the Christian Dogmas*. Two other of his works were also published: *The Glory of God* and a commentary on the satirical epistle *Alteca Boteca* which alerted the Inquisition to the double meanings of *Profiat Duran's writing.

The aim of *The Glory of God* is to create a synthesis between philosophy and religion. On the basis of a Latin version of the *Nicomachaean Ethics*, Joseph argues that Aristotle's ideas in the first and tenth book of this work are reconcilable with the Torah. In delineating his conception of the path to the supreme good as well as its nature, Joseph quotes Aristotle's texts translated from Latin (accompanied by an extensive exegesis). Throughout he advocates a return to Aristotelian principles.

In Joseph's view, by keeping God's commandments it is possible to attain perfection. Each Jew, he argues, must accept the laws governing the universe and the ideology underpining the Jewish legal system, yet it is not necessary to have a comprehensive understanding of such concepts. Just as the goldsmith has no need to understand the nature of the metal he uses or the astrologer the celestial bodies, so the Jew is under no obligation to have a profound grasp of the principles of the faith. What is required instead is dedication to the Torah.

Turning to the task of the philosopher, Joseph maintains that there are two major fields of investigation. The first is true knowledge which is derived from what exists. This science is divided into natural and divine mathematics – this is the necessary activity of the intellect and its perfection. The object of this discipline – the existents – leads to knowledge of God and dedication to him. Intellectual activity is also the path to the perfection which is bestowed by the Torah. Divine law can therefore be obtained through intellectual efforts. In the hierarchy of forms the form of the intellect is superior to the animal soul which can become more perfect in the former. Similarly, when the intellectual form is received by an individual who is religious, it functions more successfully. Hence a religious individual who achieves perfection has attained the highest level of perfection since he is able to unite in himself the perfections in both the religious and philosophical realms.

A second area of exploration concerns the Greeks who sought to contradict revealed religion. In such texts everything which does not conform to the Torah is an illusion. Nonetheless, Joseph contends, it is not possibly to deny that some Jews view intellectual perfection as the supreme good. As a consequence they despise the Torah whereas Jews who are not philosophically trained, like the inhabitants of France, have died for the faith. This does not imply that scientific study should be abandoned. However, Joseph praises those who insist that the sciences and philosophy should not be pursued until a set age; by this time religious truth would have transformed the spirit and an individual would be able to distinguish between truth and falsehood. Thus science should not be prohibited as long as its limitations are recognized. Joseph goes on to explain that it is not possible to discover the reasons for God's commands. To comprehend the truth of the mitzvot, it is obligatory to have a guide to whom God has revealed his will. The natural qualities of things exist; they are beyond doubt, and it is the same with regard to divine commandments. Their rationale exists even if it cannot be known.

Abraham Ben Shem Tov Bibago

After living at Huesca in Aragon, Abraham Ben Shem Tov Bibago became head of a religious school at Saragossa. In addition to receiving a traditional Jewish education, he learned Arabic and Latin and was familiar with the Gospels and the writings of Eusebius and Thomas Aquinas. The author of numerous works, his existing writings include *The Tree of Life* dealing with creation, letters to Moses Arondi, commentaries on Averroes' *Middle Commentaries* on the *Posterior Analytics* and *Metaphysics*, a sermon on Genesis, and his major work, *The Way of Faith*.

According to Bibago, God is absolute – he bestows existence on all things. Following Averroes and Moses of Narbonne, he declares that the plurality in the world occurs became God moves the ultimate sphere directly without relying on a supplementary Intellect. Regarding the divine attributes, he contends that they are identical with God's essence and do not entail mutliplicity. Further, Bibago asserts that these attributes are positive although they can be known only through negation. This is so because the intellect, the cognizing subject and the cognized object are one in human beings – to know the divine attibutes would involve identifying oneself with God which is impossible. Moreover, for humans to know means to comprehend the causes of existing things. God, however, has no cause.

Bibago goes on to claim that God's limits his infinity by creating the world: his actions represent his limitiations in so far as his infinity is restricted to the boundaries of the created order. This relationship between infinity and finitude can be understood solely in a negative way – human beings cannot pass beyond the point of intersection between the finite and the infinite. God, however, knows himself and thereby comprehends all of creation including the actions and thoughts of human beings.

Turning to the notion of the divine will, Bibago contends that only this concept explains the limitation of divine action as it restricts itself within the finite world. The divine will sustains the world and is mainfest in all things. Nonethleless, it does not undermine the laws of nature; on the contrary, it is identical with them. The form of everything which exists is found in all things through the action of the divine will. In this way God is manifest in the material world; further, he is the form and soul of intelligible existing things, the separate Intellects, and the soul of the angelic realm. He sets the world in motion and perpetuates its movement. Hence, God as an infinite being creates and sustains the world in its finitude,

For Bibago, the world itself is divided into three parts; these three divisions conform to the different names of God: the Name of 72 letters is equated with the world of generation and corruption; the Name of 42 letters to the world of the spheres; the Name of twelve letters to the world of separate Intellects. Elsewhere, however, Bibago argues that there is a gradual passage between absolute actuality (God) and absolute potentiality (matter). In Bibago's view, the world emerges out of God through the divine will.

Regarding miracles, Bibago contends that the material cause of such events is the object that is changed. In the case of the Nile water that was transformed into blood, liquid was the material cause. Given this conception, the object itself must have the potentiality for such alteration. To explain the formal cause of a miracle, Bibago refers to the rod Moses held which changed into a serpent. Here the formal cause is neither the rod nor the serpent, but the substance of change of one form into another – the causes of the change from rod to serpent, he argues, were not themselves present in these forms. To regard either the prophet, the Active Intellect, or the astral influx as the immediate cause of a miracle is a mistake; rather the actions of these agents are fixed whereas miraculous action is free.

In this context Bibago differentiates between four types of phenomena: (l) pele is the change which takes place according to natural law; it reinforces the truth of the miracle; (2) nes is the miracle itself which brings about the salvation of an individual or community; (3) The sign (ot) is an exception to natural law; (4) the proof (mofet) is that by which the significance of an event is expressed. All these supernatural phenomena have God as a causal agent. Nevertheless, for a miracle (nes) to occur, the Active Intellect is the intermediary agent; for the sign and the proof the prophet is the intermediary cause; and the pele is the direct act of God. The final cause of miracles, however, is the most important: it is true faith.

Turning to the purpose of human existence, Bibago argues that it is the imitation of God. Because human beings participate in the world of the intellect and the world of matter, they must attain perfection in both realms. To seek to conjoin oneself solely with the Active Intellect is insufficient – the perfection of bodily acts is of fundamental significance as well. In this connection, Bibago contends that the acquisition of intelligibles is a quest which is ultimately superseded by a second disposition which is not subject to generation and corruption. According to Bibago, at this second stage the soul is attracted by the Active Intellect: this is the degree of prophecy. Here the conjunction with the Active Intellect is not simply an automatic process; rather, it requires the influence of the divine will. For Bibago, prophecy involves the perception of what human knowledge cannot attain on its own as well as the capacity to fortell the future.

In addition to this form of prophecy which is sought after by human beings, Bibago describes another form of prophetic activity – in this case God places words into the mouth of an individual when he wishes to address himself to his people. When this takes place, the prophet serves as the instrument of divine providence. In discussing the various types of prophetic activity, Bibago asserts that the distinction of prophecy depends on the person who prophesies. In his view, Moses was the greatest of the prophets – his perfection insured that no more perfect law will be given to humankind. In this context, Bibago states that there are three kinds of providence: natural providence; providence related to the conjunction of the intellect; and providence which is concerned with the welfare of Israel.

According to Bibago, divine providence is more concerned with the Jewish people than with others because they constitute 'intellect in actu' due to the perfection of the Torah. Special providence takes more regard of individuals who have perfected their intellect, and this applies to the people of Israel as a whole. Yet, if an individual is the particular object of providential concern, this is not because he simply belongs to the Jewish nation. Rather it is because he has identified himself with Israel which has received the truths of the Torah. The definition of a Jew is therefore a person who believes in a true faith, and has natural knowledge as a person and supplementary knowledge as an adherent of the faith of Israel.

Isaac Ben Moses Arama

Born in 1420, Isaac Arama was a Spanish rabbi, philosopher and preacher. Initially he taught at Zaroma, subsequently serving as a rabbi in Tarragona and Fraga in Aragon. Later he became rabbi of Calatayud where he composed the majority of his writings. In order to counter the conversionist sermons which the Jews of Aragon were compelled to hear, he preached sermons explaining the fundamental principals of Judaism. These sermons became the basis of later works and contain important information about the history of the Spanish Jewish community. As an exponent of the Jewish faith, he participated in a number of disputations with Christian theologians. After the expulsion of the Jews of Spain in 1492, he settled in Naples.

Arama's most important work, *The Binding of Isaac*, consists of 105 'portals', and was written in the form of philosophical sermons and allegorical commentaries on the Pentateuch. Each of these 'portals' consists of a sermon divided into two parts: investigation and exposition. In the first part, Arama explores a philosophical topic in the light of biblical and rabbinic sources; the second part consists largely of Scriptural exegesis. At the end of the sermon, these two parts are harmoniously integrated. Arama's other works include a polemic dealing with the relationship between and religion, a commentary on the Five Scrolls, and commentaries on the Books of Proverbs and Esther as well as Aristotle's *Ethics*.

Critical of Maimonides, Arama argues that religious truth is superior to human reason. Our intellects, he contends, receive sense data which are incapable of providing certain knowledge of the world; similarly rational inquiry is limited. Philosophers are therefore unable to the solve fundamental metaphysical problems. Further, even though philosophy can provide information about the God of nature, it cannot penetrate the mysteries of the last things. Hence Abraham began by knowing God in the light of reason – like the philosophers, he only believed in what he could know. But, when he embraced God through faith, 'he believed in the Lord; and he counted it to him for righteousness' (Genesis 15:6). According to Arama, such an act of faith is superior to rational knowledge. Nonetheless Abraham had not attained a perfect faith. According to Genesis 15:8, Abraham asked God: 'Lord God, whereby shall I know that I shall inherit it?' In response God declared: 'Go before me and be thou perfect' (Genesis 17:1).

Critical of the scholars of his own day who wished to base their faith on the findings of reason, Arama contends that there are basic incompatibilities between faith and reason which cannot be reconciled. This does not imply, however, that the Bible must be understood literally. Rather, although faith is superior to reason it does not contradict it – instead, it surpasses it and some verses in Scripture should be interpreted allegorically. This, Arama points out, is in fact what the Talmud frequently does. Nonetheless, he states, one should not lose sight of the literal meaning of the text. In this regard, Arama is severely critical of those philosophers who engage in extensive allegorization.

In his defence of the tradition, Arama offers six principles of the faith:

1 Creation
2 Divine omnipotence
3 Prophecy and the revelation of the Torah
4 Providence
5 Penitence
6 The Immortality of the soul

In his view, these general principles do not define philosophical or divine religion, but instead serve as the basis of the Jewish faith. These principals, Arama contends, complement philosophy just as faith is added to reason.

Turning to the concept of divine omnipotence, Arama argues that God is able to suspend the laws of nature and thereby perform miracles. These laws are of two types – natural law which obeys the law of causality, and supernatural law which influences everyday existence. Philosophers such as Moses of Narbonne and *Gersonides denied the existence of supernatural nature because they placed human beings below the celestial spheres which are only dead bodies. In Arama's opinion, however, humans are created in the image of God and are therefore capable of exercising power over the natural world. Yet despite such capabilities, human error can bring about cosmic disorder. There is hence an important link between human actions and what exists: through human activity nature can be elevated or debased. In this light, he states, it is vital that there should be a correspondence between the human and natural world so that cosmic harmony is insured.

Isaac Abrabanel

Born in Lisbon in 1437, Isaac Abrabanel was a descendant of merchants and courtiers. Intially he received a Jewish and secular education; by the age of 25 he had composed a tract on providence and prophecy and gave discourses on Deuteronomy in the synagogue. Like his father Judah, he served as the treasurer to Alfonoso V of Portugal and became head of a prosperous business. However, after being accused of conspiracy by Joao II who acceded to power in 1481 he fled two years later and entered the service of Ferdinand and Isabbela of Castile. In 1492 Abrabanel unsuccesfully sought to revoke the Edict of Expulsion of the Jews of Spain; he then sailed to Naples where he undertook a similar role he had played in Castile in the court of Ferdinand I, King of Naples. Remaining at court until 1495, he settled in Venice in 1503 where he participated in diplomatic negotiations between the Venetian Senate and Portugal. During his sixteen years of residence in Italy, he composed most of his writings. His works consist of a variety of texts most of which were published in the 16th century:

1 Commentary on the Pentateuch, early prophets (Joshua, Judges, Samuel, Kings), and later prophets (Isaiah, Jeremiah, Ezekiel), and twelve minor prophets.
2 Commentaries on the *Haggadah* (Passover prayer book) and *Pirkei Avot* (Sayings of the Fathers).
3 Three studies dealing with messianic deliverance, including a commentary on the Book of Daniel.
4 A commentary on *Maimonides *Guide for the Perplexed*, as

well as answers to quieres dealing with the *Guide*, and a short treatise concerning its composition.

5 Assorted works discussing philosophical and theological issues including:

1 *The Crown of the Ancients* dealing with prophecy and providence.
2 *New Skies* on the creation of the universe.
3 *The Works of God* also dealing with creation.
4 *The Principle of Faith* treating the principles of the Jewish faith.
5 A short study on the *Form of the Elements*.
6 Two other texts on divine justice and prophecy.

In Abrabanel's writing, there are numerous references to *Maimonides whom he often bitterly criticizes; in many respects his philosophical writing is a commentary on Maimonides' *Guide for the Perplexed*. Hence Abarbanel's discussion of three major areas of interest – the creation of the cosmos, prophecy, and the principles of Judaism – was deeply influenced by Maimonides' theories even if at various points he puts forward differing interpretations. According to Abrabanel, the doctrine of creatio ex nihilo is the only viable theory of creation, even if it cannot be conclusively demonstrated through rational argument. In opposition to *Gersonides, Abrabanel maintains that the concept of pre-existent and unformed matter is unacceptable because of the necessary correlation between matter and form. Unlike Crescas, he contends that the idea of a necessary will on God's part undermines the very notion of the will. And as regards the question of the exact moment when creation is supposed to have occurred, Abarbanel maintains that this can only be resolved by appealing to the idea that God forms innumerable worlds and then destroys them after a certain period of time.

Regarding prophecy, Abarbanel endorses the first opinion Maimonides describes in his *Guide*: God chooses whomever he wishes among human beings in order to make them his prophet as long as that individual has a pure and pious heart. Prophecy is therefore a divine knowledge that God causes to descend onto the prophet either through or without an intermediary. If the prophet's intellect receives such knowledge, his words will be precise and clear; if it is bestowed on the imagination, this divine communication will be expressed through images and allegories. Thus the difference between a sage and a prophet resides in the different influx that each receives – the prophet receives a influx more abundant and eminent. Thus, the superabundance of divine emanation permits one to differentiate between the prophetic and the premonitory dream. Prophetic images impose themelves on the imagination through their intensity.

Continuing this discussion, Abarbanel argues that as a supernatural pheonomenon which is able to correct the natural weakness of the prophet's intellect and imagination, prophecy only resides in a person whose heart is constantly inclined toward God. This, he believes, only takes place in a free nation living in its own land – for the Jewish people, this is Israel. If a Jew is overwhelmed by his misfortune and dependent on the good will of gentile kings, prophecy can never occur.

Turning to the issue of Jewish dogma, Abarbanel argues for Maimonides' Thirteen priniciples in his book *The Principle of Faith*. Abarbanel sets out to defend Maimonides' conception of the thirteen central beliefs of Judaism in the first twenty-two chapters. Yet in the last chapters of this work, Abarbanel states that because the Law of Moses is of a supernatural character, no principle can in fact be more important than any other: everything contained in the Torah is of equal weight and must be accepted by the believer. In Abrabanel's view Maimonides sought to isolate the central principles of Judaism because he wished to help the ignorant to understand the underlying assumptions of the Jewish faith. In this connection, he points out that these Thirteen Principles are part of the *Mishneh Torah* which is not designed for those who are philosophically inclined.

Another important feature of Abarbanel's writing concerns politics and history. According to Maimonides, Moses was closest to the Active Intellect and therefore able to advance a divine law as a prophet-philosopher. Abrabanel, on the the other hand, views prophecy as supernatural in character: hence divine law is directly related to natural events and human history. In his view, the meeting point of the human and natural realms is biblical history where God's disclosure and intervention took place. In this context the Messiah should not be understood along Maimonidean lines as a victorious king who will be able to return the exiles to the Promised Land. Instead, he will be a person inspired by God who will act miraculously in the violent upheavals which will signify the end of the world.

Continuing this theme, Abrabanel asserts that what appears as natural history is in fact artificial. The life of the Jewish nation in the desert, for example, is like the life of Adam before the Fall. Adam's disobedience disrupted this natural state – subsequent civilized life is actually a rebellion against God. The only really natural life is that of free and equal persons who lead a rural lifestyle. Similarly, the proliferation of different languages and nations is also the consequence of human rebellion. It is in the context of this false life that Abrabanel explores the best form of government. What is at issue is the least bad sort of government since only the Messiah will be able to recreate what Abrabanel conceives as humanity's natural state.

Despite such theoretical considerations, Abrabanel lived the life of a statesman and was interested in the political realities of his day. On the basis of an analysis of Deuteronomy 17:14 and 1 Samuel 8:6, he criticizes the philosophical arguments supporting monarchy. Dismissing the principle of hierarchy, he argues that the king should serve his people. The monarch is to society what the heart is to the body. Against those who assert that only monarchy is able to assure the conditons for the proper functioning of society, he maintains that a nation can be maintained and subsit with other governments. Unity is attainable through the unanimous consent of several persons rather than the irresponsible will of only one individual. In this light continuity can be assured through the government of a succession of leaders as long as they are aware that they must provide an account of their actions. Regarding absolute power, Abrabanel insists that this is not a necessity. Furthermore, collective decision-making is advocated by the Torah. Turning to existing states, he asserts that government by elected judges, as found in Venice, Florence and Genoa is far superior to monarchial rule.

As far as Israel is concerned, Abrabanel stresses that its true guide must be the God of the Jewish nation. It does not need a king, and experience has proved that monarchy is a disasterous institution. The judges, however, were faithful servants of the Lord. The best form of government is thus that of an elite group of judges who are guided in their decisions by the will of God. The Messiah, he continues, will not be a king, but a judge and prophet. In this respect, Abrabanel anticipated the revolution in political thinking brought about by the Renaissance even though he resembles other thinkers of the Middle Ages in terms of his philosophical and theological ideas.

Elijah Ben Moses Abba Delmedigo

Born in c. 1460 Elijah Delmedigo was one of the most important Jewish figures of the Renaissance. As a teacher of philosophy at Padua and other Italian towns, he attracted a number of Christian pupils including Pico della Mirandola. His works consist largely of super-commentaries on Averroes' *Commentaries* on Aristotle. In addition he produced Latin translations of Averroes' works. Elijah's most important work, *Behinat ha-Dat* (*Examination of Religion*) was composed at Candia in 1490. In this text, based on Averroes' *Decisive Treatise*, he deals with the relation between philosophy and religion.

Science, Elijah argues, constitutes demonstrable knowledge whereas the Torah is based on principles of a different order. The philosopher who believes in the truth of the Torah must accept certain principles which cannot be demonstrated by philosophy such as the belief in prophecy, reward and punishment, and the existence of miracles. Philosophers, he contends, should study the Torah in an inquisitive spirit, but it would be a mistake for simple believers to do this. In this regard, he stresses that philosophers are misguided when they challenge such individuals.

Taking the case of anthropomorphism, Elijah points out that the belief that God has a body does not contradict Scripture – this is the view held by most believers even though it is contrary to philosophy. It would be an error for philosophers to disturb simple believers with their questioning since there is no need for them to have any grasp of such philosophical complexities. Philosophy and religion thus have no connection despite the opinions of such thinkers as *Maimonides. The aim of the Torah, he continues, is to guide human beings to the truth according to each person's abilities. However, since not everyone can attain the intellectual good, the most important purpose of the Torah is to provide the basis for a good society.

In his writing Elijah was deeply critical of the kabbalists who claimed that their tradition originated with Simeon bar Yohai who lived in the 2nd century. In fact, he points out, the Zohar was composed only three centuries previously despite the claims of Jewish mystics. Contrary to kabbalistic interpretation (as well as the opinion of philosophers), the Bible should be understood in its literal sense except in those cases where there is a conflict between verses. Yet, even here the correct exegesis must be derived from within the framework of Scripture without appealing to any external systems of thought such as Aristotelianism.

According to Elijah, everything concerning the commandments found in rabbinic sources must be accepted without question. As far as the aggadot are concerned, however, discussion is permissible. Regarding the question whether a rational explanation for the mitzvot can be given, Elijah argues that all the mitzvot have a rational basis. But, against the kabbalists, he insists that when an individual fulfils a divine commandment, this is in no way affects the harmony of the cosmos. The divine commandments simply have an effect on the state of the social order.

Throughout his writing, Elijah continually emphasizes that the Torah must be understood on its own terms without any recourse to metaphysical speculation. As he states in the *Treatises on the Intellect*:

> I do not think that the words of the Torah are explained through the method of philosophy nor does the former (Torah) need the latter (philosophy). No one thinks this way, according to my point of view, except for the man who is neither an adherent of the Torah nor a philosopher.
>
> (in Geffen, 1973–4, 82)

Judah Ben Isaac Abrabanel

Known as Leo Hebraeus, Judah Ben Isaac Abrabanel was born in Lisbon in c. 1460; the son of Isaac Abrabanel, he received a scientific and philosophical education. In 1483 he worked as a physician in Lisbon, but shortly afterwards followed his father when he fled from the city. So as to insure that his son, Issac, should avoid baptism in 1492, he sent him with a nurse to Portugal; despite such an effort, however, King John II had him baptized. After the Spanish expulsion, Judah lived in Naples, and then at Genoa, subsequently returning to Naples.

Judah's most important work, *Dialoghi d'Amore* (*Dialogues of Love*) was most probably written in Italian; between 1535 and 1607 twenty five editions were published, and from 1551–1660 it was translated into French, Latin, Spanish and Hebrew. In this work the theme of love is explored by means of dialogues between Philo and Sophia. Drawing on Neoplatonic notions, the theme of cosmic love predominates – love is conceived as the basis for the relationship between God and the universe and the universe and God:

> Since the beginning and end of the circle is the most high Creator, the first half is the descent from him to the lowest and most distant point from his supreme perfection. And first in order of descent comes the angelic nature with its ordered degrees from greater to less; then follows the heavenly, ranging from the heaven of the Empyrean, which is the greatest, to that of the moon, which is the least; and finally the circle passes to

our sphere, the lowest of all, to wit, first matter, the least perfect of the eternal substances and the farthest removed from the high perfection of the Creator. For as he is pure actuality so it is pure potentiality. And it is the terminating point of the first half of the circle of being, which descends from the Creator through the successive degrees, from greater to less, to first matter, the least of all . . . . The whole of the first half circle consists of the love of the superior for the inferior less beautiful than itself, and of successive procreation. And the producer is more beautiful than what he produces, and it is love which causes him to procreate and impart his beauty; and so it is from the highest creature down to first matter, the least of all creation, because love of the greater for the less is the means and cause of generation. In the other half circle, on the contrary, from first matter to the highest good, since it ascends the steep of perfection from inferior to superior, love must be of the less for the more beautiful to acquire greater beauty and to attain to union with it.

(Abrabanel, 1937, 450–3)

Further Reading

Abrahams, I., *Jewish Life in the Middle Ages*, New York, 1969

Agus, J., *The Evolution of Jewish Thought, From Biblical Times to the Opening of the Modern Era*, London, 1959

Altmann, A. (ed.), *Essays in Jewish Intellectual History*, London, 1981

Altmann, A. (ed.), *Jewish Medieval and Renaissance Studies*, Cambridge, Mass., 1967

Altmann, A., *Studies in Religious Philosophy and Mysticism*, London, 1969

Birnbaum, P. (ed.), *Karaite Studies*, New York, 1971

Blau, J., *The Story of Jewish Philosophy*, New York, 1962

Cohn-Sherbok, D., *The Jewish Faith*, London, 1993

Davidson, H. A., *Proofs of Eternity, Creation and the Existence of God in Medieval Islamic and Jewish Philosophy*, New York, 1987

Guttmann, J., *Philosophies of Judaism*, trans. D. W. Silverman, London, 1964

Husik, I., *A History of Medieval Jewish Philosophy*, New York, 1916

Husik, I., *Philosophical Essays, Ancient, Mediaeval and Modern*, ed. M. C. Nahon and L. Strauss, Oxford, 1952

Jacobs, L., *Principles of the Jewish Faith*, Northvale, N.J., 1988

Jacobs, L., *A Jewish Theology*, New York, 1973

Katz, S., *Jewish Philosophers*, New York, 1975

Lasker, D. L., *Jewish Philosophical Polemics against Christianity in the Middle Ages*, New York, 1977

Maccoby, H., *Judaism on Trial, Jewish-Christian Disputation in the Middle Ages*, London, 1982

Reinharz, J. and Schwetschinski, D. (eds.), *Mystics, and Politicians: Essays in Jewish Intellectual History in Honor of Alexander Altmann*, Durham, N. C., 1982

Rudavsky, T. (ed.), *Divine Omniscience and Omnipotence in Medieval Philosophy: Islamic, Jewish and Christian Perspectives*, Dordrecht, 1985

Samuelson, N. M. (ed.), *Studies in Jewish Philosophy, Collected Essays of the Academy for Jewish Philosophy*, Lanham, 1987

Schechter, S., *Aspects of Rabbinic Theology*, New York, 1961

Scholem, G., *Major Trends in Jewish Mysticism*, New York, 1961

Seltzer, R., *Jewish People Jewish Thought*, New York, 1980

Sirat, C., *A History of Jewish Philosophy in the Middle Ages*, Cambridge, 1995

185

Stein, S. and Loewe, R. (eds.), *Studies in Jewish Religious and Intellectual History, presented to Alexander Altmann*, Alabama, 1979

Twersky, I. (eds.), *Studies in Medieval Jewish History and Literature*, Cambridge, Mass., Vol. l, 1979, Vol. 2, 1984

Vajda, G, *Introduction à la pensée juive du Moyen Age*, Paris, 1947

Wolfson, H. A., *Studies in the History of Philosophy and Religion*, Cambridge, Mass, 1977

Wolfson, H. A., *The Philosophy of the Kalam*, Cambridge, Mass., 1976

Wolfson, H. A., *Repercussions of the Kalam in Jewish Philosophy*, Cambridge, Mass, 1979

References

Abrabanel, Judah ben Isaac, *The Philosophy of Love*, trans. F. Friedberg-Sealy and J. H. Barnes, London, 1937

Abrahams, I., *Hebrew Ethical Wills*, Philadelphia, 1926

Al-Barakat, Abu, *Kitab al-Mu'tabar I* in S. Pines, *Studies in Abu-l-Barakat al-Baghdadi; Physics and Metaphysics*, Collected Works, I. Jerusalem, 1979

Albalag, Issac, *Tikkun ha-De'ot*, Jerusalem, 1973 ed. G. Vajda

Al-Fayyumi, N., *The Garden of Wisdom*, ed. D. Levine, New York, 1966

Altmann, A. and Stern, S. M., *Isaac Israeli, a Neo-platonic philosopher of the early tenth century*, Oxford, 1958

Altmann, A. (ed.), *Jewish Medieval and Renaissance Studies*, Cambridge, Mass., 1967

Altmann, A., *Three Jewish Philosophers*, New York, 1969

Baer, I., *A History of the Jews in Christian Spain*, Philadelphia, 1961

Bar Hiyya, A., *Meditation of the Sad Soul*, trans. G. Wigoder, New York, 1969

Ben Solomon, Gersom, *The Gate of Heavens*, Jerusalem, 1968

Blumenthal, D. R., *The Commentary of R. Hoter Ben Shelomo to the Thirteen Principles of Maimonides*, Leyden, 1974

Carmi, T. (ed.), *The Penguin Book of Hebrew Verse*, 1981

Cohn-Sherbok, D., *Jewish Mysticism: An Anthology*, Oxford, 1995

Encyclopedia Judaica, Jerusalem, 1971

Geffen, D., 'Insights into the life and thought of Elijah del Megido based on his published and unpublished works', PAAJR 41-2, 1973–4

Gershom ben Solomon, *Sha'ar ha-Shamayim*, Jerusalem, 1968

Gordon, M.L., 'The Rationalism of Jacob Anatoli'. Ph.D. diss., Yeshiva University, New York, 1974

Halevi, J., *Book of the Kuzari*, trans. H. Hirschfeld, New York, 1946

Heinemann, I., *Three Jewish Philosophers*, New York, 1969

Husik, I., *A History of Medieval Jewish Philosophy*, New York, 1966

Ibn Daud, A., *Emunah Ramah*, Frankfort-am-Main, 1982

Ibn Gabirol, Solomon, *The Kingly Crown*, trans. B. Lewis, London, 1961

Ibn Pakuda, Bahya, *Duties of the Heart*, trans. M. Hyamson, Jerusalem, 1962

Jacobs, L., *Principles of the Jewish faith*, Northvale, N. J., 1988

Kobler, F., *Letters of Jews Through the Ages*, Philadelphia, 1952

Lorki, J., *Divrei Hakhamim*, ed. E. Ashkenazi, Metz, 1849

Nemoy, L., 'Al-Qirqisani's Account of the Jewish Sects and Christianity', *Hebrew Union College Annual* 7, Cincinnati, 1930
Nemoy, L., *Karaite Anthology*, New Haven, 1932
Pulgar, Isaac, *Ezer ha-dat*, ed. G. S. Belasco, London, 1906
Rosenblatt, S., (ed.) *The High Ways to Perfection of Abraham Maimonides*, 2 vols., New York, 1938
Sirat, C., *A History of Jewish Philosophy in the Middle Ages*, Cambridge, 1995

Glossary

Aggadah:	rabbinic teaching
Amoraim:	Jewish scholars from the 3rd-6th century
Asharyites:	medieval Islamic school of theology
Ayn Sof:	Infinite
Dayyan:	judge
Epiqoros:	heretic
Eretz Israel:	Land of Israel
Exilarch:	head of the Jewish community in Babylonia
Gan Eden:	Garden of Eden
Gaon:	head of a Babylonian academy
Gemarah:	commentary on the Mishnah
Gematria:	biblical exegesis based on the numerical value of Hebrew words
Halakhah:	Jewish law
Hasidei Ashkenaz:	German medieval religious movement
Hekhalot:	heavenly halls
Hyle:	matter
Kabbalah:	Jewish mysticism
Kahal:	congregation
Kalam:	Islamic theology
Karaites:	Jewish sect founded at the beginning of the 8th century opposed to the rabbinic tradition
Ketuvim:	Writings
Kiddush:	prayer of sanctification

Logos: word

Maaseh Bereshit: creation mysticism
Maaseh Merkavah: chariot mysticism
Masorah: principles used by textual scholars to preserve
                   the authentic text of the Bible
Merkavah: divine chariot
Metatron: angel in rabbinic literature
Midrash: interpretation of biblical texts
Mishnah: 2nd century rabbinic legal code
Mitzvot: commandments
Mutakallimun: Islamic medieval theologians
Mu'tazilia: sect of the Mutakallimun

Nasi: president of the Sanhedrin
Neviim: Prophetic books
Notarikon: system of abbreviation by shortening words or
                   writing only one letter of a word

Piyyut: liturgical poem

Sefirot: divine emanations

Torah: Five Books of Moses
Torah MiSinai: Belief that God gave the Five Books of Moses
                   to Moses on Mt. Sinai
Tosafot: explanatory notes on the Talmud

Yeshiva: rabbinical academy

Zohar: medieval mystical text

Index

191

Index